1. 완전 기초적인 단어부터 학습한다.

독해 점수가 40점 미만이라면 기본적인 단어조차 숙지하고 있지 못한 경우가 대부분입니다. 그런데 시중 단어장은 기본단어는 실려 있지 않은 경우가 많습니다. 이 교재에서는 학습 대상을 완전 노베이스를 가정하고 아주 쉬운 단어부터 학습합니다.

2. 2주 안에 13개의 해석 포인트로 130문장을 통해 해석능력을 향상한다.

만약 영어 공부할 시간이 충분하다면 8 품사를 시작으로 모든 구문을 꼼꼼하게 공부할 수 있습니다. 하지만 시간이 없는 수험생들의 상황을 고려해서 최대한의 문법 용어를 생략하고 가장 효율적으로 쉽게 해석훈련이 가능하도록 13개의 해석 포인트를 구성하였습니다.

3. 해석연습과 동의어 훈련을 동시에 학습한다.

지텔프 독해 28문항 중 8문항은 동의어 문제입니다. 지텔프 독해에서 동의어는 문맥을 파악해 야 풀 수 있게 출제됩니다. 문맥을 파악하려면 해석을 할 줄 알아야 합니다. '켈리의 지텔프 해석 포인트 13'에 나오는 130문장을 통해 문맥적으로 동의어를 파악하는 훈련을 할 것입니다.

4. 지텔프 문법에서 해석이 안 되어 포기했던 조동사와 연결어를
   풀기 위한 능력을 향상한다.

지텔프 문법 26문항 중 4문항은 문법적 지식뿐 아니라 해석까지 해야 풀 수 있는 연결어와
조동사 문제입니다. '켈리의 지텔프 해석 포인트 13'에 나오는 130문장에 필수적으로 조동사
나 연결어를 포함시켰고, 그것을 지텔프 문법과 유사한 형식으로 재구성해 문제풀이 훈련을
할 것입니다.

각 문장은 다음과 같은 단계로 진행됩니다.

STEP 1	예문의 단어를 품사와 함께 학습합니다.
STEP 2	해석 포인트를 활용하여 직독직해 훈련을 합니다.
STEP 3	예문을 통해 동의어 학습을 합니다.
STEP 4	모든 예문 학습이 끝나면 조동사와 연결어 130문제를 해결합니다.

그동안 '켈리의 G-POINT 33'을 통해 문법은 완벽하게 잡았는데 독해는 도저히 어떻게 해야 할지 감을 못 잡겠다며 수많은 수험생이 고민을 토로했었습니다. 일단 단어를 암기하고 해석을 훈련해야 한다고 조언은 해주었지만, 베이스가 없는 상태에서 단어를 암기하고 해석을 훈련하는 것이 얼마나 힘든지를 알고 있기 때문에 조언으로만 끝나는 것이 미안했습니다. 많이 고민하고 노력했습니다. 이 책이 독해점수 향상을 위한 첫 발걸음이 되리라는 것을 확신합니다. 공부하다 궁금한 점은 언제든 네이버 카페 '켈리 지텔프'에 남겨주세요. 고득점을 맞기 위해서는 결국 단어와 해석훈련에 시간을 투자해야 한다는 것을 꼭 기억하셨으면 좋겠습니다. 여러분이 원하는 모든 일을 꼭 이루시길 바랍니다.

2021년 8월

켈리 영어 연구소에서 켈리 드림

지텔프 해석 포인트에 들어가기 전 알고 가야 할 필수 사항

1. 단어 앞 품사 확인하기

[명] : 명사

[동] : 동사 ['다'로 끝남]

[형] : 형용사 [받침이 'ㄴ', 'ㄹ'로 끝나거나 '의'로 끝남]

[부] : 부사

[전] : 전치사

[접] : 접속사

2. 조동사의 해석은 알고 가자

동사 앞에 위치해 동사의 뜻을 보조해준다.

① can	할 수 있다	I can do it.
② could	할 수 있다, 할 수 있었다	I could do it.
③ will	일 것이다	He will study.
④ would	일 것이다, 였을 것이다	He would study.
⑤ must	해야 한다	You must pass the test.
⑥ should	해야 한다	We should meet him.
⑦ may	~일지 모른다	She may be sick.
⑧ have to	해야 한다	I have to go.
⑨ had to	해야 했다	I had to go.

3. 간단한 시제는 알고 가자

① 동사가 원형이거나 -s가 붙는 경우 : '~하다'로 해석 [현재]

I love you. 나는 너를 <u>사랑한다</u>.

She loves you. 그녀는 너를 <u>사랑한다</u>.

② 동사에 ed가 붙는 경우 : '~했다'로 해석 [과거]

I loved you. 나는 너를 <u>사랑했다</u>.

She loved you. 그녀는 너를 <u>사랑했다</u>.

③ 동사의 형태가 have pp이거나 has pp인 경우 : '~해오고 있다'로 해석 [현재완료]

I have loved you. 나는 당신을 <u>사랑해오고 있다</u>.

She has loved you. 그녀는 당신을 <u>사랑해오고 있다</u>.

④ 동사의 형태가 had pp인 경우 : '~해오고 있었다'로 해석 [과거완료]

I had loved you. 나는 당신을 <u>사랑해오고 있었다</u>.

She had loved you. 그녀는 당신을 <u>사랑해오고 있었다</u>.

Contents |차례|

Contents |차례|

Contents |차례|

Day 01

켈리의 지텔프 **해석 POINT** 1

① **수식어 묶기** → ② **동사 찾기 (다)** → ③ **동사 앞 주어 (은 / 는 / 이 / 가)** → ④ **동사 뒤 목적어 (을/를)**

해석의 기본은 주어와 동사를 찾는 것이다. 하지만 수식어가 많다면 진짜 주어와 동사를 찾는 것이 힘들고 이것이 해석을 힘들게 하는 가장 큰 이유라고 할 수 있다. 문장의 뼈대가 되는 주어와 동사를 찾기 위해서는 필요 없는 것들은 괄호로 묶는 연습을 해야 한다. '해석 포인트 1'에서는 "괄호로 수식어 묶기" 훈련을 할 것이며 이것이 해석의 출발점이다. 그럼 수식어구란 구체적으로 무엇일까? 이제부터 우리가 괄호로 묶는 연습을 할 기본적인 수식어는 다음과 같다.

① 전치사구

가장 흔하게 나오는 것이 전치사구이다. 전치사구란 전치사와 그 뒤에 나오는 단어(명사)를 합하여 부르는 명칭이다. 수험생들은 여기서부터 혼란을 느끼기 시작한다. 전치사가 무엇인지 공부해야 하며 그 많은 전치사를 다 외워야 할까? 라는 걱정을 하기 시작한다. 전치사 파트를 따로 떼어 문법적으로 학습하는 것은 해석 공부에 대한 흥미를 떨어뜨리며 해석훈련이 목적인 우리에게 더 많은 시간을 할애하게 한다. 우리의 목표는 문법이 아니라 정확한 해석이다. 따라서 전치사를 따로 공부하기보다는 STEP 1에 전치사 표시가 있다면 전치사와 그 뒤에 나온 단어(명사)를 묶는 연습을 먼저 하자. 핵심 전치사는 책 전반에 걸쳐 계속 나오기 때문에 외우지 않아도 모든 해석 포인트에 관한 공부가 끝나면 자연스레 암기하게 된다. 전치사의 종류는 굉장히 많지만 가장 많이 나오는 것들을 정리해 놓았으니 한 번 훑어보는 것이 도움이 될 수 있다. 또한 most of (대부분의) 처럼 묶지 않는 것이 더 자연스럽게 해석되는 경우가 있다는 것도 기억하자.

of	~의 ~에 관해 ~ 중에서	with	~와 함께 ~를 가지고	from	~로 부터
in	~에 ~안에	on	~에 ~위에	without	~없이 ~없다면
by	~에 의해	for	~를 위해 ~동안 ~에게 ~때문에	to	~에 ~에게

② 쌍 콤마

콤마 사이에 있는 단어나 구 등은 묶는다.

③ 부사(구)

부사 파트를 따로 떼어 문법적으로 학습을 하는 것은 해석 공부에 대한 흥미를 떨어뜨리며 해석훈련이 목적인 우리에게 더 많은 시간을 할애하게 한다. 우리의 목표는 문법이 아니라 정확한 해석이다. 따라서 부사(구)를 따로 공부하기 보다는 STEP 1에 부사 표시가 있다면 묶는 연습을 먼저 하자. 참고로 부사는 '다'나 '의'로 끝나지 않고 받침이 'ㄴ,ㄹ'로 끝나지 않는다. ~ly가 붙는 경우 부사인 경우가 많다. 또한 부사는 문장에서 없어도 문법적으로 오류가 없다.

기본적으로 묶어야 할 수식어를 정리하면 다음과 같다.
① 전치사구 ② 쌍 콤마 ③ 부사(구)

위에서 언급한 수식어구를 모두 묶으면 남는 단어가 있다. 남는 단어 중 '다'로 끝나는 단어가 동사이다. 우리는 주어가 아닌 동사를 먼저 찾을 것이다. 동사를 찾으면 동사 앞에 남는 단어가 있을 것인데 그 단어는 주어일 확률이 높다. 주어에는 '은/는/이/가'를 붙여 해석하면 된다. 만약 동사 뒤에 단어(명사)가 남아있다면 그것은 목적어일 가능성이 크며 보통 '을/를'로 해석하면 된다.

001

> The employer reduced my salary despite the extended work hours.
>
> 사장님은 늘어난 근무시간에도 불구하고 나의 월급을 깎았다.

STEP 01 단어 암기

The employer reduced my salary despite the extended work hours.
　(명) 사장　 (동) 감소시키다　 (명) 월급　 (전) ~에도 불구하고　 (형) 늘어난　 (명) 시간

STEP 02 구문 분석 훈련 (수식어에 표시하고 구문을 분석해보자.)

The employer reduced my salary despite the extended work hours.

STEP 03 동의어 훈련

The employer reduced my salary despite the extended work hours.

Q : In the context of the passage, reduced means _____.

(a) minimized

(b) cut

(c) narrowed

(d) shrunk

002

> **By the age of 5, many children can distinguish between reality and fantasy.**
>
> 5살 쯤 되면, 많은 아이들이 현실과 환상을 구분할 수 있다.

 STEP 01 단어 암기

By the age of 5,   many children can distinguish between reality and fantasy.
(전) ~쯤에는   (동) 구별하다   (전) ~사이에서   (명) 현실   (명) 환상

 STEP 02 구문 분석 훈련 (수식어에 표시하고 구문을 분석해보자.)

By the age of 5, many children can distinguish between reality and fantasy.

STEP 03 동의어 훈련

By the age of 5, many children can <u>distinguish</u> between reality and fantasy.

Q : In the context of the passage, <u>distinguish</u> means _____.

(a) observe

(b) acquire

(c) differentiate

(d) consolidate

필 수 문 장 003

> **Some medical volunteers will provide medical care in African communities next month.**
>
> 몇몇 의료 봉사자들이 다음 달에 시골의 아프리카 마을에 의료 서비스를 제공할 것이다.

 STEP 01 단어 암기

Some medical volunteers will provide medical care in African communities next
(형) 몇몇의 (형) 의료의 (명) 자원봉사자 (동) 제공하다 (명) 돌봄 (전) ~에서 (명)공동체, 마을 (형) 다음의

month.
(명) 달

 STEP 02 구문 분석 훈련 (수식어에 표시하고 구문을 분석해보자.)

Some medical volunteers will provide medical care in African communities next

month.

STEP 03 동의어 훈련

Some medical volunteers will <u>provide</u> medical care in African communities next

month.

Q: In the context of the passage, <u>provide</u> means _____.

(a) donate

(b) offer

(c) anticipate

(d) invest

004

In the 1990s, in a small town, a man invented numerous instruments for farmers. However, they were useless.

1990년대에 한 작은 마을에서 한 남자가 농부들을 위한 수많은 도구들을 발명했다. 그러나, 그것들은 쓸모 없었다.

 STEP 01 단어 암기

In the 1990s, in a small <u>town</u>, a man <u>invented</u> <u>numerous</u> <u>instruments</u> <u>for</u> <u>farmers</u>.
(명) 도시　　(동) 발명하다　(형) 수많은　(명) 도구　(전) ~를　(명) 농부
　　　　　　　　　　　　　　　　　　　　　　　위해

<u>However</u>, they were <u>useless</u>.
(부) 그러나　　　　　　(형) 쓸모없는

 STEP 02 구문 분석 훈련 (수식어에 표시하고 구문을 분석해보자.)

In the 1990s, in a small town, a man invented numerous instruments for farmers.

However, they were useless.

STEP 03 동의어 훈련

In the 1990s, in a small town, a man <u>invented</u> numerous instruments for farmers.

However, they were useless.

Q: In the context of the passage, <u>invented</u> means _____.

(a) adorned
(b) reinforced
(c) established
(d) made

005

> **Amy, an English author, born in Leytonstone in 1990, is one of the famous novelists. In addition, she is the drummer of a famous band in the city.**
>
> 1990년 레이턴스톤에서 태어난 영국의 작가인 에이미는 유명한 소설가 중의 한 명이다. 게다가, 그녀는 그 도시에서 가장 유명한 밴드의 드러머이기도 하다.

STEP 01 단어 암기

Amy, an English author, born in Leytonstone in 1990, is one of the famous novelists.
(형) 영국의 　(명) 작가 (형) 태어난 (전) ~에서 　　　(전) ~에 　　　~중 하나 　(형) 유명한 　(명) 소설가

In addition, she is the drummer of a famous band in the city.
(부) 게다가 　　　　　　(명) 드러머 (전) ~의 (명) 유명한 (명) 밴드 　　(명) 도시

STEP 02 구문 분석 훈련 (수식어에 표시하고 구문을 분석해보자.)

Amy, an English author, born in Leytonstone in 1990, is one of the famous novelists. In addition, she is the drummer of a famous band in the city.

STEP 03 동의어 훈련

Amy, an English author, born in Leytonstone in 1990, is one of the famous novelists. In addition, she is the drummer of a <u>famous</u> band in the city.

Q: In the context of the passage, <u>famous</u> means _____.

(a) well-known
(b) disreputable
(c) notorious
(d) dull

006

Amy announced her retirement from teaching at the age of forty. On the other hand, her co-worker, Jack, decided to continue his teaching.

에이미는 40살 때 가르치는 일에서 은퇴하기로 선언했다. 반면에, 그녀의 동료인 잭은 계속 가르치는 일을 하기로 결심했다.

STEP 01 단어 암기

Amy <u>announced</u> her <u>retirement</u> <u>from</u> teaching <u>at</u> the age <u>of</u> forty.
　　(동) 발표하다　　　　(명) 은퇴　(전) ~로 부터　　　(전) ~에　　　(전) ~의

<u>On the other hand</u>, <u>her</u> <u>co-worker</u>, Jack, <u>decided</u> to <u>continue</u> <u>his</u> <u>teaching</u>.
　(부) 반면에　　　그녀의　(명) 동료　　　　　(동) 결정하다　　(동) 계속하다　그의　(명) 수업

STEP 02 구문 분석 훈련 (수식어에 표시하고 구문을 분석해보자.)

Amy announced her retirement from teaching at the age of forty. On the other hand, her co-worker, Jack, decided to continue his teaching.

STEP 03 동의어 훈련

Amy <u>announced</u> her retirement from teaching at the age of forty. On the other hand, her co-worker, Jack, decided to continue his teaching.

Q: In the context of the passage, <u>announced</u> means _____.

(a) attracted
(b) revealed
(c) declared
(d) planned

007

For most people, money is an essential factor in happiness. However, people with high incomes are not necessarily satisfied with their lives.

대부분의 사람들에게 돈은 행복의 필수적인 요소이다. 그러나 높은 수입을 가진 사람들이 반드시 그들의 삶에 만족하는 것은 아니다.

STEP 01 단어 암기

For most people, money is an essential factor in happiness. However, people with
(전) (형) 대부분의 　　　　　　(형) 필수적인　(명) 요소 (전) ~에 (명) 행복　　(부) 그러나　　　(전) ~을 가진
~에게

high incomes are not necessarily satisfied with their lives.
(명) 수입　　　　반드시 ~는 아닌　(형) 만족한　　　그들의　(명) 삶

STEP 02 구문 분석 훈련 (수식어에 표시하고 구문을 분석해보자.)

For most people, money is an essential factor in happiness. However, people with

high incomes are not necessarily satisfied with their lives.

STEP 03 동의어 훈련

For most people, money is an essential <u>factor</u> in happiness. However, people with high incomes are not necessarily satisfied with their lives.

Q: In the context of the passage, <u>factor</u> means _____.

(a) material
(b) process
(c) element
(d) supplier

필수문장 008

Flowers use powerful tools for attracting pollinators, including bees and insects. For example, daylilies use bright colors for attracting bees and insects.

꽃은 벌과 곤충을 포함한 꽃가루 매개자를 끌어들이기 위해 강력한 도구를 사용한다. 예를 들어, 원추리는 벌과 곤충을 유인하기 위해 밝은색을 사용한다.

 STEP 01 단어 암기

Flowers <u>use</u> <u>powerful</u> <u>tools</u> for <u>attracting</u> <u>pollinators</u>, <u>including</u> <u>bees</u> and <u>insects</u>.
(동) 사용하다 (형) 강력한 (명) 도구 유혹하는 것 (명) 수분자 (전) ~을 포함하여 (명) 벌 (명) 곤충

<u>For example</u>, <u>daylilies</u> use <u>bright</u> colors <u>for</u> attracting bees and insects.
(부) 예를 들어 (명) 원추리 (형) 밝은 (전) ~위해

 STEP 02 구문 분석 훈련 (수식어에 표시하고 구문을 분석해보자.)

Flowers use powerful tools for attracting pollinators, including bees and insects.

For example, daylilies use bright colors for attracting bees and insects.

STEP 03 동의어 훈련

Flowers use powerful tools for attracting pollinators, including bees and butterflies.

For example, daylilies use bright colors for <u>attracting</u> bees and insects.

Q: In the context of the passage, <u>attracting</u> means _____.

(a) disturbing
(b) involving
(c) enticing
(d) posing

필수문장 009

Fast fashion can have a disastrous impact on humans and our environment. For example, it is responsible for global carbon emissions because of the use of fossil fuels like crude oil.

패스트 패션은 인간과 환경에 파괴적인 영향을 끼칠 수 있다. 예를 들어, 그것은 원유와 같은 화석 연료의 사용 때문에 전 세계 탄소 배출에 원인이 된다.

 단어 암기

Fast fashion can have a disastrous impact on humans and our environment
　　　　　　(동) 가지다　　(형) 막심한, 비참한　(명) 영향　(전) ~에　　　　　　우리의　　(명) 환경

For example, it is responsible for global carbon emissions because of the use of
(부) 예를 들어　　　(형) 책임이 있는, 원인이 되는　(형) 전 세계의　(명) 탄소　(명) 배출, 배출물　(전) ~ 때문에　　(명) 사용 (전) ~의

fossil fuels like crude oil.
화석연료　(전) ~같은　원유

 구문 분석 훈련 (수식어에 표시하고 구문을 분석해보자.)

Fast fashion can have a disastrous impact on humans and our environment. For example, it is responsible for global carbon emissions because of the use of fossil fuels like crude oil.

28

STEP 03 동의어 훈련

Fast fashion can have a <u>disastrous</u> impact on humans and our environment. For example, it is responsible for global carbon emissions because of the use of fossil fuels like crude oil.

Q: In the context of the passage, <u>disastrous</u> means _____.

(a) moderate
(b) unsuccessful
(c) miscarry
(d) devastating

010

One of the biggest differences between humans and other animals is the ability of inventing new tools. Also, unlike animals, humans can describe thoughts and feelings accurately.

인간과 다른 동물의 가장 큰 차이점 중 하나는 새로운 도구를 발명하는 우리의 능력이다. 또한, 동물들과 달리 인간들은 생각과 느낌을 정확하게 설명할 수 있다.

STEP 01 단어 암기

One of the biggest differences between humans and other animals is the ability
~중 하나　　(형) 가장 큰　(명) 차이점　　(전) ~사이에서　　　(형) 다른　　　(명) 능력

of inventing new tools. Also, unlike animals, humans can describe thoughts and
발명하는 것　(형) 새로운 (명) 도구 (부) 또한 (전)~와 달리　　　　(동) 설명하다　(명) 생각, 사고

feelings accurately.
(명) 감정　　(부) 정확하게

STEP 02 구문 분석 훈련 (수식어에 표시하고 구문을 분석해보자.)

One of the biggest differences between humans and other animals is the ability

of inventing new tools. Also, unlike animals, humans can describe thoughts and

feelings accurately.

STEP 03 동의어 훈련

One of the biggest differences between humans and other animals is the ability of inventing new tools. Also, unlike animals, humans can describe thoughts and feelings <u>accurately</u>.

Q: In the context of the passage, <u>accurately</u> means _____.

(a) carefully
(b) patiently
(c) undoubtedly
(d) precisely

Day 02

켈리의 지텔프 **해석** POINT **2**

접속사 + 주어 + 동사 → 접속사에 걸린 동사는 '다'로 해석하지 말고 각 접속사의 뜻에

맞춰 해석 (and, or, but, so제외)

하나의 절에는 동사가 하나 존재한다. 가령, 'I love you.'에서 동사는 'love' 하나뿐이다. 하지만 접속사가 나오면 동사가 하나 추가될 수 있다. 다음 예문을 살펴보자.

I love you because you like me.

접속사 because가 있기 때문에 동사 'like'가 하나 더 추가되었다. 문장이 길어지는 이유는 접속사로 인해 동사가 추가되기 때문이다. 접속사는 뒤에 주어와 동사를 달고 나온다. 이를 '접+주+동'이라고 암기하면 편하다. 우리는 '켈리의 해석 포인트 1'에서 수식어를 묶은 후 남는 동사를 '다'로 해석한다고 배웠다. 하지만 접속사에 걸린 동사는 '다'로 해석하면 안 된다. 접속사의 뜻을 적용해서 해석해야 한다. 가령 위의 예문에서 because는 '~ 때문에'로 해석되는 접속사이므로 because에 걸린 like는 '좋아하다'가 아닌 '좋아하기 때문에'로 해석해야 한다. 따라서 위의 예문은 '나는 너를 사랑한다 / 네가 나를 좋아하기 때문에'로 해석된다.

수험생들은 여기서부터 혼란을 느끼기 시작한다. 접속사가 무엇인지 공부해야 하며 그 많은 접속사를 다 외워야 할까? 라는 걱정을 하기 시작한다. 접속사 파트를 따로 떼어 학습하는 것은 해석 공부에 대한 흥미를 떨어뜨리며 해석훈련이 목적인 우리에게 더 많은 시간을 할애하게 한다. 우리의 목표는 문법이 아니라 정확한 해석이다. 따라서 접속사를 따로 공부하기보다는 STEP 1에 접속사 표시가 있다면 접속사 뒤에 주어와 동사를 찾은 후 접속사에 걸린 주어는 '은 / 는 / 이 / 가'로 해석하고 접속사에 걸린 동사는 접속사의 뜻을 적용해 해석하면 된다. 접속사를 따로 떼어 외우지 않아도 모든 해석 법칙에 관한 공부가 끝나면 자연스레 암기하게 될 것이다.

단, 접속사 and, or, but, so 등은 '다'로 해석된다는 것도 기억하자. 가령, 다음의 예문을 살펴보자.

I love you but I hate him.

but에 걸린 동사는 '다'로 해석된다. 따라서 위의 예문은 '나는 너를 사랑한다 / 그러나 나는 그는 싫어한다'로 해석된다.

필수문장 011

Because the boss was sick, he called off an important meeting.

사장님이 아팠기 때문에 그는 중요한 회의를 취소했다.

 STEP 01 단어 암기

Because the boss was <u>sick</u>, he <u>called off</u> an <u>important</u> meeting.
(접) ~때문에   (형) 아픈   (동) 취소했다   (형) 중요한

 STEP 02 구문 분석 훈련 (접속사와 접속사에 걸린 동사에 표시하고 구문을 분석해보자.)

Because the boss was sick, he called off an important meeting.

 STEP 03 동의어 훈련

Because the boss was sick, he <u>called off</u> an important meeting.

Q: In the context of the passage, <u>called off</u> means _____.

(a) delayed

(b) stopped

(c) canceled

(d) hampered

012

> **Police can detain people if they fail to provide a valid passport.**
>
> 만약 그들이 유효한 여권을 제공하지 않는다면 경찰은 사람들을 억류할 수 있다.

Day 02

 단어 암기

Police can <u>detain</u> people <u>if</u> they <u>fail</u> to <u>provide</u> a <u>valid</u> <u>passport</u>.
(동) 억류하다　　(접) 만약 ~하다면　(동) 실패하다　(동) 제공하다　(형) 유효한　(명) 여권

 구문 분석 훈련 (접속사와 접속사에 걸린 동사에 표시하고 구문을 분석해보자.)

Police can detain people if they fail to provide a valid passport.

STEP 03 **동의어 훈련**

Police can <u>detain</u> people if they fail to provide a valid passport.

Q: In the context of the passage, <u>detain</u> means _____.

(a) interrupt

(b) disturb

(c) defend

(d) hold

필수문장 013

A study found that outdoor play could have a positive impact on children.

한 연구는 야외 활동이 아이들에게 긍정적인 영향을 줄 수 있다는 것을 발견했다.

STEP 01 단어 암기

A <u>study</u> <u>found</u> <u>that</u> <u>outdoor</u> <u>play</u> could <u>have</u> a <u>positive</u> <u>impact</u> <u>on</u> <u>children</u>.
(명) 연구 (동) 발견했다 (접) ~것 (형) 야외의 (명) 놀이 (동) 가지다 (형) 긍정적인 (명) 영향, 효과 (전) ~에 (명) 어린이

STEP 02 구문 분석 훈련 (접속사와 접속사에 걸린 동사에 표시하고 구문을 분석해보자.)

A study found that outdoor play could have a positive impact on children.

STEP 03 동의어 훈련

A study found that outdoor play could have a <u>positive</u> impact on children.

Q: In the context of the passage, <u>positive</u> means _____.

(a) beneficial

(b) confident

(c) optimistic

(d) moderate

014

> **You need to remember that weather forecasts can be wrong.**
>
> 당신은 일기 예보가 잘못될 수 있다는 것을 기억할 필요가 있다.

Day 02

 STEP 01 단어 암기

You need to <u>remember</u> <u>that</u> <u>weather forecasts</u> can <u>be</u> <u>wrong</u>.
(동) 기억하다 (접) ~것 일기 예보 (동) 되다 (형) 잘못된

 STEP 02 구문 분석 훈련 (접속사와 접속사에 걸린 동사에 표시하고 구문을 분석해보자.)

You need to remember that weather forecasts can be wrong.

STEP 03 동의어 훈련

You need to remember that weather forecasts can be <u>wrong</u>.

Q: In the context of the passage, <u>wrong</u> means _____.

(a) changeable

(b) flexible

(c) inaccurate

(d) replaceable

015

> **Whenever Jake wanted to spend some quality time with his friends, he would go to the cozy cafe.**
>
> 제이크는 친구들과 귀중한 시간을 보내고 싶어 할 때마다 안락한 카페에 가곤 했었다.

 단어 암기

Whenever Jake wanted to spend some quality time with his friends, he would go
(접) ~할 때마다   (동) 원하다   (동) 보내다   (형) 좋은

to the cozy cafe.
(형) 안락한

 구문 분석 훈련 (접속사와 접속사에 걸린 동사에 표시하고 구문을 분석해보자.)

Whenever Jake wanted to spend some quality time with his friends, he would go

to the cozy cafe.

 동의어 훈련

Whenever Jake wanted to spend some quality time with his friends, he would go

to the cozy cafe.

Q: In the context of the passage, quality means _____.

(a) precious
(b) superior
(c) grade
(d) lazy

016

> A school counselor said that Mike should earn a bachelor's degree in a related field for his dream.
>
> 상담 선생님은 마이크가 그의 꿈을 위해 관련 분야에서 학사학위를 따야 한다고 말했다.

Day 02

 단어 암기

A school <u>counselor</u> <u>said</u> <u>that</u> Mike should <u>earn</u> a <u>bachelor</u>'s <u>degree</u> in a <u>related</u>
　　　　　(명) 상담가　(동) 말했다 (접) ~것　　　　(동) 얻다, 따다　(명) 학사　　(명) 학위　　　(형) 관련된

<u>field</u> for his dream.
(명) 분야

 구문 분석 훈련 (접속사와 접속사에 걸린 동사에 표시하고 구문을 분석해보자.)

A school counselor said that Mike should earn a bachelor's degree in a related

field for his dream.

STEP 03 **동의어 훈련**

A school counselor said that Mike should <u>earn</u> a bachelor's degree in a related

field for his dream.

Q: In the context of the passage, <u>earn</u> means _____.

(a) get

(b) collect

(c) produce

(d) create

017

> Though drinking too much carrot juice can be bad for you, some studies showed that carrot juice in your diet could have a health benefit.
>
> 당근 쥬스를 너무 많이 마시는 것이 당신에게 나쁠 수 있지만, 몇몇 연구는 당신의 식단에 당근쥬스를 포함 시키는 것이 긍정적인 건강상의 이점을 가질 수 있다는 것을 보여주었다.

 STEP 01 단어 암기

Though drinking too much carrot juice can be bad for you, some studies showed
(접) 비록   마시는 것   (부) 너무 (부) 많이 (명) 당근   (전) ~에게   (명) 연구 (동) 보여주다
~일지라도

that carrot juice in your diet could have a health benefit.
(접) ~것   (명) 식단   (동) 가지다   (명) 건강   (명) 이점

 STEP 02 구문 분석 훈련 (접속사와 접속사에 걸린 동사에 표시하고 구문을 분석해보자.)

Though drinking too much carrot juice can be bad for you, some studies showed

that carrot juice in your diet could have a health benefit.

STEP 03 동의어 훈련

Though drinking too much carrot juice can be bad for you, some studies showed

that carrot juice in your diet could have a health <u>benefit</u>.

Q: In the context of the passage, <u>benefit</u> means _____.

(a) advantage

(b) welfare

(c) comfort

(d) usability

018

A study revealed that people could build a meaningful relationship through adoption. However, it can be a challenging process.

한 연구는 사람들이 입양을 통해 의미 있는 관계를 쌓을 수 있다는 것을 보여주었다. 그러나 그것은 힘든 과정이 될 수 있다.

 STEP 01   단어 암기

A study <u>revealed</u> <u>that</u> people could <u>build</u> a <u>meaningful</u> <u>relationship</u> <u>through</u> <u>adoption</u>.
　　　　(동) 드러내다　(접) ~것　　　　　　(동) 세우다　(형) 의미 있는　　(명) 관계　　(전) ~을 통하여　(명) 입양

<u>However</u>, it can <u>be</u> a <u>challenging</u> <u>process</u>.
(부) 그러나　　　　　(동) 되다　　(형) 힘든　　(명) 과정

 STEP 02   구문 분석 훈련 (접속사와 접속사에 걸린 동사에 표시하고 구문을 분석해보자.)

A study revealed that people could build a meaningful relationship through adoption.

However, it can be a challenging process.

STEP 03   동의어 훈련

A study revealed that people could build a meaningful relationship through adoption.

However, it can be a <u>challenging</u> process.

Q: In the context of the passage, <u>challenging</u> means _____.

(a) inspiring

(b) energizing

(c) purposeful

(d) demanding

필수문장 019

> **Although carbohydrates are essential to your diet, the excessive consumption of carbohydrates can result in inconsistent blood sugar levels.**
>
> 비록 탄수화물이 당신의 식단에 필수적이지만 과도한 탄수화물 섭취는 불안정한 혈당 수치를 유발할 수 있다.

 STEP 01 단어 암기

Although carbohydrates are essential to your diet, the excessive consumption of
(접) 비록   (명) 탄수화물   (형) 필수적인   (전) ~에   (명) 식단   (형) 과도한   (명) 섭취
~일지라도

carbohydrates can result in inconsistent blood sugar levels.
                        (동) 초래하다   (형) 불안정한   혈당   (명) 수준

 STEP 02 구문 분석 훈련 (접속사와 접속사에 걸린 동사에 표시하고 구문을 분석해보자.)

Although carbohydrates are essential to your diet, the excessive consumption of

carbohydrates can result in inconsistent blood sugar levels.

 STEP 03 동의어 훈련

Although carbohydrates are essential to your diet, the excessive consumption of

carbohydrates can result in inconsistent blood sugar levels.

Q: In the context of the passage, inconsistent means _____.

(a) reconcilable

(b) unstable

(c) uncertain

(d) doubtful

020

> **The impacts of global warming are speeding up as concentrations of greenhouse gases in the atmosphere increase.**
>
> 대기 중에 온실가스의 농도가 증가함에 따라 지구 온난화의 영향이 가속화되고 있다.

 STEP 01 단어 암기

The <u>impacts</u> <u>of</u> <u>global warming</u> are <u>speeding up</u> <u>as</u> <u>concentrations</u> of <u>greenhouse</u>
　　　(명) 영향 (전) ~의 지구 온난화　　　가속화 되는 (접) ~함에 (명) 농도　　　온실
　　　　　　　　　　　　　　　　　　　　　　　　따라

<u>gases</u> in the <u>atmosphere</u> <u>increase</u>.
가스　(전) ~안에 (명) 대기 (동) 증가하다

 STEP 02 구문 분석 훈련 (접속사와 접속사에 걸린 동사에 표시하고 구문을 분석해보자.)

The impacts of global warming are speeding up as concentrations of greenhouse gases in the atmosphere increase.

STEP 03 동의어 훈련

The impacts of global warming are <u>speeding up</u> as concentrations of greenhouse gases in the atmosphere increase.

Q: In the context of the passage, <u>speeding up</u> means _____.

(a) hastening
(b) promoting
(c) accelerating
(d) simplifying

Day 03

켈리의 지텔프 **해석 POINT** **3**

① and, or, but 뒤에 나오는 단어 → ② △ 표시 → ③ 앞에서 짝 찾아 △ 표시 →

④ △ 끼리 동일하게 해석

I like him but hate her.

but 뒤에 '싫어하다'를 뜻하는 hate에 △ 표시를 한다. 마찬가지로 동사원형의 형태인 '좋아하다'를 뜻하는 'like'에 △ 표시를 하면 된다. 그 둘은 병렬관계에 있다고 말할 수 있다. 병렬 관계가 무엇인지 문법적으로 접근할 필요가 없다. 이 책이 끝날 때쯤이면 본인도 모르게 병렬에 관한 내용이 자연스레 학습되어 있을 것이다. 우리는 해석적으로 접근하면 된다. △ 표시끼리 동일한 형태로 해석하면 되는데 위의 예문에서는 '다'를 붙여 해석하면 끝이다. 즉, 위의 예문은 '나는 그를 좋아한다. 그러나 그녀는 싫어한다'로 해석하면 된다. 다음 예문도 한 번 살펴보자.

I decided to study hard and pass the test.

and 뒤에 있는 pass에 △ 표시를 하고 and 앞에서 짝을 찾아보자. pass가 동사원형이므로 동사원형의 형태를 찾아 △ 표시를 하면 된다. 동사원형 형태는 study이므로 study와 병렬관계임을 알 수 있다. 짝과 동일한 형태로 해석해야 하므로 '나는 열심히 공부하기로 결정했고, 시험에 통과하기로 결정했다'로 해석하면 된다. '나는 열심히 공부하기로 결정했고 시험에 통과했다'는 오류가 있는 해석이다.

병렬은 대표적으로 and, or, but과 관련되어 나오지만 그렇지 않은 경우도 있다. 그런 경우는 예문을 통해 학습하기로 하자.

필수문장 021

> **Because Amy wanted to be slim, she decided to get in shape and lose weight in 7 days.**
>
> 에이미는 날씬해지고 싶었기 때문에, 7일 안에 몸매를 가꾸고 살을 빼기로 결심했다.

 STEP 01 단어 암기

<u>Because</u> Amy <u>wanted</u> to be <u>slim</u>, she <u>decided</u> to <u>get in shape</u> and <u>lose</u> <u>weight</u>
(접) ~때문에   (동) 원하다   (형) 날씬한   (동) 결정하다   (동) 몸매를 가꾸다   (동) 빼다 (명) 몸무게

in 7 days.

 STEP 02 구문 분석 훈련 (and, or, but를 기준으로 짝을 찾아 표시하고 구문을 분석해보자.)

Because Amy wanted to be slim, she decided to get in shape and lose weight

in 7 days.

 STEP 03 동의어 훈련

Because Amy wanted to be slim, she <u>decided</u> to get in shape and lose weight

in 7 days.

Q: In the context of the passage, <u>decided</u> means _____.

(a) resolved

(b) executed

(c) prepared

(d) accomplished

필 수 문 장 022

> **Dogs are the best pet for many reasons. However, they can bite people and scratch furniture.**
>
> 개는 여러 가지 이유 때문에 최고의 애완동물이다. 그러나, 그들은 사람들을 물고 가구에 긁힌 자국을 낼 수 있다.

 STEP 01 단어 암기

Dogs are the best <u>pet</u> <u>for</u> many <u>reasons</u>. <u>However</u>, they can <u>bite</u> people and <u>scratch</u>
　　　　　　　(명) 애완 (전) ~때문에 　(명) 이유　(부) 그러나　　　　(동) 물다　　　　(동) 긁다
　　　　　　　동물

<u>furniture</u>.
(명) 가구

 STEP 02 구문 분석 훈련 (and, or, but를 기준으로 짝을 찾아 표시하고 구문을 분석해보자.)

Dogs are the best pet for many reasons. However, they can bite people and

scratch furniture.

 STEP 03 동의어 훈련

Dogs are the <u>best</u> pet for many reasons. However, they can bite people and scratch

furniture.

Q: In the context of the passage, <u>best</u> means _____.

(a) leading
(b) principal
(c) greatest
(d) superior

023

April gave up her vacation and canceled the flight ticket because she had to finish a project on time.

에이프릴은 프로젝트를 제 시간에 끝내야 했기 때문에 휴가를 포기하고 비행기 티켓을 취소했다.

 단어 암기

April gave up her vacation and canceled the flight ticket because she had to finish
　　(동) 포기했다　　　(명) 휴가　　(동) 취소하다　　비행기표　　　　　　(동) 마치다

a project on time.
　　　　(제 시간에

STEP 02 구문 분석 훈련 (and, or, but를 기준으로 짝을 찾아 표시하고 구문을 분석해보자.)

April gave up her vacation and canceled the flight ticket because she had to finish

a project on time.

April gave up her vacation and canceled the flight ticket because she had to <u>finish</u> a project on time.

Q: In the context of the passage, <u>finish</u> means _____.

(a) cease
(b) suspend
(c) terminate
(d) complete

Day 03

024

> **Water pollution kills a number of people every year as well as affects the health of animals. Nevertheless, most of the people don't do anything to prevent water pollution.**
>
> 수질 오염은 동물에 건강에 영향을 미칠 뿐만 아니라 매년 수많은 사람들을 죽인다. 그럼에도 불구하고, 사람들은 수질 오염을 예방하기 위해 어떤 일도 하지 않는다.

STEP 01 단어 암기

Water <u>pollution</u> kills <u>a number of</u> people <u>every year</u> <u>as well as</u> <u>affects</u> the <u>health</u>
　　　(명) 오염　　　　　　수많은　　　　　　　(부) 매년　　~뿐만 아니라　(동) 영향을 끼치다　(명) 건강

of animals. <u>Nevertheless,</u> <u>most of</u> the people don't <u>do</u> <u>anything</u> to <u>prevent</u> water pollution.
　　　　　(부) 그럼에도 불구하고　대부분의　　　　　　(동) 하다 (명) 어떤 것　　(동) 막다

STEP 02 구문 분석 훈련 (and, or, but를 기준으로 짝을 찾아 표시하고 구문을 분석해보자.)

Water pollution kills a number of people every year as well as affects the health

of animals. Nevertheless, most of the people don't do anything to prevent water pollution.

STEP 03 동의어 훈련

Water pollution kills a number of people every year as well as <u>affects</u> the health of animals. Nevertheless, most of the people don't do anything to prevent water pollution.

Q: In the context of the passage, <u>affects</u> means _____.

(a) threatens
(b) maintains
(c) profits
(d) aids

Day 03

025

Although Rachel met a man in London and had dinner with him at a fancy restaurant last year, she doesn't even remember his name.

비록 레이첼이 런던에서 한 남자를 만났고, 작년에 고급 식당에서 그와 저녁을 먹었지만, 그녀는 그의 이름조차 기억하지 못한다.

STEP 01 단어 암기

Although Rachel met a man in London and had dinner with him at a fancy restaurant
(접) 비록 ~일지라도   (동) 만났다   (명) 저녁 (전) ~와   (전) ~에서 (형) 고급의
                                                        함께

last year, she doesn't even remember his name.
(부) 작년   (부) 심지어 (동) 기억하다 그의

STEP 02 구문 분석 훈련 (and, or, but를 기준으로 짝을 찾아 표시하고 구문을 분석해보자.)

Although Rachel met a man in London and had dinner with him at a fancy restaurant last year, she doesn't even remember his name.

동의어 훈련

Although Rachel met a man in London and had dinner with him at a <u>fancy</u> restaurant last year, she doesn't even remember his name.

Q: In the context of the passage, <u>fancy</u> means _____.

(a) affordable
(b) cozy
(c) luxurious
(d) reasonable

Day
03

필수문장 026

You must present your ID card to attend tomorrow's meeting and take a special lecture. Unless you have an ID card, you can't get in.

내일 회의에 참석해서 특별 강의를 듣기 위해서는 신분증을 지참해야 한다. 만약 신분증이 없으면 들어갈 수 없다.

 STEP 01 단어 암기

You must <u>present</u> your <u>ID card</u> to <u>attend</u> tomorrow's meeting and <u>take</u> a special
　　　　　(동) 제시하다　　　(명) 신분증　　　(동) 참석하다　　　　　　　　　　　　(동) 수강하다

<u>lecture</u>. <u>Unless</u> you have an ID card, you can't <u>get in</u>.
(명) 강의　　(접) 만약 ~하지 않는다면　　　　　　　　　　　　　(동) 들어가다

 STEP 02 구문 분석 훈련 (and, or, but를 기준으로 짝을 찾아 표시하고 구문을 분석해보자.)

You must present your ID card to attend tomorrow's meeting and take a special

lecture. Unless you have an ID card, you can't get in.

STEP 03 동의어 훈련

You must <u>present</u> your ID card to attend tomorrow's meeting and take a special lecture. Unless you have an ID card, you can't get in.

Q: In the context of the passage, <u>present</u> means _____.

(a) show
(b) appear
(c) express
(d) release

Day 03

027

> **When Bill passed his road test and got his driver's license, his sister gave her car to him.**
>
> 빌이 도로 주행 테스트를 통과하고 운전면허를 땄을 때, 누나가 그에게 그녀의 차를 주었다.

STEP 01 단어 암기

When Bill <u>passed</u> his <u>road test</u> and <u>got</u> his <u>driver's license</u>, his sister <u>gave</u> her
(접) ~할 때   (동) 통과하다   도로주행시험   (동) 땄다   운전면허증   (동) 주었다

car <u>to</u> him.
(전) ~에게

STEP 02 구문 분석 훈련 (and, or, but를 기준으로 짝을 찾아 표시하고 구문을 분석해보자.)

When Bill passed his road test and got his driver's license, his sister gave her

car to him.

STEP 03 동의어 훈련

When Bill passed his road test and <u>got</u> his driver's license, his sister gave her

car to him.

Q: In the context of the passage, <u>got</u> means _____.

(a) developed
(b) earned
(c) applied
(d) prevailed

028

> **Monica was studying when she heard strange sounds and saw something through the window.**
>
> 이상한 소리를 듣고 창문을 통해 무언가를 보았을 때 모니카는 공부하는 중이었다.

 단어 암기

Monica was studying when she heard strange sounds and saw something through
　　　　　공부하는 중 (접) ~할 때 (동) 들었다 (형) 이상한 (명) 소리 (동) 보았다 (전) ~을 통해

the window.

 구문 분석 훈련 (and, or, but를 기준으로 짝을 찾아 표시하고 구문을 분석해보자.)

Monica was studying when she heard strange sounds and saw something through

the window.

STEP 03 동의어 훈련

Monica was studying when she heard strange sounds and saw something through

the window.

Q: In the context of the passage, strange means _____.

(a) unpleasant

(b) typical

(c) different

(d) unusual

필수문장 029

After archaeologists discovered and studied the tomb of a woman, they found that men and women enjoyed equal rights at that time.

고고학자들은 한 여성의 무덤을 발견했고, 그 당시 남녀가 동등한 권리를 누렸다는 것을 발견했다.

 STEP 01 단어 암기

After archaeologists discovered and studied the tomb of a woman, they found that
(접) ~후에　(명) 고고학자　(동) 발견하다　　(동) 연구했다　(명) 무덤　　　　　(동) 발견했다 (접) ~것

men and women enjoyed equal rights at that time.
(동) 즐기다,　(형) 동등한 (명) 권리　(부) 그 당시에
누리다

 STEP 02 구문 분석 훈련 (and, or, but를 기준으로 짝을 찾아 표시하고 구문을 분석해보자.)

After archaeologists discovered and studied the tomb of a woman, they found that

men and women enjoyed equal rights at that time.

After archaeologists discovered and studied the tomb of a woman, they found that men and women <u>enjoyed</u> equal rights at that time.

Q: In the context of the passage, <u>enjoyed</u> means _____.

(a) had
(b) divided
(c) appreciated
(d) allocated

Day 03

필수문장 030

Workout apps gain popularity as the interest in health is increasing. They offer workout videos and training routines for free and provide even personalized workout plans for all fitness levels.

건강에 대한 관심이 높아지면서 운동 앱이 인기를 얻고 있다. 그것은 운동 비디오와 훈련 과정을 무료로 제공한다. 게다가, 그것은 모든 건강 수준에 맞는 개인화된 운동 계획까지 제공한다.

STEP 01 단어 암기

Workout apps gain popularity as the interest in health is increasing. They offer
(명) 운동   어플   (동) 얻다   (명) 인기   (접) ~함에 따라   (명) 흥미   (명) 건강   증가하는   (동) 제공하다

workout videos and training routines for free and provide even personalized workout
(명) 과정   무료로   (동) 제공하다   (부) 심지어   (형) 개인 맞춤화된

plans for all fitness levels.
(명) 계획   (명) 건강   (명) 수준

STEP 02 구문 분석 훈련 (and, or, but를 기준으로 짝을 찾아 표시하고 구문을 분석해보자.)

Workout apps gain popularity as the interest in health is increasing. They offer

workout videos and training routines for free and provide even personalized workout

plans for all fitness levels.

STEP 03 동의어 훈련

Workout apps gain popularity as the interest in health is increasing. They offer workout videos and training routines for free and provide even <u>personalized</u> workout plans for all fitness levels.

Q: In the context of the passage, <u>personalized</u> means _____.

(a) formulaic
(b) popularized
(c) customized
(d) handy

Day
04

켈리의 지텔프 **해석** POINT **4**

명사 + 주어 + 동사

① 주어 동사 묶기 → ② 앞 명사 수식 (동사는 '~다'가 아닌 '~ㄴ'으로 해석)

다음 예문을 살펴보자.

I know a girl he likes.

과연 어떻게 해석되는 것일까? 모든 문장에는 동사가 하나라고 말했다. 동사가 또 나오려면 접속사가 나와야 하는데 접속사가 존재하지 않는다. know가 동사일까? likes가 동사일까? 둘 중에 무엇이 '다'로 해석되는 동사일까? 동사는 know이다. likes는 동사가 아니므로 '좋아하다'로 해석될 수 없다. 그 이유는

'해석 포인트 4' 때문이다. 명사 뒤에 주어와 동사가 나란히 오면 주어와 동사를 묶어야 한다. 즉 a girl(명사) 뒤에 주어 형태인 he와 동사 형태인 likes가 왔으므로 he와 likes를 묶어 a girl을 수식해주면 된다. 이때 likes는 '좋아하다'가 아닌 'ㄴ' 받침을 붙여 '좋아하는'으로 해석하면 된다. 즉 a girl he likes의 해석은 '그가 좋아하는 소녀'이며 전체 문장의 해석은 '나는 그가 좋아하는 소녀를 알고 있다'가 된다.

031

Next week, John will donate all of his prize money he received for winning the race to charity.

다음 주, 존은 경주에서 우승하여 받은 모든 상금을 자선단체에 기부할 것이다.

 STEP 01 단어 암기

Next week, John will donate all of his prize money he received for winning the
(부) 다음 주   (동) 기부하다   상금   (동) 받다   (동) 이기다

race to charity.
(명) 경주 (전) ~에 (명) 자선 단체

STEP 02 구문 분석 훈련 (명사 뒤 주어동사에 표시한 후 구문을 분석해보자.)

Next week, John will donate all of his prize money he received for winning the

race to charity.

STEP 03 동의어 훈련

Next week, John will <u>donate</u> all of his prize money he received for winning the race to charity.

Q: In the context of the passage, <u>donate</u> means _____.

(a) transfer
(b) give
(c) return
(d) assign

Day 04

032

> Jason was sure that the mobile app he had created could attract
> users. However, the app failed because it was too expensive.
>
> 제이슨은 자신이 만든 모바일 앱이 사용자들을 끌어 모을 수 있다고 확신했다. 하지만, 그 앱은 너무
> 비쌌기 때문에 실패했다.

STEP 01   단어 암기

Jason was <u>sure</u> <u>that</u> the mobile app he had <u>created</u> could <u>attract</u> <u>users</u>. However,
(형) 확신하는 (접) ~것   (동) 창조하다   (동) 끌다   (명) 사용자

the app <u>failed</u> <u>because</u> it was <u>too</u> <u>expensive</u>.
(동) 실패하다 (접) ~때문에   (부) 너무   (형) 비싼

STEP 02   구문 분석 훈련 (명사 뒤 주어동사에 표시한 후 구문을 분석해보자.)

Jason was sure that the mobile app he had created could attract users. However,

the app failed because it was too expensive.

STEP 03 동의어 훈련

Jason was sure that the mobile app he had created could <u>attract</u> users. However, the app failed because it was too expensive.

Q: In the context of the passage, <u>attract</u> means _____.

(a) include
(b) draw
(c) involve
(d) accompany

Day 04

033

Grace failed to make a delicious pasta dish because the recipe she found online was full of errors.

그레이스는 온라인에서 발견한 요리법이 오류투성이였기 때문에 맛있는 파스타 요리를 만드는 데 실패했다.

 STEP 01 단어 암기

Grace failed to make a delicious pasta dish because the recipe she found online
　　　(동) 실패하다　　(동) 만들다　　(형) 맛있는　　　(명) 요리 (접) ~때문에　　(명) 조리법　　(동) 발견했다 (부) 온라인에서

was full of errors.
　　(형) ~로 가득찬　(명) 오류

STEP 02 구문 분석 훈련 (명사 뒤 주어동사에 표시한 후 구문을 분석해보자.)

Grace failed to make a delicious pasta dish because the recipe she found online

was full of errors.

Grace failed to make a delicious pasta dish because the recipe she found online was full of errors.

Q: In the context of the passage, errors means _____.

(a) miscalculation
(b) sufficiency
(c) flaws
(d) fragility

Day 04

034

> Jason sometimes picks edible mushrooms in the mountains. He can make various dishes with the mushrooms he gathers.
>
> 제이슨은 산에서 식용 버섯을 따는 것을 즐긴다. 그는 채집한 버섯으로 다양한 요리를 만들 수 있다.

STEP 01 단어 암기

Jason <u>sometimes</u> <u>picks</u> <u>edible</u> <u>mushrooms</u> <u>in</u> the <u>mountains</u>. He can <u>make</u> <u>various</u>
      (부) 때때로 (동) 따다 (형) 식용의 (명) 버섯   (전) ~에서   (명) 산   (동) 만들다 (형) 다양한

<u>dishes</u> <u>with</u> the mushrooms he <u>gathers</u>.
(명) 요리 (전) ~를 가지고   (동) 모으다

STEP 02 구문 분석 훈련 (명사 뒤 주어동사에 표시한 후 구문을 분석해보자.)

Jason sometimes picks edible mushrooms in the mountains. He can make various

dishes with the mushrooms he gathers.

70

STEP 03 동의어 훈련

Jason sometimes picks edible mushrooms in the mountains. He can make <u>various</u> dishes with the mushrooms he gathers.

Q: In the context of the passage, <u>various</u> means _____.

(a) dissimilar
(b) disparate
(c) separate
(d) different

Day 04

필수문장 035

A few years ago, Amy lost a book her grandfather had given.
Although she searched every corner of the room, she never found
the book.

몇 년 전, 에이미는 할아버지가 주신 책을 잃어버렸다. 그녀는 방 구석구석을 뒤졌지만, 그 책을 결코
찾지 못했다.

 STEP 01 단어 암기

A few years ago, Amy lost a book her grandfather had given. Although she searched
(부) 몇 년 전에   (동) 잃어버렸다   (접) 비록 ~일지라도   (동) 살피다

every corner of the room, she never found the book.
(형) 모든 (명) 구석   결코 ~않다 (동) 발견했다

 STEP 02 구문 분석 훈련 (명사 뒤 주어동사에 표시한 후 구문을 분석해보자.)

A few years ago, Amy lost a book her grandfather had given. Although she

searched every corner of the room, she never found the book.

STEP 03 동의어 훈련

A few years ago, Amy lost a book her grandfather had given. Although she searched every corner of the room, she never <u>found</u> the book.

Q: In the context of the passage, <u>found</u> means _____.

(a) observed
(b) detected
(c) located
(d) noticed

Day 04

036

> Because Jane wants to stop wasting money on things she doesn't need and prepare for the future, she puts some money aside every month.
>
> 제인은 필요하지 않은 물건에 돈을 낭비하는 것을 멈추고 미래를 준비하기 원하기 때문에 매달 약간의 돈을 저축한다.

 단어 암기

Because Jane wants to stop wasting money on things she doesn't need and
(접) ~때문에   (동) 원하다   낭비하는 것   (명) 물건   (동) 필요로 하다

prepare for the future, she puts some money aside every month.
(동) ~을 준비하다   (명) 미래   (동) 떼어   (형) 약간의   (부) 매달
                                   놓다

STEP 02 구문 분석 훈련 (명사 뒤 주어동사에 표시한 후 구문을 분석해보자.)

Because Jane wants to stop wasting money on things she doesn't need and

prepare for the future, she puts some money aside every month.

STEP 03 동의어 훈련

Because Jane wants to stop wasting money on things she doesn't need and prepare for the future, she <u>puts</u> some money aside every month.

Q: In the context of the passage, <u>puts</u> means _____.

(a) earns
(b) invests
(c) sets
(d) funds

037

A boy the babysitter took care of was missing. Fortunately, police found him in good health and he restored emotional stability after the traumatic event.

베이비시터가 돌보던 소년이 실종되었다. 다행히, 경찰은 그를 건강한 상태로 발견했고, 그는 그 충격적인 사건 이후 정서적인 안정을 되찾았다.

STEP 01 단어 암기

A boy the babysitter <u>took care of</u> was <u>missing</u>. <u>Fortunately</u>, police <u>found</u> him in
(동) 돌보았다   (형) 실종된   (부) 다행히   (동) 발견했다

good <u>health</u> and he <u>restored</u> <u>emotional</u> <u>stability</u> <u>after</u> the <u>traumatic</u> <u>event</u>.
(명) 건강   (동) 되찾다   (형) 감정적인   (명) 안정성   (전) ~후   (형) 충격적인   (명) 사건

STEP 02 구문 분석 훈련 (명사 뒤 주어동사에 표시한 후 구문을 분석해보자.)

A boy the babysitter took care of was missing. Fortunately, police found him in

good health and he restored emotional stability after the traumatic event.

STEP 03 동의어 훈련

A boy the babysitter took care of was missing. Fortunately, police found him in good health and he <u>restored</u> emotional stability after the traumatic event.

Q: In the context of the passage, <u>restored</u> means _____.

(a) regained
(b) replaced
(c) reconstructed
(d) reconciled

Day 04

038

> One of the reasons consumers shop online is that they can compare a number of products at a time and get instant access to product reviews.
>
> 소비자들이 온라인 쇼핑을 하는 이유 중 하나는 많은 제품을 즉시 비교할 수 있고 제품 후기에 즉각적으로 접근할 수 있다는 것이다.

STEP 01 단어 암기

One of the reasons consumers shop online is that they can compare a number
~중 하나 (명) 이유 (명) 소비자 (동) 쇼핑하다 (접) ~것 (동) 비교하다 수많은

of products at a time and get instant access to product reviews.
(명) 제품 한 번에 (동) 얻다 (형) 즉각적인 (명) 접근 (전) ~에 대한 (명) 리뷰

STEP 02 구문 분석 훈련 (명사 뒤 주어동사에 표시한 후 구문을 분석해보자.)

One of the reasons consumers shop online is that they can compare a number

of products at a time and get instant access to product reviews.

STEP 03 ▶ 동의어 훈련

One of the reasons consumers shop online is that they can compare a number of products at a time and get <u>instant</u> access to product reviews.

Q: In the context of the passage, <u>instant</u> means _____.

(a) unexpected
(b) abrupt
(c) sudden
(d) immediate

039

Jack thinks that cooking is a waste of time and wants to reduce his cooking time. Therefore, he has attempted to halve the time he spends cooking by preparing the ingredients in advance.

잭은 요리가 시간 낭비라고 생각하며 요리하는 시간을 줄이고 싶어한다. 그래서 그는 미리 재료를 준비해서 요리하는 시간을 반으로 줄이려고 시도해오고 있다.

STEP 01 단어 암기

Jack thinks that cooking is a <u>waste</u> of time and wants to <u>reduce</u> his cooking time.
(명) 낭비 / (동) 감소시키다

<u>Therefore</u>, he has <u>attempted</u> to <u>halve</u> the time he <u>spends</u> cooking <u>by preparing</u>
(부) 그러므로 / (동) 시도하다 / (동) 반으로 줄이다 / (동) 보내다 / 준비함으로써

the <u>ingredients</u> <u>in advance</u>.
(명) 재료 / 미리

STEP 02 구문 분석 훈련 (명사 뒤 주어동사에 표시한 후 구문을 분석해보자.)

Jack thinks that cooking is a waste of time and wants to reduce his cooking time.

Therefore, he has attempted to halve the time he spends cooking by preparing

the ingredients in advance.

STEP 03 동의어 훈련

Jack thinks that cooking is a waste of time and wants to <u>reduce</u> his cooking time.

Therefore, he has attempted to halve the time he spends cooking by preparing

the ingredients in advance.

Q: In the context of the passage, <u>reduce</u> means _____.

(a) shorten
(b) swell
(c) remove
(d) abandon

Day
04

040

> **Technologies have brought so many changes in our lives. For example, computers have changed the way we work significantly. Similarly, smartphones have changed the way we shop.**
>
> 기술은 우리 삶에 너무 많은 변화를 가져오고 있다. 예를 들어, 컴퓨터는 우리가 일하는 방식을 상당히 변화시켜오고 있다. 유사하게, 스마트폰은 우리가 쇼핑하는 방법을 변화시켜오고 있다.

STEP 01 단어 암기

Technologies have brought so many changes in our lives. For example, computers
(명) 기술　　　(동) 가져오고 있다　(부) 너무　　(명) 변화　　　　(명) 삶　　(부) 예를 들어

have changed the way we work significantly. Similarly, smartphones have changed
(동) 변화시키다　　(명) 방식　　　(부) 상당히　　(부) 유사하게

the way we shop.
(동) 쇼핑하다

STEP 02 구문 분석 훈련 (명사 뒤 주어동사에 표시한 후 구문을 분석해보자.)

Technologies have brought so many changes in our lives. For example, computers

have changed the way we work significantly. Similarly, smartphones have

changed the way we shop.

STEP 03 동의어 훈련

Technologies have brought so many changes in our lives. For example, computers have changed the way we work <u>significantly</u>. Similarly, smartphones have changed the way we shop.

Q: In the context of the passage, <u>significantly</u> means _____.

(a) perfectly
(b) absolutely
(c) considerably
(d) ideally

Day 04

Day 05

켈리의 지텔프 **해석 POINT** **5**

관계사절 ① 관계사절 묶기

② 앞에 있는 명사를 수식하며 관계사절 안에 있는 동사는 '~다'가 아닌

'~ㄴ'으로 해석

관계사는 관계대명사와 관계부사로 분류되며 다음과 같다.

관계 대명사 : who, whom, which, that 등

관계 부사 : where, when 등

관계사는 '형용사절'이다. 형용사는 보통 'ㄴ' 받침으로 끝난다. 따라서 관계사 절에 안에 존재하는 동사의 해석은 '~다'가 아닌 'ㄴ' 받침으로 끝나야 한다. 예문을 살펴보자.

I know a girl who likes him.

관계사절은 'who likes him'인데 이때의 해석은 위에서 설명한 것처럼 '그를 좋아한다'가 아닌 '그를 좋아하는'이 된다. 'who likes him'은 앞에 있는 a girl을 수식해주며 이 문장 전체는 '나는 그를 좋아하는 소녀를 알고 있다'가 된다. 정리하면 관계사가 나오면 관계사가 속한 절을 묶은 후 앞에 있는 명사를 수식해주면 된다. 물론 관계사절이 너무 길 경우에는 다른 방법으로 해석하는 방법도 있다. 그 방법은 관계사와 관계된 10개의 필수구문을 학습하면서 공부해보도록 하자.

아마 궁금해하는 수험생이 있을 것 같다. that은 분명 '켈리의 해석 포인트 2'에서 '것'으로 해석되는 접속사로 알고 있었는데 'that'이 관계대명사 역할도 한다고? '켈리의 지텔프 해석 포인트' 중 겨우 4개의 법칙만 공부했지만, 문법적인 궁금증이 혹시 생겼을 수험생들을 위해 that에 대해 문법적인 이야기를 조심스럽게 꺼내려고 한다. 만약 여기에서 혼란스럽거나 머리가 아파지기 시작한다면 일단 이 부분은 스킵하도록 하자. that은 하는 역할이 굉장히 많다. 그 중 '해석 포인트 2'에서 나온 접속사 that과 '해석 포인트 4'에 나올 관계대명사 that을 설명할 것이다. 도대체 접속사 that과 관계대명사 that의 차이는 무엇일까?

접속사 that의 특징은 다음과 같다.
① 접속사에 걸린 동사의 해석 : 것   ② 뒷문장 완전 ③ 보통 동사 뒤에 위치

관계 대명사 that의 특징은 다음과 같다.
① 관계사에 걸린 동사의 해석 : 'ㄴ' ② 뒷문장 불완전 (주어나 목적어가 없음) ③ 보통 명사 뒤에 위치

'I know that she is kind.'에서 that은 무엇일까? that 뒷문장에 'she is kind'라는 완전한 문장이 왔기 때문에 접속사이며 이 때의 해석은 '나는 그녀가 친절하다는 것을 안다'이다.

'I have a book that is interesting.'에서 that은 무엇일까? that 뒷문장에 주어가 빠진 'is interesting'이라는 불완전한 문장이 왔기 때문에 관계대명사이며 이 때의 해석은 '나는 흥미로운 책을 가지고 있다'이다. 어려워할 것 없다. 우리는 이제 관계사를 묶고 앞에 있는 명사를 수식하는 훈련을 할 것이다.

필수문장 041

> Whenever Molly is not able to sleep well at night, she takes sleeping pills which help to induce sleep.
>
> 몰리는 밤에 잠을 제대로 잘 수 없을 때마다 잠을 유도하는데 도움이 되는 수면제를 먹는다.

 STEP 01 단어 암기

Whenever Molly is not able to sleep well at night, she takes sleeping pills which
(접) ~할 때마다   ~할 수 있는 (동) 자다 (부) 잘   (동) 복용하다   수면제

help to induce sleep.
      (동) 유도하다 (명) 잠

 STEP 02 구문 분석 훈련

Whenever Molly is not able to sleep well at night, she takes sleeping pills which

help to induce sleep.

STEP 03 동의어 훈련 (관계사절과 선행사를 표시한 후 구문을 분석해보자.)

Whenever Molly is not able to sleep well at night, she takes sleeping pills which help to <u>induce</u> sleep.

Q: In the context of the passage, <u>induce</u> means _____.

(a) persuade
(b) facilitate
(c) inspire
(d) disdain

042

> **People who want to get plastic surgery should understand the potential medical risks and get enough information to avoid harmful effects.**
>
> 성형수술을 받기 원하는 사람들은 잠재적인 의료적 위험에 대해 이해하고 해로운 영향을 피할 수 있도록 충분한 정보를 얻어야 한다.

STEP 01 단어 암기

People who want to get <u>plastic surgery</u> should <u>understand</u> the <u>potential</u> <u>medical</u>
　　　　　　　　　　　　성형수술　　　　　　　　　(동) 이해하다　　(형) 잠재적인　(형) 의료의

<u>risks</u> and get <u>enough</u> <u>information</u> to <u>avoid</u> <u>harmful</u> effects.
(명) 위험　　　　　(형) 충분한　　(명) 정보　　　(동) 피하다　(형) 해로운

STEP 02 구문 분석 훈련 (관계사절과 선행사를 표시한 후 구문을 분석해보자.)

People who want to get plastic surgery should understand the potential medical

risks and get enough information to avoid harmful effects.

동의어 훈련

People who want to get plastic surgery should understand the potential medical risks and get enough information to avoid <u>harmful</u> effects.

Q: In the context of the passage, <u>harmful</u> means _____.

(a) painful
(b) bothersome
(c) irritating
(d) detrimental

043

> People who spend long hours on computers may experience a
> headache. You should take a break when you are on a computer.
>
> 컴퓨터에서 오랜 시간을 보내는 사람들은 두통을 겪을지도 모른다. 당신은 컴퓨터를 사용 할 때 휴식
> 을 취해야 한다.

STEP 01 단어 암기

People who spend long hours on computers may experience a headache. You
          (형) 긴 (명) 시간   (동) 경험하다   (명) 두통

should take a break when you are working on a computer.
    휴식을 취하다

STEP 02 구문 분석 훈련 (관계사절과 선행사를 표시한 후 구문을 분석해보자.)

People who spend long hours on computers may experience a headache. You

should take a break when you are on a computer.

STEP 03 동의어 훈련

People who spend long hours on computers may <u>experience</u> a headache. You should take a break when you are on a computer.

Q: In the context of the passage, <u>experience</u> means _____.

(a) have
(b) confront
(c) meet
(d) approach

Day
05

044

Jack is a famous pianist. However, he is also a comic book writer who has won many awards in comic book contests.

잭은 유명한 피아니스트이다. 하지만 그는 만화책 대회에서 많은 상을 받은 만화책 작가이기도 하다.

 STEP 01 단어 암기

Jack is a <u>famous</u> pianist. However, he is <u>also</u> a comic book writer who <u>has won</u>
　　　　　(형) 유명한　　　　　　　　　　　(부) 또한　　　　　　　　　(동) 타오고 있다

many <u>awards</u> in <u>comic book</u> <u>contests</u>.
　　　(명) 상　　　　(명) 만화책　　(명) 경기, 대회

STEP 02 구문 분석 훈련 (관계사절과 선행사를 표시한 후 구문을 분석해보자.)

Jack is a famous pianist. However, he is also a comic book writer who has won

many awards in comic book contests.

STEP 03 동의어 훈련

Jack is a famous pianist. However, he is also a comic book writer who has won many awards in comic book <u>contests</u>.

Q: In the context of the passage, <u>contests</u> means _____ .

(a) finals
(b) games
(c) competitions
(d) occurrence

Day 05

필수문장 045

A boy who physically hurt a man on purpose and went to jail managed to get out of jail after he paid the full bail amount.

고의로 한 남자를 다치게 하고 감옥에 간 소년은 보석금 전액을 지불한 후 가까스로 감옥에서 나왔다.

 STEP 01 단어 암기

A boy who <u>physically</u> <u>hurt</u> a man <u>on purpose</u> and went to <u>jail</u> <u>managed to</u>
(부) 신체적으로　(동) 다치게 했다　　의도적으로　　　　　　(명) 감옥　(동) 가까스로 ~했다

<u>get out of</u> jail after he <u>paid</u> the <u>full</u> <u>bail</u> <u>amount</u>.
(동) ~에서 나오다　　　　　(동) 지불했다　(형) 완전한 (명) 보석금 (명) 총액, 양

STEP 02 구문 분석 훈련 (관계사절과 선행사를 표시한 후 구문을 분석해보자.)

A boy who physically hurt a man on purpose and went to jail managed to get out of jail after he paid the full bail amount.

STEP 03 동의어 훈련

A boy who physically <u>hurt</u> a man on purpose and went to jail managed to get out of jail after he paid the full bail amount.

Q: In the context of the passage, <u>hurt</u> means _____.

(a) destroyed
(b) ruined
(c) crashed
(d) injured

Day 05

046

> Jack is crazy about spicy Mexican food which has a strong flavor from spices. However, his mom suggested that he avoid eating too much spicy food because it is harmful to his health.
>
> 잭은 향신료를 사용한 강한 향을 함유한 멕시코 음식에 열광한다. 하지만, 그의 엄마는 그에게 건강에 해롭기 때문에 너무 매운 음식을 먹는 것을 피해야 한다고 제안했다.

 단어 암기

Jack is <u>crazy</u> <u>about</u> spicy Mexican food which has a strong <u>flavor</u> <u>from</u> <u>spices</u>.
(형) 열광한 (전) ~에 대해   (명) 맛   (전) ~로부터 (명) 향신료

However, his mom <u>suggested</u> that he <u>avoid</u> eating too much spicy food because
(동) 제안하다   (동) 피하다

it is <u>harmful</u> <u>to</u> his <u>health</u>.
(형) 형용사   (전) ~에   (명) 건강

STEP 02 구문 분석 훈련 (관계사 절을 괄호로 묶고 선행사와 연결해주세요.)

Jack is crazy about spicy Mexican food which has a strong flavor from spices.

However, his mom suggested that he avoid eating too much spicy food because

it is harmful to his health.

STEP 03 동의어 훈련

Jack is crazy about spicy Mexican food which has a strong flavor from spices. However, his mom suggested that he <u>avoid</u> eating too much spicy food because it is harmful to his health.

Q: In the context of the passage, <u>avoid</u> means _____.

(a) stop
(b) keep
(c) illegalize
(d) persist

Day 05

필수문장 047

Ross didn't pay back his student loan when he earned a salary. Instead, he bought a company's stock which a colleague recommended.

로스는 월급을 받았을 때 학자금 대출금을 갚지 않았다. 대신, 그는 동료가 추천한 회사의 주식을 샀다.

 STEP 01 단어 암기

Ross didn't <u>pay back</u> his student <u>loan</u> when he <u>earned</u> a <u>salary</u>. <u>Instead</u>, he <u>bought</u>
(동) 상환하다   (명) 대출   (동) 벌다   (명) 월급   (부) 대신에   (동) 샀다

a <u>company</u>'s <u>stock</u> which a <u>colleague</u> <u>recommended</u>.
(명) 회사   (명) 주식   (명) 동료   (동) 추천하다

 STEP 02 구문 분석 훈련 (관계사절과 선행사를 표시한 후 구문을 분석해보자.)

Ross didn't pay back his student loan when he earned a salary. Instead, he

bought a company's stock which a colleague recommended.

STEP 03 동의어 훈련

Ross didn't pay back his student loan when he was earning a salary. Instead, he <u>bought</u> a company's stock which a colleague recommended.

Q: In the context of the passage, <u>bought</u> means _____.

(a) preserved
(b) secured
(c) purchased
(d) picked

Day 05

048

> Even though the girl who had lost three times in a row in a card game suggested changing the rule in her favor, everyone didn't accept her suggestion.
>
> 카드 게임에서 세 번 연패한 소녀가 그녀에게 유리하게 규칙을 바꾸자고 제안했지만, 모두가 그녀의 제안을 받아들이지 않았다.

 단어 암기

Even though the girl who had lost three times in a row in a card game suggested
(접) 비록 ~일지라도 　　　 (동) 졌다 　　　 연속으로 　　　 (동) 제안하다

changing the rule in her favor, everyone didn't accept her suggestion.
　　　 (명) 규칙 그녀에게 유리하게 (명) 모든 사람 　　 (동) 받아들이다 (명) 제안

STEP 02 구문 분석 훈련 (관계사절과 선행사를 표시한 후 구문을 분석해보자.)

Even though the girl who had lost three times in a row in a card game suggested

changing the rule in her favor, everyone didn't accept her suggestion.

STEP 03 · 동의어 훈련

Even though the girl who had lost three times in a row in a card game suggested changing the rule in her favor, everyone didn't <u>accept</u> her suggestion.

Q: In the context of the passage, <u>accept</u> means _____.

(a) obtain
(b) take
(c) pick
(d) determine

Day 05

필수문장 049

The car offers the option to select a driving mode. Those who want to immerse themselves in the exciting driving experience can select sport mode. In contrast, those who want a smoother ride can select comfort mode.

그 자동차는 주행 모드를 선택할 수 있는 옵션을 제공한다. 신나는 운전 경험을 하고 싶은 사람들은 스포츠 모드를 선택할 수 있다. 반면에, 더 부드러운 승차감을 원하는 사람들은 컴포트 모드를 선택할 수 있다.

STEP 01 단어 암기

The car <u>offers</u> the option to <u>select</u> a driving mode. <u>Those</u> who want to <u>immerse</u>
       (동) 제안하다   (동) 선택하다   (명) 사람들   (동) 몰두하다

<u>themselves</u> in the <u>exciting</u> driving <u>experience</u> can select sport mode. <u>In contrast</u>,
  그들 자신   (형) 신나는   (명) 경험   (부) 대조적으로

those who want a <u>smoother</u> ride can select for <u>comfort</u> mode.
          (형) 더 부드러운   (명) 안락, 편안

STEP 02 구문 분석 훈련 (관계사절과 선행사를 표시한 후 구문을 분석해보자.)

The car offers the option to select a driving mode. Those who want to immerse

themselves in the exciting driving experience can select sport mode. In contrast,

those who want a smoother ride can select comfort mode.

STEP 03 동의어 훈련

The car <u>offers</u> the option to select a driving mode. Those who want to immerse themselves in the exciting driving experience can select sport mode. In contrast, those who want a smoother ride can select comfort mode.

Q: In the context of the passage, <u>offers</u> means _____.

(a) provides
(b) supports
(c) improves
(d) awards

Day 05

필수문장 050

Some retail stores that have suffered sharp sales drop because of the emergence of e-commerce are going through tough times. On the other hand, some retail stores have survived the crisis because they offer things e-commerce cannot replace, including the shopping experience.

전자상거래 등장으로 매출이 급감한 일부 유통점들이 힘든 시간을 겪고 있다. 반면에 일부 소매점들은 쇼핑 경험을 포함하여 전자상거래가 대체할 수 없는 것들을 제공함으로써 위기에서 살아남았다.

 STEP 01 **단어 암기**

Some retail stores that have suffered sharp sales drop because of the emergence
(형) 몇몇의   소매점   (동) 겪다   (형) 급격한   (명) 감소   (전) ~ 때문에   (명) 출현

of e-commerce are going through tough times. On the other hand, some retail
(명) 전자상거래   겪는   (형) 힘든   (부) 반면에

stores have survived the crisis because they offer things e-commerce cannot
(동) 살아남다   (명) 위기   (동) 제공하다

replace, including the shopping experience.
(동) 대체하다 (전) ~을 포함하여   (명) 경험

 STEP 02 **구문 분석 훈련 (관계사절과 선행사를 표시한 후 구문을 분석해보자.)**

Some retail stores that have suffered sharp sales drop because of the emergence

of e-commerce are going through tough times. On the other hand, some retail

stores have survived the crisis because they offer things e-commerce cannot

replace, including the shopping experience.

STEP 03 동의어 훈련

Some retail stores that have suffered sharp sales drop because of the emergence of e-commerce are going through <u>tough</u> times. On the other hand, some retail stores have survived the crisis because they offer things e-commerce cannot replace, including the shopping experience.

Q: In the context of the passage, <u>tough</u> means _____.

(a) resistant
(b) resilient
(c) hard
(d) destructive

Day 05

Day
06

켈리의 지텔프 **해석 POINT 6**

> (준)동사 + 목적어 + 목적 보어 → 목적어의 해석 ① 은/는/이/가 ② 을/를

동사 뒤에 나오는 목적어는 보통 '을/를'이라고 해석한다고 배웠다. 하지만 목적어에 무조건 '을/를'을 붙이면 어색한 경우가 있고 대표적인 경우가 목적어 뒤에 목적보어가 나오는 경우이다. 목적보어라는 것은 목적어를 보충해 주기 위해 나온 것이다. 목적 보어는 목적어의 상태나 행위를 설명해주기 때문에 목적어와만 관련이 있다. 다음 예문을 살펴보자.

I want him to study.

목적어는 him이고 목적 보어는 to study이다. 만약 him이 목적어라서 '을/를'을 붙인다면 해석이 어색해질 것이다. 가령 '나는 그를 원한다 공부하게' 정도로 해석되어 정확한 의미를 파악하기 힘들다. 목적 보어가

있는 경우 목적어의 해석은 1차적으로 '은/는/이/가'로 해석하는 것이 적절하다. 이를 적용하면 '나는 그가 공부하기를 원한다'로 명확히 해석된다. 물론 때로는 목적 보어가 있더라도 목적어의 해석을 '을/를'로 하는 것이 적절한 경우도 있다. 다음 예문을 살펴보자.

I made her happy.

목적어는 her이고 목적 보어는 happy이다. 이 경우에는 '나는 그녀를 행복하게 만들었다'로 해석하는 것이 더 정확하다. 정리하면, 목적 보어 앞에 나오는 목적어의 해석은 대부분 '은/는/이/가'이고 때로는 '을/를'이 적절한 경우도 있다.

필수문장 051

You should choose the right kindergarten if you want your kids to develop valuable social skills.

만약 자녀들이 가치 있는 유용한 사회적 기술을 개발하기 원한다면 올바른 유치원을 선택해야 한다.

 STEP 01 단어 암기

You should <u>choose</u> the <u>right</u> <u>kindergarten</u> if you want your <u>kids</u> to <u>develop</u> <u>valuable</u>
(동) 선택하다　(형) 올바른　(명) 유치원　　　　　　　　　(명) 아이　(동) 발달시키다　(형) 소중한, 유용한

<u>social</u> <u>skills</u>.
(형) 사회적 (명) 기술

 STEP 02 구문 분석 훈련 (목적어와 목적보어에 표시한 후 구문을 분석해 보자.)

You should choose the right kindergarten if you want your kids to develop

valuable social skills.

STEP 03 동의어 훈련

You should choose the right kindergarten if you want your kids to develop <u>valuable</u> social skills.

Q: In the context of the passage, <u>valuable</u> means _____.

(a) lucrative
(b) profitable
(c) useful
(d) extravagant

052

An expert recommends that we stop working from home because it could cause the line between our personal lives and work to blur.

한 전문가는 우리가 집에서 일하는 것을 그만둘 것을 권하는데 그것이 우리의 개인적인 삶과 일 사이의 경계를 흐리게 할 수 있기 때문이다.

STEP 01 단어 암기

An expert recommends that we stop working from home because it could cause
　　(명) 전문가　　(동) 권고하다　　　　　　　　　　　　　　　　　　　　　　　　　　　　　(동) 야기하다

the line between our personal lives and work to blur.
　　(명) 경계　(전) ~사이에　　　(형) 사적인　　　　　　　　　　　(동) 흐리게 하다

STEP 02 구문 분석 훈련 (목적어와 목적보어에 표시한 후 구문을 분석해 보자.)

An expert recommends that we stop working from home because it could cause

the line between our personal lives and work to blur.

STEP 03 동의어 훈련

An expert recommends that we stop working from home because it could cause the <u>line</u> between our personal lives and work to blur.

Q: In the context of the passage, <u>line</u> means _____.

(a) frontier
(b) limit
(c) boundary
(d) edge

053

Jane was under stress because of a colleague interfering with her work. Eventually, she asked her boss to move him to another department.

제인은 자신의 일에 간섭하는 동료 때문에 스트레스를 받았다. 결국, 그녀는 상사에게 그를 다른 부서로 옮겨달라고 부탁했다.

 STEP 01 단어 암기

Jane was under stress <u>because of</u> a <u>colleague</u> <u>interfering with</u> her work. <u>Eventually</u>,
　　　　　　　　　　　　(전) ~때문에　　　(명) 동료　　　~를 방해하는　　　　　　(부) 결국

she <u>asked</u> her <u>boss</u> to <u>move</u> him to <u>another</u> <u>department</u>.
　　(동) 요청하다　　(명) 상사　(동) 옮기다　　　(형) 또 다른　(명) 부서

STEP 02 구문 분석 훈련 (목적어와 목적보어에 표시한 후 구문을 분석해 보자.)

Jane was under stress because of a colleague interfering with her work.

Eventually, she asked her boss to move him to another department.

STEP 03 동의어 훈련

Jane was under stress because of a colleague interfering with her work. Eventually, she <u>asked</u> her boss to move him to another department.

Q: In the context of the passage, <u>asked</u> means _____.

(a) requested
(b) inquired
(c) questioned
(d) forced

054

> Because many people found harmful materials in a popular convenience food, the local health department required supermarkets to stop the sales of the food.
>
> 많은 사람들이 대중적인 편의 음식에서 해로운 물질을 발견했기 때문에, 지역 보건부는 슈퍼마켓에 음식 판매를 중단하도록 요구했다.

STEP 01 단어 암기

Because many people <u>found</u> <u>harmful</u> <u>materials</u> in a <u>popular</u> <u>convenience food</u>, the
　　　　　　　　　(동) 발견했다　(형) 해로운　(명) 물질　　　　(형) 유명한　　　편의 식품

<u>local</u> health <u>department</u> <u>required</u> supermarkets to stop the <u>sales</u> of the food.
(형) 지역의　　　　(명) 부서　　(동) 요구하다　　　　　　　　　　　(명) 판매

STEP 02 구문 분석 훈련 (목적어와 목적보어에 표시한 후 구문을 분석해 보자.)

Because many people found harmful materials in a popular convenience food, the

local health department required supermarkets to stop the sales of the food.

STEP 03 동의어 훈련

Because many people <u>found</u> harmful materials in a popular convenience food, the local health department required supermarkets to stop the sales of the food.

Q: In the context of the passage, <u>found</u> means _____.

(a) diagnosed
(b) perceived
(c) marked
(d) detected

Day 06

필수문장 055

> Mark assigned too much work to Rachel, which caused her to become depressed. Furthermore, she had a problem with her coworker.
>
> 마크는 레이첼에게 너무 많은 일을 할당했고, 그것은 레이첼을 우울하게 만들었다. 게다가, 그녀는 동료와 문제가 있었다.

 STEP 01 단어 암기

Mark <u>assigned</u> too <u>much</u> work to Rachel, which <u>caused</u> her to <u>become</u> <u>depressed</u>.
     (동) 할당하다   (형) 많은   (동) 야기하다   (동) 되다   (형) 우울한

<u>Furthermore</u>, she had a <u>problem</u> with her <u>coworker</u>.
     (부) 게다가   (명) 문제   (명) 동료

 STEP 02 구문 분석 훈련 (목적어와 목적보어에 표시한 후 구문을 분석해 보자.)

Mark assigned too much work to Rachel, which caused her to become depressed.

Furthermore, she had a problem with her coworker.

STEP 03 동의어 훈련

Mark <u>assigned</u> too much work to Rachel, which caused her to become depressed.

Furthermore, she had a problem with her coworker.

Q: In the context of the passage, <u>assigned</u> means _____.

(a) determined
(b) empowered
(c) transferred
(d) gave

필수문장 056

> A company will release a new version of its software next month.
> Its various features will allow you to experience amazing things.
>
> 한 회사가 다음 달에 새로운 버전의 소프트웨어를 출시할 것이다. 그것의 다양한 특징들은 여러분이
> 놀라운 것들을 경험할 수 있게 해 줄 것이다.

 단어 암기

A company will <u>release</u> a new version of its software next month. <u>Its</u> <u>various</u> <u>features</u>
　　　　　　　(동) 출시하다　　　　　　　　　　　　　　　　　　　　그것의 (형) 다양한　(명) 특징

will <u>allow</u> you to <u>experience</u> <u>amazing</u> <u>things</u>.
　　　(동) 허락하다　　　　(동) 경험하다　(형) 놀라운　(명) 것

 구문 분석 훈련 (목적어와 목적보어에 표시한 후 구문을 분석해 보자.)

A company will release a new version of its software next month. Its various

features will allow you to experience amazing things.

STEP 03 동의어 훈련

A company will release a new version of its software next month. Its various _features_ will allow you to experience amazing things.

Q: In the context of the passage, _features_ means _____.

(a) drawbacks
(b) themes
(c) characteristics
(d) appearance

Day 06

필수문장 057

> Parents should teach their children to respect each other and encourage lifelong friendships between siblings because a positive relationship between siblings can lead to higher levels of self-esteem.
>
> 형제간의 긍정적인 관계가 더 높은 수준의 자존감으로 이어질 수 있기 때문에 부모는 자녀들이 서로를 존중하도록 가르치고 형제간의 평생의 우정을 장려해야 한다.

 STEP 01 단어 암기

Parents should teach their children to <u>respect</u> <u>each other</u> and <u>encourage</u> <u>lifelong</u>
(동) 존중하다 서로서로 (동) 장려하다 (형) 평생의

<u>friendships</u> <u>between</u> <u>siblings</u> because a <u>positive</u> <u>relationship</u> between siblings can
(명) 우정 (전) ~사이에서 (명) 형제자매 (형) 긍정적인 (명) 관계

<u>lead to</u> <u>higher</u> levels of <u>self-esteem</u>.
(동) ~로 (형) 더 높은 (명) 자존감
이어지다

 STEP 02 구문 분석 훈련 (목적어와 목적보어에 표시한 후 구문을 분석해 보자.)

Parents should teach their children to respect each other and encourage lifelong

friendships between siblings because a positive relationship between siblings can

lead to higher levels of self-esteem.

Parents should teach their children to <u>respect</u> each other and encourage lifelong friendships between siblings because a positive relationship between siblings can lead to higher levels of self-esteem.

Q: In the context of the passage, <u>respect</u> means _____.

(a) praise
(b) deify
(c) value
(d) admire

058

Employees should attend the training program, which will encourage them to cultivate creativity. Moreover, the program can motivate employees to increase innovation in products and work hard.

직원들은 연수 프로그램에 참석해야 하는데 이것은 그들이 창의성을 기르도록 장려할 것이다. 게다가, 이 프로그램은 직원들의 제품 혁신을 증가시키고 열심히 일하도록 동기를 부여할 수 있다.

 단어 암기

Employees should attend the training program, which will encourage them to cultivate
(명) 직원 　　　　　(동) 참석하다 　　　　　　　　　　　　　　(동) 장려하다 　　　　　(동) 기르다

creativity. Moreover, the program can motivate employees to increase innovation
(명) 창의성 　　(부) 게다가 　　　　　　　　　　(동) 동기부여하다 　　　　(동) 증가시키다 　(명) 혁신

in products and work hard.
　　(명) 제품 　　　　　　(부) 열심히

STEP 02 구문 분석 훈련 (목적어와 목적보어에 표시한 후 구문을 분석해 보자.)

Employees should attend the training program, which will encourage them to

cultivate creativity. Moreover, the program can motivate employees to increase

innovation in products and work hard.

Employees should attend the training program, which will encourage them to cultivate creativity. Moreover, the program can motivate employees to increase innovation in products and work hard.

Q: In the context of the passage, cultivate means _____.

(a) fertilize
(b) foster
(c) learn
(d) absorb

Day
06

필수문장 059

> Some adoptive parents have urged young couples to adopt a child. However, those who want to adopt a child must be financially stable. Unless they meet the financial requirements of adoption, they can't adopt a child.

일부 양부모들은 젊은 부부들에게 아이를 입양하라고 권해오고 있다. 하지만, 아이를 입양하고 싶은 사람들은 재정적으로 안정되어야 한다. 만약 그들이 입양의 재정적 요구사항을 충족시키지 못하면 그들은 입양할 수 없다.

STEP 01 단어 암기

Some <u>adoptive parents</u> have <u>urged</u> young <u>couples</u> to <u>adopt</u> a child.
　　　양부모　　　　　　　(동) 권하다　　　　(명) 부부　　　(동) 입양하다

<u>However</u>, those who want to adopt a child must be <u>financially</u> <u>stable</u>. <u>Unless</u> they
(부) 그러나　　　　　　　　　　　　　　　　　　　　(부) 재정적으로　(명) 안정적인 (접) 만약 ~가 아니라면

<u>meet</u> the <u>financial</u> <u>requirements</u> of <u>adoption</u>, they can't adopt a child.
(동) 충족시키다　(형) 재정적인　(명) 요구조건　　　(명) 입양

STEP 02 구문 분석 훈련 (목적어와 목적보어에 표시한 후 구문을 분석해 보자.)

Some adoptive parents have urged young couples to adopt a child. However, those who want to adopt a child must be financially stable. Unless they meet the financial requirements of adoption, they can't adopt a child.

STEP 03 동의어 훈련

Some adoptive parents have <u>urged</u> young couples to adopt a child. However, those who want to adopt a child must be financially stable. Unless they meet the financial requirements of adoption, they can't adopt a child.

Q: In the context of the passage, <u>urged</u> means _____.

(a) encouraged
(b) pressured
(c) pleaded
(d) forced

Day 06

필수문장 060

> Suzy, a wedding florist, takes a lot of pride in her work and tries to make her customers feel special. Instead of choosing flowers for the wedding by herself, she always allows brides to choose flowers they want for their wedding.
>
> 웨딩 플로리스트인 수지는 자신의 일에 큰 자부심을 갖고 있으며, 고객들이 특별하게 느끼도록 노력한다. 그녀는 결혼식을 위해 꽃을 고르는 대신에, 항상 신부가 결혼식에서 원하는 꽃을 고르도록 한다.

STEP 01 단어 암기

Suzy, a wedding florist, <u>takes</u> <u>a lot of</u> <u>pride</u> in her work and <u>tries to</u> make her
(동) 가지다　(형) 많은　(명) 자부심　　　　(동) 애쓰다

<u>customers</u> feel <u>special</u>. <u>Instead of</u> <u>choosing</u> flowers for the wedding <u>by herself</u>,
(명) 고객　　(형) 특별한　(전) ~대신에　선택하는 것　　　　　　그녀 스스로

she <u>always</u> <u>allows</u> <u>brides</u> to <u>choose</u> flowers they want for their wedding.
(부) 항상　(동) 허락하다 (명) 신부　(동) 선택하다

STEP 02 구문 분석 훈련 (목적어와 목적보어에 표시한 후 구문을 분석해 보자.)

Suzy, a wedding florist, takes a lot of pride in her work and tries to make her

customers feel special. Instead of choosing flowers for the wedding by herself,

she always allows brides to choose flowers they want for their wedding.

STEP 03 동의어 훈련

Suzy, a wedding florist, takes a lot of pride in her work and tries to make her customers feel <u>special</u>. Instead of choosing flowers for the wedding by herself, she always allows brides to choose flowers they want for their wedding.

Q: In the context of the passage, <u>special</u> means _____.

(a) exceptional
(b) superb
(c) arrogant
(d) important

Day 06

Day 07

켈리의 지텔프 **해석** POINT **7**

> **to 부정사의 해석**
> ① ~하기 위해서 ② ~할, ~하는 ③ 것 ④ ~해서 ⑤ ~하기에

to 뒤에 동사원형이 나오면 to 부정사라고 부른다. 품사가 정해져 있지 않기 때문에 부정사라는 이름이 붙었다. 더 쉽게 말하면 하는 역할이 엄청 많다는 것이다. 부정사가 하는 역할은 문법적으로 매우 다양하다. 문법적인 역할이 달라짐에 따라 해석도 달라진다. 부정사의 문법적 역할은 매우 다양하기 때문에 빠른 시간 안에 해석을 훈련하는 것이 목적인 우리에게 to 부정사를 문법적으로 접근하는 것은 비효율적이다. 따라서 '켈리의 지텔프 해석 포인트 7'에서는 부정사를 문법적으로 접근하지 않고 해석적으로 접근할 것이다. 단, 문법적인 것이 궁금한 수험생들을 위해 최소한의 문법적인 설명은 추가하기로 했다.

부정사의 다양한 해석 중에 '켈리의 해석 포인트 7'에서는 가장 많이 나오는 5개의 해석을 학습할 것이다. 그중에서도 '① ~하기 위해서 ② ~할, ~하는 ③ 것' 은 가장 많이 나오는 해석이므로 꼭 암기해야 한다.

① ~하기 위해서

'~하기 위해서'는 to 부정사가 부사로 기능할 때의 해석이다. 보통 문법적으로는 to 부정사의 부사적 용법 중 '목적'으로 분류된다. 부사이기 때문에 괄호로 묶더라도 전체 문장에는 전혀 영향이 없다. 다음의 예문을 살펴보자.

I studied English to pass the exam.

이 문장은 '주어:I 동사:studied 목적어: English'로 분석된다. to pass the exam은 부사로써 수식어이므로 괄호로 묶는다. 영어를 공부한 목적이 시험을 통과하기 위해서이며 '나는 영어를 공부했다 / 시험에 통과하기 위해서'로 해석된다.

② ~할, ~하는

'~할, ~하는'은 to 부정사가 형용사로 기능할 때의 해석이다. 보통 받침이 'ㄴ', 'ㄹ'로 끝나거나 '의'로 끝나면 형용사라고 한다. 따라서 to 부정사의 해석이 'ㄴ', 'ㄹ'로 끝날 때 형용사적 용법으로 분류한다. 형용사의 역할 중 하나가 명사를 수식하는 것이다. 형용사 또한 수식어이므로 괄호로 묶더라도 전체 문장에는 영향이 없다. to 부정사가 '~할, ~하는'으로 해석될 때에는 앞에 있는 명사를 수식해준다. 다음의 예문을 살펴보자.

I have a friend to play with.

to play with가 앞에 있는 명사인 a friend를 수식해주기 때문에 '나는 친구 한 명이 있다 / 함께 놀'이라고 해석된다.

③ 것

'것'은 to 부정사가 명사로 기능할 때의 해석이다. 보통 문법적으로는 to 부정사의 명사적 용법으로 분류된다. 명사는 문장 내에서 '주어, 목적어, 보어'의 역할을 한다. 따라서 '것'으로 해석되는 to 부정사 역시 문장 내에서 '주어, 목적어, 보어'의 역할을 한다. 다음의 예문을 살펴보자.

I want to buy the book.

to buy가 want의 목적어로 쓰였으며 '나는 원한다 / 그 책을 사는 것을(사기를)'로 해석된다.

④ ~해서

'~해서'는 to 부정사가 부사로 기능할 때의 해석이다. 보통 문법적으로는 to 부정사의 부사적 용법 중 '감정의 원인'으로 분류된다. 부사이기 때문에 괄호로 묶더라도 전체 문장에는 전혀 영향이 없다. 감정을 나타내는 형용사 뒤에 나올 경우 '~해서'로 해석된다. 다음의 예문을 살펴보자.

I am pleased to meet you.

pleased '기쁜'을 뜻하는 형용사이다. to 부정사가 감정을 나타내는 형용사 뒤에 왔으므로 '나는 기쁘다 / 당신을 만나서'로 해석된다.

⑤ ~하기에

'~하기에'는 to 부정사가 부사로 기능할 때의 해석이다. 보통 문법적으로는 to 부정사의 부사적 용법 중 '형용사 수식'으로 분류된다. 부사이기 때문에 괄호로 묶더라도 전체 문장에는 전혀 영향이 없다. 형용사 뒤에 나올 경우 '~하기에'로 해석된다. 다음의 예문을 살펴보자.

The book is easy to read.

easy는 '쉬운'을 뜻하는 형용사이다. to 부정사가 형용사 뒤에 왔으므로 '이 책은 쉽다 / 읽기에'로 해석된다.

이 외에도 to 부정사는 '~하다니, (결국)~하다'등의 해석이 있고, 암기해야 할 다양한 표현들도 있다. 하지만 우리의 목표는 가장 많이 나오는 to 부정사의 해석을 단시간에 공부하는 것이므로 to 부정사는 여기까지 정리하기로 한다.

필수문장 061

> Although Mike tried to keep his old dog healthy, the dog vomited several times and refused to eat.
>
> 마이크는 그의 늙은 개를 건강하게 하려고 노력했지만, 그 개는 하루에 여러 번 구토를 했고 먹는 것을 거부했다.

 STEP 01 단어 암기

Although Mike tried to keep his old dog healthy, the dog vomited several times
(접) 비록 ~일지라도　　(동) ~하려고　(동) 유지하다　　　　　(형) 건강한　　　　　(동) 구토하다　(형) 몇 번의
　　　　　　　　　　노력했다

and refused to eat.
　　(동) 거절하다

 STEP 02 구문 분석 훈련 (to 부정사에 표시한 후 구문을 분석해 보자.)

Although Mike tried to keep his old dog healthy, the dog vomited several times

and refused to eat.

 STEP 03 동의어 훈련

Although Mike tried to keep his old dog healthy, the dog vomited several times

and refused to eat.

Q: In the context of the passage, tried means _____.

(a) attempted
(b) ventured
(c) experimented
(d) forced

Day 07

131

필수문장 062

> You should develop the ability to organize your thoughts and support your point logically to express your ideas clearly.
>
> 당신의 아이디어를 분명하게 표현하기 위해서 생각을 정리하는 능력을 개발하고 당신이 말하고자 하는 요점을 논리적으로 뒷받침해야 한다.

 STEP 01 단어 암기

You should <u>develop</u> the <u>ability</u> to <u>organize</u> your <u>thoughts</u> and <u>support</u> your <u>point</u>
(동) 발달시키다 　 (명) 능력 　 (동) 정리하다 　 (명) 생각 　 (동) 뒷받침하다 　 (명) 요점

<u>logically</u> to <u>express</u> your ideas <u>clearly</u>.
(부) 논리적으로 　 (동) 표현하다 　 (부) 분명하게

 STEP 02 구문 분석 훈련 (to 부정사에 표시한 후 구문을 분석해 보자.)

You should develop the ability to organize your thoughts and support your point

logically to express your ideas clearly.

STEP 03 · 동의어 훈련

You should develop the ability to organize your thoughts and support your point

logically to <u>express</u> your ideas clearly.

Q: In the context of the passage, <u>express</u> means _____.

- (a) prove
- (b) extract
- (c) conceal
- (d) communicate

필수문장 063

Judy knows that vacation is an excellent opportunity to read books. She ordered some books online and will read them all this vacation.

주디는 휴가가 책을 읽을 수 있는 좋은 기회라는 것을 안다. 그녀는 인터넷으로 책을 몇 권 주문했고 이번 휴가 때 그것들을 모두 읽을 것이다.

 단어 암기

Judy <u>knows</u> <u>that</u> <u>vacation</u> is an <u>excellent</u> <u>opportunity</u> to read books. She <u>ordered</u>
(동) 알다 (접) ~것 (명) 휴가   (형) 훌륭한   (명) 기회   (동) 주문하다

some books online and will read them all this vacation.

 구문 분석 훈련 (to 부정사에 표시한 후 구문을 분석해 보자.)

Judy knows that vacation is an excellent opportunity to read books. She ordered

some books online and will read them all this vacation.

STEP 03 동의어 훈련

Judy knows that vacation is an excellent <u>opportunity</u> to read books. She ordered some books online and will read them all this vacation.

Q: In the context of the passage, <u>opportunity</u> means _____.

(a) possibility
(b) prospect
(c) chance
(d) anticipation

Day 07

필수문장 064

Many children who live in extreme poverty struggle to meet the basic living expenses. We should take some measures to provide assistance for them.

극심한 빈곤 속에 사는 많은 어린이들이 기본 생활비를 충족하기 위해 고군분투한다. 우리는 그들을 돕기 위해 몇 가지 조치를 취해야 한다.

 단어 암기

Many children who live in <u>extreme</u> <u>poverty</u> <u>struggle</u> to <u>meet</u> the <u>basic</u> living <u>expense</u>.
                               (형) 극심한   (명) 빈곤   (동) 고군분투하다   (동) 충족시키다 (형) 기본적인   (명) 지출

We should <u>take</u> some <u>measures</u> to <u>provide</u> <u>assistance</u> <u>for</u> them.
               (동) 취하다   (명) 조치   (동) 제공하다   (명) 도움   (전) ~를 위해

 구문 분석 훈련 (to 부정사에 표시한 후 구문을 분석해 보자.)

Many children who live in extreme poverty struggle to meet the basic living expense. We should take some measures to provide assistance for them.

STEP 03 동의어 훈련

Many children who live in extreme poverty struggle to meet the basic living expense. We should take some measures to provide <u>assistance</u> for them.

Q: In the context of the passage, <u>assistance</u> means _____.

(a) intervention
(b) service
(c) compensation
(d) support

065

Because the boss always ignores Amy, she is under too much stress, which is causing hair loss. She is going to buy a special shampoo which strengthens each strand of hair to stop hair loss.

상사가 항상 에이미를 무시해서 그녀는 너무 많은 스트레스를 받고 있고, 이것이 탈모를 유발하고 있다. 그녀는 탈모를 막기 위해 머리카락의 각 가닥을 강화해주는 특별한 샴푸를 살 것이다.

STEP 01 단어 암기

Because the boss <u>always</u> <u>ignores</u> Amy, she <u>is</u> <u>under</u> too much stress, which is
(부) 항상   (동) 무시하다   (동) 있다 (전) ~중에, ~아래

<u>causing</u> hair <u>loss</u>. She <u>is</u> <u>going to</u> <u>buy</u> a <u>special</u> shampoo which <u>strengthens</u>
유발하는   탈모   (동) ~할 예정이다 (동) 사다 (형) 특별한   (동) 강화시키다

<u>each</u> <u>strand</u> of hair to <u>stop</u> hair loss.
(형) 각각의 (명) 가닥   (동) 멈추다

STEP 02 구문 분석 훈련 (to 부정사에 표시한 후 구문을 분석해 보자.)

Because the boss always ignores Amy, she is under too much stress, which is

causing hair loss. She is going to buy a special shampoo which strengthens each

strand of hair to stop hair loss.

STEP 03 동의어 훈련

Because the boss always ignores Amy, she is under too much stress, which is causing hair loss. She is going to buy a special shampoo which strengthens each strand of hair to <u>stop</u> hair loss.

Q: In the context of the passage, <u>stop</u> means _____.

(a) prevent
(b) finish
(c) pause
(d) complete

066

> To make the best salad dressing, Ross tried mixing various ingredients such as vinegar and olive oil. Finally, he could make the perfect dressing by using yogurt and Dijon mustard.
>
> 로스는 최고의 샐러드 드레싱을 만들기 위해, 식초와 올리브 오일과 같은 다양한 재료들을 섞었다. 마침내, 그는 요거트와 디종 머스타드를 사용함으로써 완벽한 드레싱을 만들 수 있었다.

STEP 01 단어 암기

To make the best salad dressing, Ross <u>tried</u> <u>mixing</u> <u>various</u> <u>ingredients</u> <u>such as</u>
　　　　　　　　　　　　　　　　　　　(동) 시도했다　섞는 것　(형) 다양한　(명) 재료　가령

<u>vinegar</u> and olive oil. <u>Finally,</u> he could make the <u>perfect</u> dressing <u>by using</u> yogurt
(명) 식초　　　　　　　　(부) 마침내　　　　　　　(형) 완벽한　　사용함으로써

and Dijon mustard.

STEP 02 구문 분석 훈련 (to 부정사에 표시한 후 구문을 분석해 보자.)

To make the best salad dressing, Ross tried mixing various ingredients such as

vinegar and olive oil. Finally, he could make the perfect dressing by using yogurt

and Dijon mustard.

STEP
03 동의어 훈련

To make the best salad dressing, Ross tried <u>mixing</u> various ingredients such as vinegar and olive oil. Finally, he could make the perfect dressing by using yogurt and Dijon mustard.

Q: In the context of the passage, <u>mixing</u> means _____.

(a) combining
(b) shaking
(c) constructing
(d) synthesizing

필수문장 067

The doctor recommended that Jenny take essential nutrients through the diet to maintain optimal health and enjoy her life. Nevertheless, she keeps on eating only a single food item for each meal to lose weight.

의사는 제니가 최적의 건강을 유지하고 인생을 즐기기 위해서 식단을 통해 필수적인 영양소를 섭취할 것을 권고했다. 그럼에도 불구하고, 그녀는 살을 빼기 위해 매 끼니마다 단 하나의 음식만을 먹는다.

 단어 암기

The doctor <u>recommended</u> <u>that</u> Jenny <u>take</u> <u>essential</u> <u>nutrients</u> <u>through</u> the <u>diet</u>
　　　　(동) 권고하다　(접) ~것　　　(동) 섭취하다 (형) 필수적인 (명) 영양소　(전) ~을 통해서　(명) 식단

to <u>maintain</u> <u>optimal</u> health and <u>enjoy</u> her life. <u>Nevertheless</u>, she <u>keeps on</u> eating
　　(동) 유지하다 (형) 최적의　　　　(동) 즐기다　　　(부) 그럼에도 불구하고　　(동) 계속 ~하다

<u>only</u> a <u>single</u> food <u>item</u> for each meal to <u>lose</u> <u>weight</u>.
(부) 오직　(형) 하나의　　(명) 품목, 항목　　　　　　　(동) 빼다 (명) 몸무게

 구문 분석 훈련 (to 부정사에 표시한 후 구문을 분석해 보자.)

The doctor recommended that Jenny take essential nutrients through the diet to

maintain optimal health and enjoy her life. Nevertheless, she keeps on eating only

a single food item for each meal to lose weight.

동의어 훈련

The doctor recommended that Jenny <u>take</u> essential nutrients through the diet to maintain optimal health and enjoy her life. Nevertheless, she keeps on eating only a single food item for each meal to lose weight.

Q: In the context of the passage, <u>take</u> means _____.

(a) devour
(b) swallow
(c) consume
(d) digest

Day
07

068

My father had wanted to build a factory to make custom furniture in London. However, he gave up because he didn't have enough money to build a factory.

아버지는 런던에 맞춤 가구를 만들기 위해 공장을 짓고 싶어 한다. 하지만, 그는 공장을 지을 충분한 돈이 없었기 때문에 포기했다.

STEP 01 단어 암기

My father had wanted to <u>build</u> a <u>factory</u> to make <u>custom furniture</u> in London.
(동) 짓다, 세우다   (명) 공장   맞춤 가구

However, he <u>gave up</u> because he didn't have <u>enough</u> money to build a factory.
(동) 포기했다   (형) 충분한

STEP 02 구문 분석 훈련 (to 부정사에 표시한 후 구문을 분석해 보자.)

My father had wanted to build a factory to make custom furniture in London.

However, he gave up because he didn't have enough money to build a factory.

STEP 03 동의어 훈련

My father had wanted to build a factory to <u>make</u> custom furniture in London.

However, he gave up because he didn't have enough money to build a factory.

Q: In the context of the passage, <u>make</u> means _____.

(a) design
(b) plan
(c) exhibit
(d) manufacture

Day 07

필수문장 069

Many small companies need to take a new approach to overcome the financial crisis and achieve their goal. Otherwise, they would stop operating and go out of business.

많은 중소기업들이 금융위기를 극복하고 목표를 달성하기 위해 새로운 접근법을 취해야 한다. 그렇지 않으면, 그들은 운영을 그만두고 폐업할 것이다.

 STEP 01 단어 암기

Many small companies need to <u>take</u> a new <u>approach</u> to <u>overcome</u> the <u>financial</u>
　　　　　　　　　　　　　　　(동) 취하다　　　　(명) 접근법　　　(동) 극복하다　　　(형) 재정적인

<u>crisis</u> and <u>achieve</u> <u>their</u> <u>goal</u>. <u>Otherwise</u>, they would stop <u>operating</u> and <u>go out</u>
(명) 위기　　　(동) 성취하다　그들의　(명) 목표　(부) 만약 그렇지 않으면　　　　　　운영하는 것

<u>of business</u>.
(동) 폐업하다

 STEP 02 구문 분석 훈련 (to 부정사에 표시한 후 구문을 분석해 보자.)

Many small companies need to take a new approach to overcome the financial

crisis and achieve their goal. Otherwise, they would stop operating and go out

of business.

STEP 03 동의어 훈련

Many small companies need to <u>take</u> a new approach to overcome the financial

crisis and achieve their goal. Otherwise, they would stop operating and go out

of business.

Q: In the context of the passage, <u>take</u> means _____.

(a) exclude
(b) adopt
(c) acquire
(d) keep

Day 07

필수문장 070

Because Rachel's father promised to give some money to her if she solved a difficult math problem, she made an effort to work through the problem.

레이첼의 아버지가 어려운 수학 문제를 풀면 돈을 주겠다고 약속했기 때문에, 그녀는 그 문제를 해결하려고 노력했다.

 STEP 01 단어 암기

Because Rachel's father <u>promised</u> to give some money to her if she <u>solved</u> a <u>difficult</u>
(동) 약속하다 　　　　　　　　　　　　　　　　　　(동) 해결하다 　(형) 어려운

<u>math</u> problem, she made an <u>effort</u> to <u>work through</u> the problem.
(명) 수학 　　　　　　　　　(명) 노력 　(동) 해치우다, 해결하다

 STEP 02 구문 분석 훈련 (to 부정사에 표시한 후 구문을 분석해 보자.)

Because Rachel's father promised to give some money to her if she solved a

difficult math problem, she made an effort to work through the problem.

동의어 훈련

Because Rachel's father promised to give some money to her if she solved a difficult math problem, she made an effort to work through the problem.

Q: In the context of the passage, difficult means _____.

(a) challenging
(b) punishing
(c) stressful
(d) cruel

Day 08

켈리의 지텔프 **해석** POINT **8**

> V-ing (동명사) → '것'으로 해석

동사에 ing가 붙은 형태를 동명사라고 부른다. '것'으로 해석되며 명사의 기능을 한다. 사실 동사에 ing가 붙었다고 해서 무조건 동명사는 아니다. 현재분사일 수도 있는데 이것은 '켈리의 지텔프 해석 포인트 9'에서 학습할 예정이다. '켈리의 지텔프 해석 포인트 8' 에서는 주어나 목적어 자리에 동명사가 와서 '것'으로 해석되는 경우를 공부할 것이다. 다음 예문을 살펴보자.

Studying English is hard.

주어는 studying이며 '공부하다'가 아닌 '공부하는 것은'으로 해석되기 때문에 전체 문장은 '영어를 공부하는 것은 / 어렵다'로 해석된다. 이번에는 동명사가 목적어 자리에 온 예문을 살펴보자.

I enjoy studying English.

동명사인 studying이 목적어 자리에 왔다. 이 경우 '공부하는 것을'로 해석되기 때문에 전체 문장은 '나는 즐긴다 / 영어를 공부하는 것을'로 해석된다.

071

A doctor warns that drinking too much can cause serious health problems.

한 의사는 술을 너무 많이 마시는 것은 심각한 건강 문제를 일으킬 수 있다고 경고한다.

 단어 암기

A doctor <u>warns</u> that <u>drinking</u> too much can <u>cause</u> <u>serious</u> health problem.
　　　　　(동) 경고하다　　　　마시는 것　　　　　　　　(동) 유발하다 (형) 심각한

STEP 02 구문 분석 훈련 (V-ing에 표시한 후 구문을 분석해 보자.)

A doctor warns that drinking too much can cause serious health problem.

STEP 03 동의어 훈련

A doctor warns that drinking too much can cause <u>serious</u> health problem.

Q: In the context of the passage, <u>serious</u> means _____.

(a) abrupt
(b) severe
(c) common
(d) insignificant

Day 08

072

Involving children in household chores has many advantages. For example, getting children to clean their room can make them feel needed.

아이들을 집안일에 참여시키는 것은 많은 이점이 있다. 예를 들어, 아이들이 방을 청소하도록 하는 것은 그들이 필요한 존재라고 느끼게 할 수 있다.

 STEP 01 단어 암기

Involving children in household chores has many advantages. For example, getting
참여시키는 것　　　　　　　가족의　(명) 잡일　　　　(명) 이점　　(부) 예를 들어　시키는 것

children to clean their room can make them feel needed.
(동) 청소하다　　　　　　　　　　　　　　　(형) 필요로 되는

STEP 02 구문 분석 훈련 (V-ing에 표시한 후 구문을 분석해 보자.)

Involving children in household chores has many advantages. For example,

getting children to clean their room can make them feel needed.

Involving children in household chores has many advantages. For example, getting children to clean their room can make them feel needed.

Q: In the context of the passage, Involving means _____.

(a) Excluding
(b) Engaging
(c) Forcing
(d) Withdrawing

073

> When you start a restaurant, finding the perfect location for it is so important. Unless it is in a good location, you will fail to attract many customers.
>
> 식당을 시작할 때, 완벽한 장소를 찾는 것은 매우 중요하다. 좋은 위치에 있지 않다면, 많은 손님들을 끌어들이는 데 실패할 것이다.

STEP 01 단어 암기

When you start a restaurant, finding the perfect location for it is so important. Unless
(접) ~할 때   (형) 완벽한   (명) 위치   (부) 너무 (형) 중요한   (접) 만약
  ~가 아니라면

it is in a good location, you will fail to attract many customers.
(동) 실패하다   (동) 끌어들이다   (명) 고객

STEP 02 구문 분석 훈련 (V-ing에 표시한 후 구문을 분석해 보자.)

When you start a restaurant, finding the perfect location for it is so important.

Unless it is in a good location, you will fail to attract many customers.

STEP 03 **동의어 훈련**

When you start a restaurant, finding the <u>perfect</u> location for it is so important. Unless it is in a good location, you will fail to attract many customers.

Q: In the context of the passage, <u>perfect</u> means _____.

(a) eminent
(b) infamous
(c) ideal
(d) majestic

필수문장 074

Until a doctor warned that drinking too much coffee could be harmful to the body by increasing the heartbeat, Judy took in too much caffeine through coffee. The doctor advised her to find alternatives to coffee.

한 의사가 너무 많은 커피를 마시는 것이 심장 박동을 높임으로써 몸에 해로울 수 있다고 경고하기 전까지, 주디는 커피를 통해 너무 많은 카페인을 섭취했다. 의사는 그녀에게 커피 대체재를 찾아보라고 권고했다.

 STEP 01 단어 암기

Until a doctor warned that drinking too much coffee could be harmful to the body
(접) ~까지   (동) 경고하다   (형) 해로운   (전) ~에

by increasing the heartbeat, Judy took in too much caffeine through coffee.
증가시킴으로써   (명) 심장 박동   (동) 섭취했다   (전) ~을 통해서

The doctor advised her to find alternatives to coffee.
        (동) 권고하다   (동) 발견하다   (명) 대체제

 STEP 02 구문 분석 훈련 (V-ing에 표시한 후 구문을 분석해 보자.)

Until a doctor warned that drinking too much coffee could be harmful to the body

by increasing the heartbeat, Judy took in too much caffeine through coffee. The

doctor advised her to find alternatives to coffee.

STEP 03 동의어 훈련

Until a doctor warned that drinking too much coffee could be harmful to the body by increasing the heartbeat, Judy took in too much caffeine through coffee. The doctor advised her to find <u>alternatives</u> to coffee.

Q: In the context of the passage, <u>alternatives</u> means _____.

(a) additives
(b) complements
(c) replacements
(d) ingredients

Day 08

필수문장 075

Because spending too much time playing computer games could lead to migraines, Molly advised her brother to stop playing them. Nevertheless, he ignored her advice and played more intensely to escape reality.

컴퓨터 게임을 하는 것에 너무 많은 시간을 보내는 것은 편두통으로 이어질 수 있기 때문에 몰리는 남동생에게 게임을 그만하라고 충고했다. 그럼에도 불구하고, 그는 그녀의 충고를 무시하고 현실에서 벗어나기 위해 더 강도높게 게임을 했다.

 STEP 01 단어 암기

Because <u>spending</u> too much time playing computer games could <u>lead to</u> <u>migraines</u>,
　　　　　보내는 것　　　　　　　　　　　　　　　　　　　　　　　　(동) ~로 이어지다　(명) 편두통

Molly <u>advised</u> her brother to stop playing them. Nevertheless, he ignored her advice
　　　(동) 조언하다, 충고하다

and played <u>more</u> <u>intensely</u> to <u>escape</u> <u>reality</u>.
　　　　　더욱　(부) 강도높게　　(동) 탈출하다　(명) 현실

 STEP 02 구문 분석 훈련 (V-ing에 표시한 후 구문을 분석해 보자.)

Because spending too much time playing computer games could lead to migraines, Molly advised her brother to stop playing them. Nevertheless, he ignored her advice and played more intensely to escape reality.

STEP 03 동의어 훈련

Because spending too much time playing computer games could lead to migraines, Molly advised her brother to stop playing them. Nevertheless, he <u>ignored</u> her advice and played more intensely to escape reality.

Q: In the context of the passage, <u>ignored</u> means _____.

(a) disregarded
(b) forgot
(c) overlooked
(d) undertook

076

> Amy helps her son to develop responsibility. For example, she always gets him to do chores like mowing the lawn and setting the table because she believes that giving household chores helps him to learn responsibility.
>
> 에이미는 그녀의 아들이 책임감을 발달시키도록 돕는다. 예를 들어, 그녀는 항상 그에게 잔디를 깎고 식탁을 차리는 것과 같은 집안일을 하게 하는데 집안일을 할당해주는 것이 책임감을 배우는 데 도움이 된다고 믿기 때문이다.

STEP 01 단어 암기

Amy helps her son to <u>develop</u> <u>responsibility</u>. <u>For example</u>, she <u>always</u> <u>gets</u> him
　　　　　　　　　　　(동) 발달시키다　　(명) 책임감　　　　　(부) 예를 들어　　　(부) 항상　(동) 시키다

to <u>do</u> chores <u>like</u> <u>mowing</u> the <u>lawn</u> and setting the table because she <u>believes</u>
　(동) 하다　　　(전) ~처럼 (동) 깎다　　(명) 잔디　　　　　　　　　　　　　　　　　(동) 믿다

that giving household chores helps him to <u>learn</u> responsibility.
　　　　　　　　　　　　　　　　　　　　　(동) 알다, 배우다

STEP 02 구문 분석 훈련 (V-ing에 표시한 후 구문을 분석해 보자.)

Amy helps her son to develop responsibility. For example, she always gets him

to do chores like mowing the lawn and setting the table because she believes

that giving household chores helps him to learn responsibility.

STEP 03 동의어 훈련

Amy helps her son to develop responsibility. For example, she always gets him to do chores like mowing the lawn and setting the table because she believes that <u>giving</u> household chores helps him to learn responsibility.

Q: In the context of the passage, <u>giving</u> means _____.

(a) determining
(b) reserving
(c) assigning
(d) permitting

Day
08

필수문장 077

Taking some time to research a company you want to work for online in advance is necessary before you attend a job interview. By doing so, you can make a good impression on your potential employer.

취업 면접에 참석하기 전에 온라인으로 일하고 싶은 회사를 미리 조사하기 위한 시간을 갖는 것이 필요하다. 그렇게 함으로써, 당신은 잠재적인 고용주에게 좋은 인상을 줄 수 있다.

 STEP 01 단어 암기

Taking some time to <u>research</u> a company you want to work for online <u>in advance</u>
(동) 조사하다   미리

is <u>necessary</u> <u>before</u> you <u>attend</u> a <u>job interview</u>. <u>By doing</u> <u>so</u>, you can make a
(형) 필수적인   (접) ~전에   (동) 참석하다   면접   ~함으로써   (부) 그렇게

good <u>impression</u> on your <u>potential</u> <u>employer</u>.
(명) 인상   (형) 잠재적인   (명) 고용인

 STEP 02 구문 분석 훈련 (V-ing에 표시한 후 구문을 분석해 보자.)

Taking some time to research a company you want to work for online in advance

is necessary before you attend a job interview. By doing so, you can make a

good impression on your potential employer.

STEP 03 동의어 훈련

Taking some time to research a company you want to work for online in advance is necessary before you attend a job interview. By doing so, you can make a good impression on your <u>potential</u> employer.

Q: In the context of the passage, <u>potential</u> means _____.

(a) prospective
(b) capable
(c) accessible
(d) pliable

078

> Because a doctor said that eating too much red meat could increase the risk of getting heart disease, Judy decided to choose plant—based diets instead of eating a large amount of meat.
>
> 한 의사가 육류를 너무 많이 섭취하면 심장병에 걸릴 위험을 증가시킬 수 있다고 말했기 때문에, 주디는 많은 양의 고기를 먹는 대신에 식물 위주의 식사를 선택하기로 결정했다.

STEP 01 단어 암기

Because a doctor said that eating too much red <u>meat</u> could <u>increase</u> the <u>risk</u> of
(명) 고기   (동) 증가시키다   (명) 위험

getting <u>heart disease</u>, Judy <u>decided</u> to <u>choose</u> <u>plant—based</u> <u>diets</u> <u>instead of</u> eating
심장병   (동) 결정하다   (동) 선택하다   (형) 식물 기반의   (명) 식단   (전) ~대신에

a large <u>amount</u> of meat.
(명) 양

STEP 02 구문 분석 훈련 (V-ing에 표시한 후 구문을 분석해 보자.)

Because a doctor said that eating too much red meat could increase the risk of

getting heart disease, Judy decided to choose plant—based diets instead of eating

a large amount of meat.

STEP 03 동의어 훈련

Because a doctor said that eating too much red meat could increase the risk of <u>getting</u> heart disease, Judy decided to choose plant−based diets instead of eating a large amount of meat.

Q: In the context of the passage, <u>getting</u> means _____.

(a) mitigating
(b) developing
(c) improving
(d) flourishing

Day 08

079

> **Because Rachel spent too much money on her hobbies, she was short on rent last month. Although having a hobby made her happy, her boyfriend asked her to save money instead of spending on expensive hobbies.**
>
> 레이첼은 취미에 너무 많은 돈을 썼기 때문에, 지난 달에는 집세가 부족했다. 비록 취미를 가지는 것이 그녀를 행복하게 만들었지만, 그녀의 남자친구는 비싼 취미에 많은 돈을 쓰는 대신에 돈을 모으라고 요청했다.

STEP 01 단어 암기

Because Rachel <u>spent</u> too much money on her <u>hobbies</u>, she <u>was short on</u> <u>rent</u> <u>last month</u>.
(동) 썼다   (명) 취미들   ~가 부족하다   (명) 집세   지난 달

<u>Although</u> having a hobby made her happy, her boyfriend <u>asked</u> her to <u>save</u> money
(접) 비록 ~일지라도   (동) 요청하다   (동) 절약하다

instead of spending on <u>expensive</u> hobbies.
(형) 비싼

STEP 02 구문 분석 훈련 (V-ing에 표시한 후 구문을 분석해 보자.)

Because Rachel spent too much money on her hobbies, she was short on rent last month. Although having a hobby made her happy, her boyfriend asked her to save money instead of spending on expensive hobbies.

STEP 03 동의어 훈련

Because Rachel spent too much on her hobbies, she was short on rent last month.

Although having a hobby made her happy, her boyfriend asked her to save

money instead of spending on <u>expensive</u> hobbies.

Q: In the context of the passage, <u>expensive</u> means _____.

(a) costly
(b) abundant
(c) economical
(d) moderate

Day
08

080

> Molly bans employees from wasting time on social media by blocking social networking sites while they are working because she thinks that using social media in the workplace has a negative effect on productivity.
>
> 몰리는 직장에서 소셜 미디어를 사용하는 것이 생산성에 부정적인 영향을 미친다고 생각하기 때문에 직원들이 일하는 동안 소셜 네트워킹 사이트를 차단함으로써 소셜 미디어에서 시간을 낭비하는 것을 금지하고 있다.

STEP 01 단어 암기

Molly bans employees from wasting time on social media by blocking social
     (동) 금지하다 (명) 직원   낭비하는 것   막음으로써

networking sites while they are working because she thinks that using social media
         (접) ~동안   (접) 왜냐하면   사용하는 것

in the workplace has a negative effect on productivity.
   (명) 일터   (형) 부정적인 (명) 영향 (명) 생산성

STEP 02 구문 분석 훈련 (V-ing에 표시한 후 구문을 분석해 보자.)

Molly bans employees from wasting time on social media by blocking social

networking sites while they are working because she thinks that using social

media in the workplace has a negative effect on productivity.

STEP 03 동의어 훈련

Molly bans employees from wasting time on social media by blocking social networking sites while they are working because she thinks that using social media in the workplace has a negative <u>effect</u> on productivity.

Q: In the context of the passage, <u>effect</u> means _____.

(a) result
(b) process
(c) conclusion
(d) evaluation

Day 08

Day 09

켈리의 지텔프 **해석 POINT** **9**

~ing (현재분사)의 해석

① ~하는 ② ~하는 중 ③ ~하면서

'켈리의 해석 포인트 8'에서 V-ing 형태를 동명사라고 부르며 '것'으로 해석된다고 배웠다. 하지만 동사에 ing가 붙으면 현재 분사일 수도 있다. 현재분사를 문법적으로 접근하는 것은 빠른 시간 안에 해석을 훈련하는 것이 목적인 우리에게 비효율적이다. 따라서 '켈리의 지텔프 해석 포인트 9'에서는 현재분사를 문법적으로 접근하지 않고 해석적으로 접근할 것이다. 현재분사의 해석 중 가장 많이 나오는 3개의 해석은 다음과 같다.

① ~하는

V-ing가 명사 앞이나 뒤에 나와 명사를 수식하면 '~(하)는'으로 해석된다. 다음 예문을 살펴보자.

I met a crying boy.

crying은 뒤에 나온 명사 boy를 수식해주며 '나는 만났다 / 울고 있는 소년을'이라고 해석된다.

② ~하는 중

V-ing가 be 동사 (am, are, is, was, were, be, been) 뒤에 나오면 '~하는 중'으로 해석된다. 다음 예문을 살펴보자.

She is studying English now.

studying이 be 동사 뒤에 나왔으므로 '그녀는 공부하는 중이다 / 영어를 / 지금'으로 해석된다.

③ ~하면서

분사구문이라고 불릴 때의 해석이다. 분사구문은 원래 존재하던 접속사를 생략한 표현이다. 따라서 우리는 분사구문을 보고 생략된 접속사가 무엇인지 판단해야 한다. 접속사는 무수히 많지만, 보통 '~하면서'를 뜻하는 as가 생략되었다고 생각하면 쉽다. 물론 자세히 파고 들어가면 굉장히 다양한 해석이 가능하지만, 빠른 시간안에 해석법을 훈련해야 하는 수험생들은 분사구문이 나오는 경우 '~하면서' 정도로 해석하면 된다. 가장 많이 나오는 분사구문의 형태는 다음의 2가지이다. 아래와 같은 형태가 나오면 V-ing를 '~하면서' 정도로 해석하면 대부분 적절하다.

- '주어 + 동사 , V-ing'
- 'V-ing, 주어 + 동사' 일 경우가 대부분 분사구문이다. 다음 예문을 살펴보자.

She is studying English, eating cookies.

, 뒤에 V-ing가 나온 경우 대부분 분사구문이므로 '그녀는 영어를 공부하는 중이다 / 쿠키를 먹으면서' 정도로 해석된다.

081

> Chris wants to get along with his girlfriend's friends, hoping to meet them. However, she hides their current relationship from them.
>
> 크리스는 여자친구의 친구들과 사이좋게 지내고 싶어하고 그들을 만나고 싶어한다. 하지만, 그녀는 그들의 현재 관계를 친구들에게 숨긴다.

 STEP 01 단어 암기

Chris wants to <u>get along with</u> his girlfriend's friends, hoping to <u>meet</u> them.
~와 사이좋게 지내다   (동) 만나다

<u>However,</u> she <u>hides</u> <u>their</u> <u>current</u> <u>relationship</u> <u>from</u> them.
(부) 그러나   (동) 숨기다   그들의   (형) 현재의   (명) 관계   (전) ~로 부터

STEP 02 구문 분석 훈련 (V-ing에 표시한 후 구문을 분석해 보자.)

Chris wants to get along with his girlfriend's friends, hoping to meet them.

However, she hides their current relationship from them.

STEP 03 동의어 훈련

Chris wants to get along with his girlfriend's friends, hoping to meet them. However, she <u>hides</u> their current relationship from them.

Q: In the context of the passage, <u>hides</u> means _____.

(a) conceals
(b) ceases
(c) suspends
(d) deteriorates

082

> Amy is eager to travel around the world, experiencing new ways of living and broadening her horizons. Unfortunately, she doesn't have enough money to travel.
>
> 에이미는 새로운 삶의 방식을 경험하고, 시야를 넓히면서 세계를 여행하길 열망하고 있다. 안타깝게도, 그녀는 여행할 충분한 돈이 없다.

STEP 01 단어 암기

Amy is eager to travel around the world, experiencing new ways of living and
　　　~하길 열망하다　(동) 여행하다　(전) ~주변을　　　　경험하면서　　　　(명) 방식　(명) 생활

broadening her horizons. Unfortunately, she doesn't have enough money to travel.
넓히면서　　　　(명) 시야　　(부) 불행하게도　　　　　　　(형) 충분한

STEP 02 구문 분석 훈련 (V-ing에 표시한 후 구문을 분석해 보자.)

Amy is eager to travel around the world, experiencing new ways of living and

broadening her horizons. Unfortunately, she doesn't have enough money to travel.

STEP 03 동의어 훈련

Amy is eager to travel around the world, experiencing new ways of living and broadening her horizons. Unfortunately, she doesn't have enough money to travel.

Q: In the context of the passage, broadening means _____.

(a) inflating
(b) filling
(c) contracting
(d) expanding

필수문장 083

An aircraft mechanic reported the serious problem with the left engine, adding that the plane must make an emergency landing immediately.

한 항공기 정비사는 왼쪽 엔진에 심각한 문제가 있다고 보고했으며, 비행기가 즉시 비상 착륙해야 한다고 덧붙였다.

 단어 암기

An aircraft mechanic reported the serious problem with the left engine, adding that
　　　(명) 항공기　(명) 정비공　(동) 보고하다　　(형) 심각한　　　　　　　(형) 왼쪽의　　　덧붙이면서　(접) ~것

the plane must make an emergency landing immediately.
　　　　　　　　　　　　　(명) 비상　　　(명) 착륙　　(부) 즉시

 구문 분석 훈련 (V-ing에 표시한 후 구문을 분석해 보자.)

An aircraft mechanic reported the serious problem with the left engine, adding that

the plane must make an emergency landing immediately.

STEP 03 동의어 훈련

An aircraft mechanic reported the serious problem with the left engine, adding that the plane must make an emergency landing <u>immediately</u>.

Q: In the context of the passage, <u>immediately</u> means _____.

(a) punctually
(b) instantly
(c) diligently
(d) prudently

Day 09

084

> **Despite financial problems, E&K has grown into the largest beverage company, generating approximately $500 million of revenue over the last two quarters.**
>
> 재정적인 문제에도 불구하고, E&K는 지난 2분기 동안 약 5억 달러의 매출을 올리며 가장 큰 음료 회사로 성장했다.

 STEP 01 단어 암기

Despite financial problems, E&K has grown into the largest beverage company,
(전) ~에도 불구하고　(형) 재정적인　　　　　　　　(동) 성장해오고 있다　(전) ~로　(형) 가장 큰　(명) 음료　(명) 회사

generating approximately $500 million of revenue over the last two quarters.
만들어내면서　　　(부) 대략　　　(명) 백만　　(명) 수익　(전) ~에 걸쳐　(형) 지난　　(명) 분기

STEP 02 구문 분석 훈련 (V-ing에 표시한 후 구문을 분석해 보자.)

Despite financial problems, E&K has grown into the largest beverage company,

generating approximately $500 million of revenue over the last two quarters.

STEP 03 동의어 훈련

Despite financial problems, E&K has grown into the largest beverage company, generating <u>approximately</u> $500 million of revenue over the last two quarters.

Q: In the context of the passage, <u>approximately</u> means _____.

(a) precisely
(b) roughly
(c) exactly
(d) conservatively

Day 09

085

The new concealer helps men to cover their skin flaws, addressing the specific needs of men. However, in case that it causes skin irritation, stop using it and consult your doctor.

그 새로운 컨실러는 남성들의 특정 욕구를 다루면서 피부 결점을 커버할 수 있도록 도와준다. 만약 그 것이 피부 염증을 일으키는 경우에는 사용을 중지하고 의사와 상담해라.

STEP 01 단어 암기

The new <u>concealer</u> helps men to <u>cover</u> their skin <u>flaws</u>, <u>address</u>ing the <u>specific</u>
      (명) 컨실러   (동) 덮다, 감추다   (명) 결점   다루면서   (형) 특정한

<u>need</u>s of men. <u>However</u>, <u>in case that</u> it <u>causes</u> skin <u>irritation</u>, stop using it and
(명) 욕구   (부) 그러나   (접) ~하는 경우에   (동) 유발하다   (명) 염증

<u>consult</u> your doctor.
(동) 상담하다

STEP 02 구문 분석 훈련 (V-ing에 표시한 후 구문을 분석해 보자.)

The new concealer helps men to cover their skin flaws, addressing the specific

needs of men. However, in case that it causes skin irritation, stop using it and

consult your doctor.

동의어 훈련

The new concealer helps men to cover their skin flaws, <u>addressing</u> the specific needs of men. However, in case that it causes skin irritation, stop using it and consult your doctor.

Q: In the context of the passage, <u>addressing</u> means _____.

(a) withstanding
(b) treating
(c) neglecting
(d) maintaining

필수문장 086

> Using sport mode in your car will make your driving experience more exciting, making your car go faster. However, leaving your car in sport mode all the time could cause some problems.
>
> 자동차에서 스포츠 모드를 사용하는 것은 당신의 차가 더 빨리 가도록 만들면서 당신의 운전 경험을 더욱 흥미진진하게 만들 것이다. 하지만, 항상 스포츠 모드로 두는 것은 문제를 일으킬 수 있다.

STEP 01 단어 암기

Using sport mode in your car will make your driving experience more exciting,
사용하는 것   (명) 경험   더욱   (형) 흥미진진한

making your car go faster. However, leaving your car in sport mode all the time
(부) 더 빠르게   (부) 그러나   두는 것   (부) 항상

could cause some problems.

STEP 02 구문 분석 훈련 (V-ing에 표시한 후 구문을 분석해 보자.)

Using sport mode in your car will make your driving experience more exciting,

making your car go faster. However, leaving your car in sport mode all the time

could cause some problems.

184

STEP 03 동의어 훈련

Using sport mode in your car will make your driving experience more exciting, making your car go faster. However, leaving your car in sport mode all the time can <u>cause</u> some problems.

Q: In the context of the passage, <u>cause</u> means _____.

(a) make
(b) discover
(c) find
(d) resolve

필 수 문 장 087

Matthew had to cancel his summer vacation to Varanasi due to some reasons, giving up his hope of walking along the Ganges River. Instead, he decided to take a break at home, relaxing on the couch and watching movies.

매튜는 몇몇 이유로 인해 갠지스 강을 따라 걷겠다는 희망을 버리고 바라나시로 가는 여름휴가를 취소해야만 했다. 대신, 그는 소파 위에서 느긋하게 쉬면서 영화를 보며 집에서 휴식을 취하기로 결심했다.

 STEP 01 단어 암기

Matthew had to <u>cancel</u> his summer vacation to Varanasi <u>due to</u> some <u>reasons</u>,
　　　　　　　(동) 취소하다　　　　　　　　　　　　　　　　　　(전) ~ 때문에　　　(명) 이유

<u>giving up</u> his hope of walking along the Ganges River. <u>Instead</u>, he <u>decided</u> to
포기하면서　　　　　　　　　　　　　　　　　　　　　　　　(부) 대신에　　　(동) 결정하다

<u>take a break</u> at home, <u>relaxing</u> on the <u>couch</u> and watching movies.
휴식을 취하다　　　　　　　느긋하게 쉬면서　　　(명) 소파

 STEP 02 구문 분석 훈련 (V-ing에 표시한 후 구문을 분석해 보자.)

Matthew had to cancel his summer vacation to Varanasi due to some reasons,

giving up his hope of walking along the Ganges River. Instead, he decided to

take a break at home, relaxing on the couch and watching movies.

Matthew had to cancel his summer vacation to Varanasi due to some reasons, giving up his hope of walking along the Ganges River. Instead, he <u>decided</u> to take a break at home, relaxing on the couch and watching movies.

Q: In the context of the passage, <u>decided</u> means _____.

(a) chose
(b) executed
(c) implemented
(d) proceeded

Day 09

필수문장 088

> Because while a man was doing his shopping, his phone was missing, he requested CCTV footage to locate his phone. CCTV footage showed that a little girl glancing around the store and browsing through a magazine stole the phone from his bag.
>
> 한 남성이 쇼핑을 하던 중 휴대전화가 없어졌기 때문에 휴대전화 위치 파악을 위해 CCTV 영상을 요청했다. CCTV영상은 가게를 둘러보고 잡지를 뒤적이는 한 소녀가 그의 가방에서 전화기를 훔치는 모습을 보여주었다.

 STEP 01 단어 암기

Because <u>while</u> a man was doing his shopping, his phone was <u>missing</u>, he <u>requested</u>
　　　　(접) ~동안　　　　　　　　　　　　　　　　　　　　　　　(형) 분실된　　　(동) 요청하다
CCTV <u>footage</u> to <u>locate</u> his phone. CCTV footage <u>show</u>ed that a little girl <u>glancing</u>
　　　　(명) 화면　　　(동) 찾다　　　　　　　　　　　　　(동) 보여주다　　　　　　　　　　훑어보는
<u>around</u> the <u>store</u> and <u>browsing through</u> a <u>magazine</u> <u>stole</u> the phone from his bag.
(전) ~주변　　　(명) 가게　　　~를 여기저기 훑어보던　　　(명) 잡지　　(동) 훔쳤다

 STEP 02 구문 분석 훈련 (V-ing에 표시한 후 구문을 분석해 보자.)

Because while a man was doing his shopping, his phone was missing, he

requested CCTV footage to locate his phone. CCTV footage showed that a little

girl glancing around the store and browsing through a magazine stole the phone

from his bag.

STEP 03 동의어 훈련

Because while a man was doing his shopping, his phone was missing, he requested CCTV footage to locate his phone. CCTV footage showed that a little girl glancing around the store and browsing through a magazine stole the phone from his bag.

Q: In the context of the passage, stole means _____.

(a) detected
(b) took
(c) surveyed
(d) observed

필수문장 089

Some people take many different supplements at the same time without thinking, which can increase the risk of adverse drug reactions, leading to dangerous effects. Therefore, you should be careful when you are taking them, reading the label carefully.

몇몇 사람들은 다양한 보충제를 생각하지 않고 동시에 복용하는데, 이것은 약물유해반응의 위험을 증가시켜 위험한 결과로 이어질 수 있다. 따라서, 보충제를 복용할 때에는 라벨을 주의 깊게 읽어야 한다.

 STEP 01 단어 암기

Some people <u>take</u> many <u>different</u> <u>supplements</u> <u>at the same time</u> <u>without</u> thinking,
　　　　　　　(동) 복용하다　　　(형) 다양한　　(명) 보충제　　　　　동시에　　　　　(전) ~하지 않고

which can <u>increase</u> the <u>risk</u> of <u>adverse</u> drug <u>reactions</u>, <u>leading to</u> <u>dangerous</u> <u>effects</u>.
　　　　　　(동) 증가시키다　　(명) 위험　(형) 해로운　　　(명) 반응　　~로 이어지면서　(형) 위험한　(명) 영향

<u>Therefore</u>, you should be <u>careful</u> when you are taking them, reading the <u>label</u>
(부) 그러므로　　　　　　　　(형) 신중한　　　　　　　　　　　　　　　　　　　(명) 라벨

<u>carefully</u>.
(부) 주의깊게

 STEP 02 구문 분석 훈련 (V-ing에 표시한 후 구문을 분석해 보자.)

Some people take many different supplements at the same time without thinking,

which can increase the risk of adverse drug reactions, leading to dangerous

effects. Therefore, you should be careful when you are taking them, reading the

label carefully.

STEP 03 동의어 훈련

Some people take many different supplements at the same time without thinking, which can increase the risk of adverse drug reactions, leading to <u>dangerous</u> effects. Therefore, you should be careful when you are taking them, reading the label carefully.

Q: In the context of the passage, <u>dangerous</u> means _____.

(a) devastating
(b) unpleasant
(c) prospective
(d) adequate

Day
09

090

> A non-profit organization is working to offer various academic
> programs for the most vulnerable students. As a result, many
> students who otherwise would not have access to quality
> education have the opportunity to learn.
>
> 한 비영리 단체가 가장 취약한 학생들에서 다양한 학술 프로그램을 제공하기 위해 노력하고 있다. 그
> 결과 그렇지 않았다면 양질의 교육을 받을 수 없었을 많은 학생들이 배울 기회를 가진다.

STEP 01 단어 암기

A <u>non-profit</u> <u>organization</u> is <u>working</u> to <u>offer</u> <u>various</u> <u>academic</u> programs for <u>the</u>
　　비영리의　　　(명) 조직　　　　(동) 노력하다　(동) 제공하다 (형) 다양한　(명) 학문의

<u>most</u> <u>vulnerable</u> students. <u>As a result,</u> many students who <u>otherwise</u> would not
가장　　(형) 취약한　　　　　　(부) 그 결과　　　　　　　　　　(부) 만약 그렇지 않다면

have <u>access</u> to <u>quality</u> <u>education</u> have the <u>opportunity</u> to <u>learn.</u>
　　(명) 접근　　(형) 양질의　(명) 교육　　　　　(명) 기회　　　(동) 배우다

STEP 02 구문 분석 훈련 (V-ing에 표시한 후 구문을 분석해 보자.)

A non-profit organization is working to offer various academic programs for the

most vulnerable students. As a result, many students who otherwise would not

have access to quality education have the opportunity to learn.

STEP 03 동의어 훈련

A non-profit organization is <u>working</u> to offer various academic programs for the most vulnerable students. As a result, many students who otherwise would not have access to quality education have the opportunity to learn.

Q: In the context of the passage, <u>working</u> means _____.

(a) trying
(b) toiling
(c) unwilling
(d) reluctant

Day
09

Day 10

켈리의 지텔프 **해석** POINT **10**

① it (가주어) : 해석 안 함 – to 부정사 (진주어) : '~것은'

② it (가주어) : 해석 안 함 – that 주어 + 동사 (진주어) : '~것은'

영어에서는 주어가 너무 길 경우 주어 자리에 가짜 주어인 'it'을 쓴다. 그리고 진짜 주어를 뒤쪽으로 보내는데 이때 진주어 자리에 'to 부정사'를 쓰거나 'that 주어 + 동사'를 쓴다. 진주어에 'to 부정사'를 쓰는 경우와 'that 주어+동사'를 쓰는 경우를 나누어서 공부해보자.

① 진주어에 to 부정사를 쓰는 경우

It is difficult to learn English.

이때의 it은 가짜이므로 '그것'이라고 해석하지 않는다. 뒤에 있는 'to learn'가 진짜 주어이다. 진짜 주어의 해석은 '~것은'을 붙이면 된다. 따라서 전체 문장은 '어렵다 / 영어를 배우는 것은'으로 해석된다. 그러나 it이 '그것'으로 해석될 때도 있으므로 it과 to가 함께 나왔다고 하여 무조건 가주어-진주어 구문으로 보면 안된다. 다음의 예문을 살펴보자.

I have a book. It is interesting to read.

it은 앞 문장의 a book을 지칭하는 것이므로 '그것'이라고 해석되며 가주어가 아니다. it이 지칭하는 단어나 표현이 없고 뒤에 to 부정사가 나올 경우에만 '켈리의 지텔프 해석 포인트 10'을 활용해야 한다.

② 진주어에 'that + 주어 + 동사'를 쓰는 경우

It is true that he is kind.

이때의 it은 가짜이므로 '그것'이라고 해석하지 않는다. 뒤에 'that he is kind'가 진짜 주어이다. 진짜 주어의 해석은 '~것은'을 붙이면 된다. 따라서 전체 문장은 '사실이다 / 그가 친절하다는 것은'으로 해석된다.

091

> **It is well known that the restaurant is good for a first date because of the perfect lighting.**
>
> 그 식당은 조명이 완벽해서 첫 데이트에 좋다는 사실이 잘 알려져 있다.

 단어 암기

It is <u>well</u> <u>known</u> that the restaurant is good for a first date <u>because of</u>
　　(부) 잘　(형) 알려진　　　　　　　　　　　　　　　　　　　　　　　(전) ~ 때문에

the <u>perfect</u> <u>lighting</u>.
　　(형) 완벽한　(명) 조명

STEP 02 구문 분석 훈련 (가주어와 진주어에 표시한 후 구문을 분석해 보자.)

It is well known that the restaurant is good for a first date because of the perfect

lighting.

STEP 03 동의어 훈련

It is well known that the restaurant is <u>good</u> for a first date because of the perfect lighting.

Q: In the context of the passage, <u>good</u> means _____.

(a) suitable
(b) efficient
(c) admissible
(d) precious

Day 10

필 수 문 장 092

Money may be necessary for happiness. However, it is more important to be satisfied with your life to live a happy life.

돈은 행복을 위해 필요할지도 모른다. 하지만, 행복한 삶을 살기 위해서는 자신의 삶에 만족하는 것이 더 중요하다.

 STEP 01 단어 암기

Money may be <u>necessary</u> for <u>happiness</u>. However, it is more <u>important</u> to be <u>satisfied</u>
         (형) 필수적인   (명) 행복   (형) 중요한   (형) 만족한

with your <u>life</u> to <u>live</u> a happy life.
      (명) 삶   (동) 살다

 STEP 02 구문 분석 훈련 (가주어와 진주어에 표시한 후 구문을 분석해 보자.)

Money may be necessary for happiness. However, it is more important to be satisfied with your life to live a happy life.

STEP 03 동의어 훈련

Money may be necessary for happiness. However, it is more important to be satisfied with your life to live a happy life.

Q: In the context of the passage, satisfied means _____.

(a) proud
(b) prominent
(c) plentiful
(d) contented

Day 10

093

> **It is necessary to prevent global warming from becoming worse.**
> **Therefore, we should do something to save the planet.**
>
> 지구 온난화가 더 심해지는 것을 막을 필요가 있다. 그러므로, 우리는 지구를 구하기 위해 무언가를
> 해야 한다.

STEP 01 단어 암기

It is <u>necessary</u> to <u>prevent</u> <u>global warming</u> from <u>becoming</u> <u>worse</u>. <u>Therefore</u>, we should
　　　(형) 필수적인　　　(동) 막다　　　지구 온난화　　　　　되는것　　(형) 더 악화된　 (부) 그러므로

<u>do</u> <u>something</u> to <u>save</u> the <u>planet</u>.
(동) 하다　(명) 무언가　　(동) 구하다　　(명) 지구, 행성

STEP 02 구문 분석 훈련 (가주어와 진주어에 표시한 후 구문을 분석해 보자.)

It is necessary to prevent global warming from becoming worse. Therefore, we

should do something to save the planet.

STEP 03 동의어 훈련

It is necessary to prevent global warming from becoming worse. Therefore, we should do something to <u>save</u> the planet.

Q: In the context of the passage, <u>save</u> means _____.

(a) reserve
(b) retain
(c) conquer
(d) rescue

094

Although Kate is wealthy enough not to work, she always works hard instead of being lazy. "It is important to continue working to feel alive.", she says.

케이트는 평생 일을 하지 않을 만큼 충분히 부유하지만, 게으름을 피우는 대신에 열심히 일한다. "살아 있다고 느끼기 위해 계속 일하는 것은 중요합니다."라고 그녀는 말한다.

STEP 01 단어 암기

Although Kate is <u>wealthy</u> <u>enough</u> not to work, she always works <u>hard</u> <u>instead of</u>
(접) 비록 ~일지라도 　 (형) 부유한　(부) 충분히　　　　　　　　 (부) 열심히　(전) ~대신에

being <u>lazy</u>. "It is <u>important</u> to <u>continue</u> working to feel <u>alive</u>.", she says.
　　(형) 게으른　　(형) 중요한　　(동) 계속하다　　　　　(형) 살아있는

STEP 02 구문 분석 훈련 (가주어와 진주어에 표시한 후 구문을 분석해 보자.)

Although Kate is wealthy enough not to work, she always works hard instead of

being lazy. "It is important to continue working to feel alive.", she says.

STEP 03 동의어 훈련

Although Kate is wealthy enough not to work, she always works <u>hard</u> instead of being lazy. "It is important to continue working to feel alive.", she says.

Q: In the context of the passage, <u>hard</u> means _____.

(a) necessarily
(b) diligently
(c) roughly
(d) accurately

Day 10

095

> It is beneficial to talk and listen to babies. For example, talking to babies from birth makes them hear different and more words, improving their understanding of language and encouraging them to build communication skills.
>
> 아기들에게 말하고 아기들의 말을 들어주는 것은 이점이 있다. 예를 들어, 태어날 때부터 아기들에게 말하는 것은 그들로 하여금 많은 다양하고 많은 단어들을 들을 수 있게 하고, 언어에 대한 그들의 이해를 향상시키고 의사소통 기술을 쌓도록 장려한다.

STEP 01 단어 암기

It is beneficial to talk and listen to babies. For example, talking to babies from birth
　　　　(형) 이로운　　 (동) 말하다　　(동) 귀를 기울이다　　　　　(부) 예를 들어　　　　　　　　　　　(명) 탄생

makes them hear different and more words, improving their understanding of
　　　　　　　　(형) 다양한　　　　　(명) 낱말, 말　　 향상시키면서　　　　(명) 이해

language and encouraging them to build communication skills.
(명) 언어　　　　장려하면서　　　　　　　(동) 쌓다　 (명) 의사소통　　 (명) 기술

STEP 02 구문 분석 훈련 (가주어와 진주어에 표시한 후 구문을 분석해 보자.)

It is beneficial to talk and listen to babies. For example, talking to babies from

birth makes them hear different and more words, improving their understanding

of language and encouraging them to build communication skills.

STEP 03 동의어 훈련

It is <u>beneficial</u> to talk and listen to babies. For example, talking to babies from birth makes them hear different and more words, improving their understanding of language and encouraging them to build communication skills.

Q: In the context of the passage, <u>beneficial</u> means _____.

(a) advantageous
(b) fundamental
(c) evitable
(d) outstanding

Day 10

필수문장 096

It was found that serious problems with tires after the car run over a sharp object occurred. Because Joey thought that these could cause a car accident, he replaced the tires immediately.

차량이 날카로운 물체에 부딪힌 뒤 타이어에 심각한 문제가 발생한 것으로 드러났다. 조이는 이런 것들이 교통사고를 일으킬 수 있다고 생각했기 때문에 즉시 교체했다.

 STEP 01 단어 암기

It was <u>found</u> that <u>serious</u> problems with tires <u>after</u> the car <u>run over</u> a <u>sharp</u> <u>object</u>
(형) 발견된　(형) 심각한　　　　　　　(접) ~후에　　(동) ~를 치다　(형) 날카로운　(명) 물체

<u>occurred</u>. <u>Because</u> Joey <u>thought</u> that these could <u>cause</u> a car <u>accident</u>, he <u>replaced</u>
(동) 발생하다　(접) ~ 때문에　(동) 생각했다　　　　　　(동) 유발하다　　(명) 사고　　(동) 대체하다

the tires <u>immediately</u>.
(부) 즉시

 STEP 02 구문 분석 훈련 (가주어와 진주어에 표시한 후 구문을 분석해 보자.)

It was found that serious problems with tires after the car run over a sharp object

occurred. Because Joey thought that these could cause a car accident, he

replaced the tires immediately.

STEP 03 동의어 훈련

It was found that serious <u>problems</u> with tires after the car run over a sharp object occurred. Because Joey thought that these could cause a car accident, he replaced the tires immediately.

Q: In the context of the passage, <u>problems</u> means _____.

(a) obstacles
(b) eradication
(c) troubles
(d) features

097

> To make a successful presentation, it is especially important to examine information about your listeners and analyze it. In addition, you should know how to keep audience's attention during your presentation.
>
> 성공적인 발표를 하기 위해서는 특히 청중 대한 정보를 조사하고 그것을 분석하는 것이 중요하다. 게다가, 청중들이 당신의 프레젠테이션에 집중할 수 있도록 하는 방법을 알아야 한다.

STEP 01 단어 암기

To make a <u>successful</u> <u>presentation</u>, it is <u>especially</u> important to <u>examine</u> <u>information</u>
　　　　　(형) 성공적인　　(명) 발표　　　　　(부) 특히　　　　　　　　(동) 조사하다　　(명) 정보

about your listeners and <u>analyze</u> it. <u>In addition</u>, you should know <u>how to</u> keep
　　　　　　　　　　　　　(동) 분석하다　　　(부) 게다가　　　　　　　　　　~하는 방법

<u>audience</u>'s <u>attention</u> <u>during</u> your presentation.
(명) 청중　　　(명) 관심　　(전) ~동안

STEP 02 구문 분석 훈련 (가주어와 진주어에 표시한 후 구문을 분석해 보자.)

To make a successful presentation, it is especially important to examine information

about your listeners and analyze it. In addition, you should know how to keep

audience's attention during your presentation.

STEP 03 동의어 훈련

To make a successful presentation, it is especially important to examine information about your listeners and analyze it. In addition, you should know how to <u>keep</u> audience's attention during your presentation.

Q: In the context of the passage, <u>keep</u> means _____.

(a) maintain
(b) prove
(c) support
(d) establish

필수문장 098

> It is normal to lose between 50 and 100 hairs a day because they are naturally replaced and return to normal levels. However, if you are losing too much hair, see your doctor to do something about it.
>
> 머리카락은 자연스럽게 대체되고 정상 수준으로 돌아오기 때문에 하루에 50에서 100개의 머리카락이 빠지는 것은 정상이다. 하지만, 만약 머리카락이 너무 많이 빠지고 있다면, 그것에 대해 뭔가를 하기 위해 의사에게 가봐라.

 단어 암기

It is <u>normal</u> to <u>lose</u> between 50 and 100 hairs <u>a day</u> because they are <u>naturally</u>
(형) 정상적인   (동) 줄다, 잃다   (부) 하루에   (부) 자연스럽게

<u>replaced</u> and <u>return</u> <u>to</u> normal <u>levels</u>. However, if you are losing too much hair,
(형) 대체되는   (동) 돌아가다 (전) ~로   (명) 수준

<u>see</u> your doctor to do <u>something</u> about it.
(동) 보다   (명) 무언가, 어떤 것

 구문 분석 훈련 (가주어와 진주어에 표시한 후 구문을 분석해 보자.)

It is normal to lose between 50 and 100 hairs a day because they are naturally

replaced and return to normal levels. However, if you are losing too much hair,

see your doctor to do something about it.

STEP 03 동의어 훈련

It is <u>normal</u> to lose between 50 and 100 hairs a day because they are naturally replaced and return to normal levels. However, if you are losing too much hair, see your doctor to do something about it.

Q: In the context of the passage, <u>normal</u> means _____.

(a) typical
(b) peculiar
(c) primary
(d) grave

099

It is essential that Betty get some rest because she feels burned out and exhausted after work, losing her passion she once had in her work. Getting more sleep and enough rest can relax her mind and body, also improving her mood and relieving stress.

베티는 한때 일에서 느꼈던 열정을 잃어버리면서 일을 마친 후 피곤하고 지쳤으므로 휴식을 취하는 것이 필수적이다. 잠을 더 자고 충분한 휴식을 취하는 것은 그녀의 몸과 마음을 편하게 하고, 또한 그녀의 기분을 좋게 하고 스트레스를 완화시킬 수 있다.

STEP 01 단어 암기

It is <u>essential</u> that Betty <u>get</u> some <u>rest</u> because she feels <u>burned out</u> and <u>exhausted</u>
(형) 필수적인　　　　(동) 얻다　　(명) 휴식　　　　　　(형) 지친　　(형) 진이 빠진, 기진맥진한

after work, <u>losing</u> her <u>passion</u> she <u>once</u> had in her work. Getting more sleep and
　　　　　잃어버리면서　　(명) 열정　　(부) 한 때

<u>enough</u> rest can <u>relax</u> her mind and body, <u>also</u> <u>improving</u> her <u>mood</u> and <u>relieving</u>
(형) 충분한　　　　(동) 쉬게하다　　　　　　(부) 또한　향상시키면서　　(명) 기분　　완화시키면서

stress.

STEP 02 구문 분석 훈련 (가주어와 진주어에 표시한 후 구문을 분석해 보자.)

It is essential that Betty get some rest because she feels burned out and exhausted

after work, losing her passion she once had in her work. Getting more sleep and

enough rest can relax her mind and body, also improving her mood and relieving

stress.

동의어 훈련

It is essential that Betty get some rest because she feels burned out and exhausted after work, losing her passion she once had in her work. Getting more sleep and enough rest can relax her mind and body, also improving her mood and relieving stress.

Q: In the context of the passage, enough means _____.

(a) adequate
(b) expanding
(c) brief
(d) compulsory

Day
10

필수문장 100

> It is known that uniforms function as a visual marker of identities and strengthen cohesion among group members. However, people wearing uniforms can lose their individuality because others are wearing the same outfit.
>
> 유니폼은 신분을 시각적으로 표시하는 역할을 하며 단체 구성원 간 결속력을 강화하는 것으로 알려졌다. 하지만, 유티폼을 입는 사람들은 다른 사람들이 같은 옷을 입기 때문에 그들의 개성을 잃을 수 있다.

 STEP 01 단어 암기

It is <u>known</u> that <u>uniforms</u> <u>function</u> <u>as</u> <u>a</u> <u>visual</u> <u>marker</u> of <u>identities</u> and <u>strengthen</u>
　　　(형) 알려진　　　(명) 유니폼　　(동) 기능하다 (전) ~로써 (형) 시각적인 (명) 표시,　　(명) 정체성　　　(동) 강화시키다
　　　　　　　　　　　　　　　　　　　　　　　　　　　　　표시해주는 것

<u>cohesion</u> <u>among</u> group members. However, people <u>wearing</u> uniforms can <u>lose</u> their
(명) 결속력　·　(전) ~사이에서　　　　　　　　　　　　　(형) 입는　　　　　　　　　(동) 잃다

<u>individuality</u> because others are wearing the <u>same</u> <u>outfit</u>.
(명) 개성　　　　　　　　　　　　　　　　　　　　　(형) 같은　(명) 옷

 STEP 02 구문 분석 훈련 (가주어와 진주어에 표시한 후 구문을 분석해 보자.)

It is known that uniforms function as a visual marker of identities and strengthen

cohesion among group members. However, people wearing uniforms can lose

their individuality because others are wearing the same outfit.

STEP 03 · 동의어 훈련

It is known that uniforms function as a visual marker of identities and strengthen cohesion among group members. However, people wearing uniforms can lose their individuality because others are wearing the same outfit.

Q: In the context of the passage, cohesion means _____.

(a) separation
(b) combination
(c) cooperation
(d) unity

Day 11

켈리의 지텔프 **해석 POINT** 11

명사 앞이나 뒤에 나오는 과거분사 (pp) : '~된, ~되는, ~당하는' 으로 해석

과거분사 (pp) 는 형용사이다. 형용사는 보통 받침이 'ㄴ'으로 끝나기 때문에 과거분사 역시 받침이 'ㄴ'으로 끝난다고 생각해도 좋다.

혹시 중학교 때 동사의 3단 변화를 암기한 수험생들이 있을 것이다. 3단 변화 중 세 번째에 나오는 단어가 과거분사(pp)이다. 보통 동사원형에 ed를 붙인 형태이지만 때로는 전혀 다른 형태일 수도 있다. 만약 시간이 충분하다면 'V-ed' 형태가 아닌 과거분사(불규칙형)를 암기하는 것이 좋다. 과거분사가 무엇인지 전혀 감이 안 오는 수험생들을 위해 약간의 문법적인 설명을 추가하도록 하겠다. 다음 예문을 살펴보자.

I have a bag made in Korea.

위의 예문은 '나는 한국에서 만들어진 가방을 가지고 있다'라고 해석된다.

동사 make의 3단 변화는 '① make – ② made – ③ made'이다. 이를 좀 더 자세히 살펴보면 다음과 같다.

① make : 만들다 (현재 동사)

② made : 만들었다 (과거 동사)

③ made : 만들어진 (과거분사)

과거분사는 '③ made' 이다. 과거분사는 형용사라고 했으므로 'ㄴ' 받침으로 끝난다. 형용사는 명사를 수식해주는 특징을 지니고 있는데 과거분사 역시 형용사이므로 앞에 나온 명사나 뒤에 나온 명사를 수식해준다. 예문에서는 made는 앞에 나온 명사인 'a bag'을 수식하기 때문에 '만들어진 가방'으로 해석하면 된다.

필 수 문 장 101

Because of toxic substances found in a processed food, the authority banned the sale of the product.

한 가공식품에서 발견된 독성물질 때문에 당국은 그 제품의 판매를 금지했다.

 단어 암기

Because of toxic substances found in a processed food, the authority banned the
(전) ~ 때문에　　(형) 독성의　　(명) 물질　　(형) 발견된　　(형) 가공된　　　　　(명) 당국　　(동) 금지하다

sale of the product.
(명) 판매

 구문 분석 훈련 (과거분사에 표시한 후 구문을 분석해 보자.)

Because of toxic substances found in a processed food, the authority banned the

sale of the product.

STEP 03 동의어 훈련

Because of toxic substances found in a processed food, the authority <u>banned</u> the sale of the product.

Q: In the context of the passage, <u>banned</u> means _____.

(a) renovated
(b) prohibited
(c) inspected
(d) facilitated

필수문장 102

A company will provide cash bonuses next week. That's because sales of products released by the company have been soaring.

한 회사가 다음 주에 현금 보너스를 제공할 것이다. 이 회사가 출시한 제품 판매가 급증하고 있기 때문이다.

 STEP 01 단어 암기

A <u>company</u> will <u>provide</u> <u>cash</u> bonuses next week. That's because <u>sales</u> of <u>products</u>
(명) 회사　　　(동) 제공하다　(명) 현금　　　　　　　　　　　　　　(명) 판매　　(명) 제품

<u>released</u> <u>by</u> the company have been <u>soaring</u>.
(형) 출시된　(전) ~에 의해　　　　　　　　　　(형) 급증하는

 STEP 02 구문 분석 훈련 (과거분사에 표시한 후 구문을 분석해 보자.)

A company will provide cash bonuses next week. That's because sales of products

released by the company have been soaring.

STEP 03 동의어 훈련

A company will provide cash bonuses next week. That's because sales of products

released by the company have been <u>soaring</u>.

Q: In the context of the passage, <u>soaring</u> means _____.

(a) developing
(b) skyrocketing
(c) reinforcing
(d) supporting

103

> Kevin plans to make a chocolate cake topped with flowers for mom this Mother's Day. Because he didn't know how to make a cake, he tried finding secrets for a perfect cake online.
>
> 케빈은 이번 어머니 날에 엄마를 위해 꽃으로 토핑된 초콜릿 케이크를 만들 계획이다. 그는 케이크를 만드는 법을 몰랐기 때문에 온라인에서 완벽한 케이크를 만들기 위한 비법을 찾으려고 시도했다.

STEP 01 단어 암기

Kevin <u>plans</u> to make a chocolate cake <u>topped</u> with flowers for mom this Mother's
　　　(동) 계획하다　　　　　　　　　(형) 덮힌

Day. Because he didn't know <u>how to</u> make a cake, he <u>tried</u> finding <u>secrets</u> for
　　　　　　　　　　　　　　　　～하는 방법　　　　　　　(동) 시도했다　　(명) 비결, 비밀

a <u>perfect</u> cake <u>online</u>.
　(형) 완벽한　　　(부) 온라인에서

 STEP 02 구문 분석 훈련 (과거분사에 표시한 후 구문을 분석해 보자.)

Kevin plans to make a chocolate cake topped with flowers for mom this Mother's

Day. Because he didn't know how to make a cake, he tried finding secrets for

a perfect cake online.

STEP 03 동의어 훈련

Kevin plans to make a chocolate cake topped with flowers for mom this Mother's Day. Because he didn't know how to make a cake, he tried finding secrets for a perfect cake online.

Q: In the context of the passage, secrets means _____.

(a) tips
(b) procedures
(c) instruction
(d) strategies

필 수 문 장 104

Jennifer often goes to a restaurant and enjoys a special meal made by famous chefs with her boyfriend. They drink a glass of wine whenever they go to the restaurant.

제니퍼는 종종 레스토랑에 가서 그녀의 남자친구와 함께 유명한 요리사들이 만든 특별한 식사를 하는 것을 즐긴다. 그들은 식당에 갈 때마다 와인 한 잔을 마신다.

STEP 01 단어 암기

Jennifer <u>often</u> goes to a restaurant and <u>enjoys</u> a special <u>meal</u> <u>made</u> by <u>famous</u>
　　　　(부) 종종　　　　　　　　　　　　　(동) 즐기다　　　　　　(명) 식사 (형) 만들어진　 (형) 유명한

<u>chef</u>s with her boyfriend. They drink a glass of wine <u>whenever</u> they go to the
(명) 요리사　　　　　　　　　　　　　　　　　　　　　　　(접) ~할 때마다

restaurant.

STEP 02 구문 분석 훈련 (과거분사에 표시한 후 구문을 분석해 보자.)

Jennifer often goes to a restaurant and enjoys a special meal made by famous

chefs with her boyfriend. They drink a glass of wine whenever they go to the

restaurant.

STEP 03 동의어 훈련

Jennifer often goes to a restaurant and enjoys a special meal <u>made</u> by famous chefs with her boyfriend. They drink a glass of wine whenever they go to the restaurant.

Q: In the context of the passage, <u>made</u> means _____.

(a) prepared
(b) manufactured
(c) generated
(d) constructed

105

We should not believe everything presented in the media.
Sometimes stories delivered as news can be false information,
deliberately deceiving people.

우리는 매체에 보여진 모든 것을 믿어서는 안 된다. 때때로 뉴스로 전달되는 이야기들은 사람들을 고의로 속이고 잘못된 정보일 수 있다.

STEP 01 단어 암기

We should not <u>believe</u> everything <u>presented</u> in the <u>media</u>. <u>Sometimes</u> stories
               (동) 믿다   (형) 보여진   (명) 매체   (부) 때때로

<u>delivered</u> <u>as</u> news can be <u>false</u> <u>information</u>, <u>deliberately</u> <u>deceiving</u> people.
(형) 전달된   (전) ~로써   (형) 잘못된   (명) 정보   (부) 의도적으로   속이면서

STEP 02 구문 분석 훈련 (과거분사에 표시한 후 구문을 분석해 보자.)

We should not believe everything presented in the media. Sometimes stories

delivered as news can be false information, deliberately deceiving people.

STEP 03 동의어 훈련

We should not believe everything presented in the media. Sometimes stories delivered as news can be false information, <u>deliberately</u> deceiving people.

Q: In the context of the passage, <u>deliberately</u> means _____.

(a) intentionally
(b) unknowingly
(c) accidentally
(d) systematically

필 수 문 장 106

> When a work environment makes workers uncomfortable, creativity is likely to decrease. On the other hand, a comfortable work environment leads to increased creativity and innovation in employees.
>
> 근무환경이 근로자들을 불편하게 할 때 창의력이 떨어지기 쉽다. 반면에, 편안한 근무 환경은 근로자들에게 증진된 창의력과 혁신으로 이어진다.

STEP 01 단어 암기

When a work <u>environment</u> makes <u>workers</u> <u>uncomfortable</u>, <u>creativity</u> <u>is likely to</u>
　　　　　　　(명) 환경　　　　　　(명) 근로자　　(형) 불편한　　(명) 창의성　～할 가능성이 있다

<u>decrease</u>. <u>On the other hand</u>, a <u>comfortable</u> work environment <u>leads to</u> <u>increased</u>
(동) 감소시키다　　(부) 반면에　　　　　(형) 편안한　　　　　　　　　　(동) ～로 이어지다　(형) 증가된

creativity and <u>innovation</u> in <u>employees</u>.
　　　　　　　(명) 혁신　　　　(명) 근로자

 STEP 02 구문 분석 훈련 (과거분사에 표시한 후 구문을 분석해 보자.)

When a work environment makes workers uncomfortable, creativity is likely to

decrease. On the other hand, a comfortable work environment leads to increased

creativity and innovation in employees.

STEP 03 동의어 훈련

When a work environment makes workers uncomfortable, creativity is <u>likely</u> to

decrease. On the other hand, a comfortable work environment leads to increased

creativity and innovation in employees.

Q: In the context of the passage, <u>likely</u> means _____.

(a) apt
(b) reasonable
(c) suitable
(d) acceptable

필수문장 107

> When the devastating earthquake hit the city, Emily tried to provide assistance for people affected by the earthquake. In fact, she always helps others in need.
>
> 파괴적인 지진이 도시를 강타했을 때, Emily는 지진의 피해를 입은 사람들을 돕기 위해 노력했다. 사실, 그녀는 항상 어려움에 처한 다른 사람들을 돕는다.

 STEP 01 단어 암기

When the <u>devastating</u> <u>earthquake</u> <u>hit</u> the city, Emily <u>tried to</u> <u>provide</u> <u>assistance</u>
      (형) 파괴적인   (명) 지진   (동) 쳤다   (동) 노력했다 (동) 제공하다   (명) 도움

for people <u>affected</u> by the earthquake. <u>In fact</u>, she always helps <u>others</u> <u>in need</u>.
      (형) 영향을 받은   (부) 사실   (명) 다른 사람 어려움에 처한

 STEP 02 구문 분석 훈련 (과거분사에 표시한 후 구문을 분석해 보자.)

When the devastating earthquake hit the city, Emily tried to provide assistance

for people affected by the earthquake. In fact, she always helps others in need.

STEP 03 동의어 훈련

When the devastating earthquake hit the city, Emily tried to provide <u>assistance</u>

for people affected by the earthquake. In fact, she always helps others in need.

Q: In the context of the passage, <u>assistance</u> means _____.

(a) instruction
(b) inspiration
(c) endurance
(d) aid

필수문장 108

Right after a car hit a boy walking with his mother, she took him to the hospital. Fortunately, he miraculously survived the fatal car accident caused by a drunk driver.

차가 엄마와 함께 걷고 있는 소년을 친 직후, 그녀는 그를 병원으로 데려갔다. 다행히 그는 음주 운전자가 낸 치명적인 교통사고에서 기적적으로 살아남았다.

 STEP 01 단어 암기

Right after a car hit a boy walking with his mother, she took him to the hospital.
(접) ~ 직후   (동) 데려갔다

Fortunately, he miraculously survived the fatal car accident caused by a drunk
(부) 다행히   (부) 기적적으로   (동) 살아남다   (형) 치명적인   (명) 사고   (형) 유발된   (전) ~에 의해

driver.

 STEP 02 구문 분석 훈련 (과거분사에 표시한 후 구문을 분석해 보자.)

Right after a car hit a boy walking with his mother, she took him to the hospital.

Fortunately, he miraculously survived the fatal car accident caused by a drunk

driver.

STEP 03 동의어 훈련

Right after a car hit a boy walking with his mother, she took him to the hospital. Fortunately, he miraculously survived the <u>fatal</u> car accident caused by a drunk driver.

Q: In the context of the passage, <u>fatal</u> means _____.

(a) tolerable
(b) trivial
(c) superficial
(d) deadly

필수문장 109

It is debatable whether the ancient city built 1,800 years ago really existed or not. Although some archeologists can't find written records of the city, they believe that the city really existed.

1800년 전에 지어진 이 고대 도시가 실제로 존재했는지는 논쟁의 여지가 있다. 어떤 고고학자들은 그 도시에 대한 기록을 찾을 수 없음에도 그 도시가 실제로 존재했다고 확신하고 있다.

 STEP 01 단어 암기

It is debatable whether the ancient city built 1,800 years ago really existed or not.
(형) 논쟁의 여지가 있는   (접) ~인지 아닌지   (형) 고대의   (형) 세워진   (동) 존재하다

Although some archeologists can't find written records of the city, they believe that
(접) 비록 ~일지라도   (명) 고고학자   (동) 발견하다 (형) 쓰여진 (명) 기록   (동) 믿는다

the city really existed.

 STEP 02 구문 분석 훈련 (과거분사에 표시한 후 구문을 분석해 보자.)

It is debatable whether the ancient city built 1,800 years ago really existed or not.

Although some archeologists can't find written records of the city, they believe that

the city really existed.

STEP 03 동의어 훈련

It is <u>debatable</u> whether the ancient city built 1,800 years ago really existed or not. Although some archeologists can't find written records of the city, they believe that the city really existed.

Q: In the context of the passage, <u>debatable</u> means _____.

(a) resistant
(b) advocating
(c) arguable
(d) agreeable

필수문장 110

Some organisms called keystone species are essential in determining the structure of the entire ecosystem. Therefore, we should protect keystone species in order to maintain ecosystems in the right condition.

몇몇 유기체는 핵심종이라고 불리는데, 이것은 생태계 전체의 구조를 결정하는 데 필수적이다. 그러므로, 우리는 생태계가 적절한 상태로 유지되도록 핵심종을 보호해야 한다.

단어 암기

Some <u>organisms</u> <u>called</u> <u>keystone species</u> are <u>essential</u> in <u>determining</u> the <u>structure</u>
　　　(명) 유기체　(형) 불리는　　핵심종　　　　(형) 필수적인　　결정하는 것　　　(동) 구조

of the <u>entire</u> <u>ecosystem.</u> <u>Therefore,</u> we should <u>protect</u> keystone species <u>in order to</u>
　　　(형) 전체의　(명) 생태계　(부) 그러므로　　　　(동) 보호하다　　　　　　～하기 위해서

<u>maintain</u> ecosystems in the <u>right</u> <u>condition.</u>
(동) 유지하다　　　　　　　(형) 적절한　(명) 상태

구문 분석 훈련 (과거분사에 표시한 후 구문을 분석해 보자.)

Some organisms called keystone species are essential in determining the structure

of the entire ecosystem. Therefore, we should protect keystone species in order

to maintain ecosystems in the right condition.

STEP 03 동의어 훈련

Some organisms called keystone species are essential in determining the structure of the entire ecosystem. Therefore, we should protect keystone species in order to maintain ecosystems in the <u>right</u> condition.

Q: In the context of the passage, <u>right</u> means _____.

(a) significant
(b) vicious
(c) unrivaled
(d) appropriate

Day 12

be 동사 + 과거분사 (pp) : '**되다, 당하다' 등으로 해석**

'해석 포인트 11'에서 우리는 명사 앞이나 뒤에 나오는 과거분사 (pp)를 '~된, ~되는, ~당하는' 으로 해석한다는 것을 배웠다. '해석 포인트 12'에서는 그를 활용하여 더 확장할 것이다. 과거분사 앞에 be 동사가 와서 be 동사와 결합하는 경우가 있다. 동사는 '다'로 해석되므로 만약 'be/been/being + 과거분사'의 형태가 있다면 '되다, 당하다' 등으로 해석되면 된다. be 동사의 형태는 다양하기 때문에 해석은 조금씩 차이가 있다. 그 부분을 문법적으로 공부하려고 한다면 시제부터 태까지 우리에게는 엄청나게 많은 시간이 요구된다. 단시간에 해석하는 것이 목표인 우리에게 그러한 공부 방법은 너무 비효율적이므로 효율적인 학습을 위해 be 동사가 과거분사와 결합할 때 각각 어떻게 해석되는지 다음의 표를 암기하자.

형태	해석	예문
① was / were + 과거분사	~되었다 ~당했다	The bag was made in Korea. [그 가방은 한국에서 만들어졌다.]
② am / is / are + 과거분사	~되다 ~당하다	The bag is made in Korea. [그 가방은 한국에서 만들어진다.]
③ will be + 과거분사	~될 것이다 ~당할 것이다	The bag will be made in Korea. [그 가방은 한국에서 만들어질 것이다.]
④ was/were + being + 과거분사	~되는 중이었다 ~당하는 중이었다	The bag was being made in Korea. [그 가방은 한국에서 만들어지고 있는 중이었다.]
⑤ am/is/are + being + 과거분사	~되는 중이다 ~당하는 중이다	The bag is being made in Korea. [그 가방은 한국에서 만들어지고 있는 중이다.]
⑥ will + be + being + 과거분사	~되는 중일 것이다 ~당하는 중일 것이다	The bag will be being made in Korea. [그 가방은 한국에서 만들어지고 있는 중일 것이다.]
⑦ had been + 과거분사	~되어 오고 있었다 ~당해오고 있었다	The bag had been made in Korea. [그 가방은 한국에서 만들어져왔다.]
⑧ have(has) been + pp	~되어오고 있다 ~당해오고 있다	The bag have been made in Korea. [그 가방은 한국에서 만들어져 오고 있다.]
⑨ will have been + pp	~되어 오고 있을 것이다 ~당해오고 있을 것이다	The bag will have been made in Korea. [그 가방은 한국에서 만들어지고 있을 것이다.]

111

After more than three people were killed in a house fire, police said that unknown suspects entered the house and lit it on fire, adding that the investigation was still ongoing.

경찰은 주택 화재로 3명 이상이 숨진 뒤 알려지지 않은 용의자들이 집에 들어와 불을 붙였다며 여전히 조사가 진행 중이라고 밝혔다.

STEP 01 단어 암기

After <u>more than</u> three people were <u>killed</u> in a house fire, police said that <u>unknown</u>
　　　이상　　　　　　　　　　　(동) 죽이다　　　　　　　　　　　　　　　　(형) 알려지지 않은

<u>suspects</u> <u>entered</u> the house and <u>lit</u> it on fire, <u>adding</u> that the <u>investigation</u> was
(명) 용의자　(동) 들어가다　　　　　　　(동) 불을 붙였다　　(동) 덧붙이다　　　　(명) 조사

still <u>ongoing</u>.
　　(형) 진행 중인

STEP 02 구문 분석 훈련 (be + 과거분사에 표시한 후 구문을 분석해 보자.)

After more than three people were killed in a house fire, police said that unknown

suspects entered the house and lit it on fire, adding that the investigation was

still ongoing.

Day
12

STEP 03 동의어 훈련

After more than three people were killed in a house fire, police said that unknown suspects entered the house and lit it on fire, adding that the investigation was still <u>ongoing</u>.

Q: In the context of the passage, <u>ongoing</u> means _____.

(a) emerging
(b) consistent
(c) persistent
(d) underway

112

A number of polar bears left in the world have been pushed on the verge of extinction. We should do something to protect them from extinction.

전 세계에 남겨진 수많은 북극곰들이 멸종위기에 처해있다. 우리는 멸종으로부터 그들을 보호하기 위해 무언가를 해야 한다.

STEP 01 단어 암기

A number of polar bears left in the world have been pushed on the verge of extinction.
수많은   (형) 북극의 (명) 곰 (형) 남겨진   (동) 압박하다   ~의 직전에   (명) 멸종

We should do something to protect them from extinction.
            (동) 하다   (동) 보호하다   (전) ~로 부터

STEP 02 구문 분석 훈련 (be + 과거분사에 표시한 후 구문을 분석해 보자.)

A number of polar bears left in the world have been pushed on the verge of extinction. We should do something to protect them from extinction.

STEP 03 동의어 훈련

A number of polar bears left in the world have been pushed on the verge of extinction. We should do something to <u>protect</u> them from extinction.

Q: In the context of the passage, <u>protect</u> means _____.

(a) maintain
(b) save
(c) increase
(d) breed

필수문장 113

An organization that has been working to safeguard the health of people with disabilities will be financed by a conglomerate starting next year.

장애인의 건강을 지키기 위해 노력해 온 단체가 내년부터 대기업의 후원을 받게 된다.

 STEP 01 단어 암기

An <u>organization</u> that has been <u>working</u> to <u>safeguard</u> the <u>health</u> of people with
(명) 조직, 단체   (동) 노력하다   (동) 지키다   (명) 건강

<u>disabilities</u> will be <u>financed</u> <u>by</u> a <u>conglomerate</u> <u>starting</u> next year.
(명) 장애, 무력   (동) 자금을 대다 (전) ~에 의해   (명) 대기업   ~부터

 STEP 02 구문 분석 훈련 (be + 과거분사에 표시한 후 구문을 분석해 보자.)

An organization that has been working to safeguard the health of people with

disabilities will be financed by a conglomerate starting next year.

동의어 훈련

An organization that has been working to safeguard the health of people with disabilities will be <u>financed</u> by a conglomerate starting next year.

Q: In the context of the passage, <u>financed</u> means _____.

(a) operated
(b) invested
(c) sponsored
(d) regulated

필수문장 114

To use public spaces as event venues, you must register your event with the council and comply with relevant regulations and safety measures. Otherwise, you are not allowed to hold events.

공공장소를 행사장으로 이용하려면 해당 행사를 시의회에 등록하고 관련 규정과 안전조치를 준수해야 한다. 그렇지 않으면 행사를 개최할 수 없다.

 STEP 01 단어 암기

To use <u>public</u> <u>spaces</u> as <u>event</u> <u>venues</u>, you must <u>register</u> your <u>event</u> with the <u>council</u>
(형) 공공의　(명) 공간　(명) 행사　(명) 장소　(동) 등록하다　(명) 행사　(명) 시의회

and <u>comply with</u> <u>relevant</u> <u>regulations</u> and <u>safety</u> <u>measures</u>. <u>Otherwise</u>, you are not
(동) ~를 준수하다　(형) 관련있는　(명) 규정　(명) 안전　(명) 조치　(부) 만약 그렇지 않으면

<u>allowed</u> to <u>hold</u> events.
(동) 허락하다　(동) 열다, 개최하다

 STEP 02 구문 분석 훈련 (be + 과거분사에 표시한 후 구문을 분석해 보자.)

To use public spaces as event venues, you must register your event with the council and comply with relevant regulations and safety measures. Otherwise, you are not allowed to hold events.

동의어 훈련

To use public spaces as event venues, you must register your event with the council and comply with relevant regulations and safety measures. Otherwise, you are not <u>allowed</u> to hold events.

Q: In the context of the passage, <u>allowed</u> means _____.

(a) permitted
(b) legal
(c) contracted
(d) advised

Day 12

필수문장 115

Although a leader worked hard to create a positive work environment, making his team members comfortable and encouraging them to achieve the goal they set, productivity was decreased.

리더가 긍정적인 업무 환경을 조성해 팀원들을 편안하게 해주고, 자신이 설정한 목표를 달성하도록 격려해 주었지만 생산성이 떨어졌다.

 STEP 01 단어 암기

Although a leader worked hard to <u>create</u> a <u>positive</u> work <u>environment</u>, making
(접) 비록 ~일지라도　　　　　　　　(동) 창조하다　　(형) 긍정적인　　　　　(명) 환경

his team members <u>comfortable</u> and encouraging them to <u>achieve</u> the <u>goal</u> they
　　　　　　　　　　(형) 편안한　　　　　　　　　　　　　　　(동) 달성하다　　(명) 목표

<u>set</u>, <u>productivity</u> was <u>decreased</u>.
(동) 설정하다　(명) 생산성　　　　(동) 감소시키다

 STEP 02 구문 분석 훈련 (be + 과거분사에 표시한 후 구문을 분석해 보자.)

Although a leader worked hard to create a positive work environment, making

his team members comfortable and encouraging them to achieve the goal they

set, productivity was decreased.

STEP 03 동의어 훈련

Day 12

Although a leader worked hard to create a positive work environment, making his team members comfortable and encouraging them to <u>achieve</u> the goal they set, productivity was decreased.

Q: In the context of the passage, <u>achieve</u> means _____.

(a) acquire
(b) secure
(c) accomplish
(d) cease

필수문장 116

Various organizations have been established to cope with food insecurity and provide people in developing countries with food in a sustainable way. In addition, they aim to break down the barriers to education by improving the education of poor children.

식량 불안정에 대처하고 개발도상국 사람들에게 지속 가능한 방법으로 식량을 제공하기 위해 다양한 기관들이 설립되었다. 게다가, 그들은 가난한 아이들의 교육을 향상함으로써 교육의 장벽을 부수는 것을 목표로 하고 있다.

 STEP 01 단어 암기

Various organizations have been established to cope with food insecurity and
(형) 다양한　　(명) 조직, 단체　　　　　　(동) 설립하다　　　(동) ~을 다루다　　　(명) 불안정

provide people in developing countries with food in a sustainable way. In addition,
(동) 제공하다　　　　　　개발 도상국　　　　　　　　　(형) 지속적인　(명) 방법　(부) 게다가

they aim to break down the barriers to education by improving the education of
(동) ~를　　(동) 부수다　　(명) 장벽　　(명) 교육　　　향상함으로써　　　(명) 교육
목표로 하다

poor children.
(형) 가난한

 STEP 02 구문 분석 훈련 (be + 과거분사에 표시한 후 구문을 분석해 보자.)

Various organizations have been established to cope with food insecurity and

provide people in developing countries with food in a sustainable way. In addition,

they aim to break down the barriers to education by improving the education of

poor children.

STEP 03 동의어 훈련

Various organizations have been established to <u>cope</u> with food insecurity and provide people in developing countries with food in a sustainable way. In addition, they aim to break down the barriers to education by improving the education of poor children.

Q: In the context of the passage, <u>cope</u> means _____.

(a) deal
(b) solve
(c) get
(d) remove

Day
12

필수문장 117

The scheduled final exam is going to be pushed back because teachers need extra teaching time. Some students insist that it follow the original final exam schedule.

교사들이 추가적인 수업 시간을 필요로 하기 때문에 예정된 기말고사는 미뤄질 것이다. 일부 학생들은 시험이 원래의 기말고사 일정을 따라야 한다고 주장한다.

STEP 01 단어 암기

The <u>scheduled</u> <u>final exam</u> <u>is going to</u> be <u>pushed back</u> because teachers <u>need</u>
　　(형) 예정된　　기말고사　　～ 할 예정이다　　(형) 미뤄진　　　　　　　　(동) 필요로 하다

<u>extra</u> teaching time. Some students <u>insist</u> that it <u>follow</u> the <u>original</u> final exam <u>schedule</u>.
(형) 추가의　　　　　　　　　　　　(동) 주장하다　　(동) 따르다　(형) 원래의　　　　　　(명) 일정

STEP 02 구문 분석 훈련 (be + 과거분사에 표시한 후 구문을 분석해 보자.)

The scheduled final exam is going to be pushed back because teachers need

extra teaching time. Some students insist that it follow the original final exam

schedule.

STEP 03 동의어 훈련

The scheduled final exam is going to be pushed back because teachers <u>need</u> extra teaching time. Some students insist that it follow the original final exam schedule.

Q: In the context of the passage, <u>need</u> means _____.

(a) force
(b) require
(c) entail
(d) inquire

118

Since some parents can't afford to pay for the tuition, a number of students living in poverty are being forced to drop out of school. In fact, the problems persist in poor countries in spite of taking measures to reduce school dropout.

일부 부모들은 수업료를 낼 여유가 없기 때문에, 빈곤 속에 사는 많은 학생들이 학교를 중퇴하도록 강요받고 있다. 사실, 그 문제는 학교 중퇴를 줄이기 위한 조치를 취했음에도 불구하고 가난한 나라들에서 지속되고 있다.

 STEP 01 단어 암기

Since some parents can't afford to pay for the tuition, a number of students living
(접) ~ 때문에　(동) 여유가 있다　(동) 지불하다　(명) 수업료　수많은

in poverty are being forced to drop out of school. In fact, the problems persist
(명) 빈곤　(형) 강요받는　~에서 중도 하차하다　(부) 사실　(동) 지속되다

in poor countries in spite of taking measures to reduce school dropout.
(전) ~에도 불구하고　(명) 조치　(동) 감소시키다　(명) 중퇴자

STEP 02 구문 분석 훈련 (be + 과거분사에 표시한 후 구문을 분석해 보자.)

Since some parents can't afford to pay for the tuition, a number of students living

in poverty are being forced to drop out of school. In fact, the problems persist

in poor countries in spite of taking measures to reduce school dropout.

STEP 03 동의어 훈련

Since some parents can't afford to pay for the tuition, a number of students living

in poverty are being forced to drop out of school. In fact, the problems persist

in poor countries in spite of taking <u>measures</u> to reduce school dropout.

Q: In the context of the passage, <u>measures</u> means _____.

(a) deeds
(b) operations
(c) standards
(d) steps

필수문장 119

Grace had been injured and fallen into a coma in a hit—and—run car accident. Although her husband made an effort to find witnesses who saw the accident and consulted with a car accident attorney, the hit—and—run driver wasn't caught.

그레이스는 뺑소니 교통사고로 부상을 입고 혼수상태에 빠졌다. 남편이 사고를 본 목격자를 찾기 위해 노력했고 교통사고 변호사와 상담했지만, 뺑소니 운전자는 잡히지 않았다.

STEP 01 단어 암기

Grace had been <u>injured</u> and <u>fallen</u> <u>into</u> a <u>coma</u> in a <u>hit—and—run car accident</u>.
(형) 부상 당한   (형) 빠진 (전) ~에 (명) 혼수상태   뺑소니 교통 사고

<u>Although</u> her <u>husband</u> made an <u>effort</u> to <u>find</u> <u>witness</u>es who <u>saw</u> the accident
(접) 비록 ~일지라도   (명) 남편   (명) 노력 (동) 찾다 (명) 목격자   (동) 봤다

and <u>consulted</u> with a car accident <u>attorney</u>, the hit—and—run driver wasn't <u>caught</u>.
(동) 상담하다   (명) 변호사   (형) 붙잡힌

STEP 02 구문 분석 훈련 (be + 과거분사에 표시한 후 구문을 분석해 보자.)

Grace had been injured and fallen into a coma in a hit—and—run car accident.

Although her husband made an effort to find any witnesses who saw the accident

and consulted with a car accident attorney, the hit—and—run driver wasn't caught.

STEP 03 동의어 훈련

Grace had been injured and fallen into a coma in a hit-and-run car accident. Although her husband made an <u>effort</u> to find witnesses who saw the accident and consult with a car accident attorney, the hit-and-run driver wasn't caught.

Q: In the context of the passage, <u>effort</u> means _____.

(a) endeavor
(b) fruitful
(c) labor
(d) toil

필수문장 120

Some pollutants that contain extremely hazardous substances, such as industrial waste and plastic debris, are being dumped into the ocean. Unless proper measures to solve this problem are taken, there will be a considerable threat to the survival of marine mammals.

산업폐기물과 플라스틱 파편 등 극히 유해한 물질이 포함된 일부 오염물질이 바다에 버려지고 있다. 이 문제를 해결하기 위한 적절한 조치가 취해지지 않으면 해양 포유류의 생존에 상당한 위협이 될 것이다.

 STEP 01 단어 암기

Some <u>pollutants</u> that <u>contain</u> <u>extremely</u> <u>hazardous</u> <u>substances</u>, <u>such as</u> <u>industrial</u>
　(명) 오염물질　　　　(동) 포함하다　(부) 극도로　　(형) 유해한　　(명) 물질　　　(전) ~와 같은　(형) 산업의

<u>waste</u> and plastic <u>debris</u>, are being <u>dumped</u> into the ocean. <u>Unless</u> <u>proper</u> <u>measures</u>
(명) 폐기물　　　　　　(명) 파편　　　　　　(동) 버리다　　　　　　　　(접) 만약 ~가　(형) 적절한　(명) 조치
　　　　　　　　　　　　　　　　　　　　　　　　　　　　　　　　　아니라면

to <u>solve</u> this problem are <u>taken</u>, <u>there will be</u> a <u>considerable</u> <u>threat</u> to the <u>survival</u>
　(동) 해결하다　　　　　　　　(형) 취해진　　있을 것이다.　　　(형) 상당한　　　(명) 위협　　　　(명) 생존

of <u>marine</u> <u>mammals</u>.
　(형) 해양의　(명) 포유류

 STEP 02 구문 분석 훈련 (be + 과거분사에 표시한 후 구문을 분석해 보자.)

Some pollutants that contain extremely hazardous substances, such as industrial

waste and plastic debris, are being dumped into the ocean. Unless proper

measures to solve this problem are taken, there will be a considerable threat to

the survival of marine mammals.

동의어 훈련

Some pollutants that contain extremely hazardous substances, such as industrial waste and plastic debris, are being dumped into the ocean. Unless proper measures to solve this problem are taken, there will be a <u>considerable</u> threat to the survival of marine mammals.

Q: In the context of the passage, <u>considerable</u> means _____.

(a) important
(b) huge
(c) fancy
(d) persistent

Day 13

give의 해석   ① ~을 주다   ② ~에게 ~을 주다

give는 '~을 주다'의 뜻을 가지는 동사이다. 다음 예문을 살펴보자.

I gave some money.

동사는 gave이고 목적어는 some money이므로 '나는 / 주었다 / 약간의 돈을'이라고 해석된다. 다음 예문도 살펴보자.

I gave her some money.

이 문장에서도 동사는 gave이며 목적어는 her이다. 하지만 '나는 / 주었다 / 그녀를 / 약간의 돈을'이라고 해석하면 어색하고 틀린 문장이 된다. 이 예문에서 gave는 목적어를 두 개 가지며 첫 번째 목적어가 'her'이고 두 번째 목적어가 some money이다. 이 경우 첫 번째 목적어를 간접목적어라고 부르며 '~에게'라고 해석한다. 두 번째 목적어는 직접목적어라고 부르며 '~을, ~를'이라고 해석한다. 따라서 '나는 / 주었다 / 그녀에게 / 약간의 돈을'이라고 해석하는 것이 적절하다.

give처럼 목적어를 두 개 가지는 동사를 4형식 동사라고 하며 대표적인 4형식 동사는 다음과 같다.

	목적어가 1개인 경우	목적어가 2개인 경우
give	~를 주다	~에게 -을 주다
teach	~를 가르치다	~에게 -을 가르치다
show	~를 보여주다	~에게 -을 보여주다
tell	~를 말하다	~에게 -을 말하다
buy	~를 사다	~에게 -을 사주다
make	~를 만들다	~에게 -을 만들어주다
ask	~를 묻다	~에게 -을 물어보다

필수문장 121

Because Amy was so depressed, avoiding contact with people and isolating herself, Mike gave her some tips for handling depression and encouraged her to seek therapy.

에이미가 사람들과의 접촉을 피하고 자신을 고립시키면서 너무 우울했기 때문에, 마이크는 그녀에게 우울증을 다루기 위한 몇 가지 팁을 주었고 그녀에게 치료를 받으라고 권했다.

 STEP 01 단어 암기

Because Amy was so depressed, avoiding contact with people and isolating herself,
(형) 우울한　　　피하면서　(명) 접촉　　　　　　　　　고립시키면서　그녀 자신

Mike gave her some tips for handling depression and encouraged her to seek
다루는 것　　(명) 우울증　　　　(동) 장려하다　　(동) 구하다, 추구하다

therapy.
(명) 치료

 STEP 02 구문 분석 훈련 (4형식 동사, 간접목적어, 직접목적어를 표시하고 구문을 분석해보자.)

Because Amy was so depressed, avoiding contact with people and isolating

herself, Mike gave her some tips for handling depression and encouraged her

to seek therapy.

STEP 03 동의어 훈련

Because Amy was so depressed, avoiding contact with people and isolating herself, Mike gave her some tips for <u>handling</u> depression and encouraged her to seek therapy.

Q: In the context of the passage, <u>handling</u> means _____ .

(a) operating
(b) addressing
(c) manipulating
(d) reacting

Day 13

122

If you want to thank servers for their services, just tell them a quick "thank you" and be kind and courteous. However, the best way to show appreciation is to give them a generous tip.

만약 당신이 서비스에 대해 종업원에게 감사하고 싶다면, 단지 "감사합니다" 라고 빨리 말하고 친절하고 공손해라. 그러나 감사를 보여주는 가장 좋은 방법은 그들에게 후한 팁을 주는 것이다.

STEP 01 단어 암기

If you want to <u>thank</u> <u>servers</u> for their services, just tell them a <u>quick</u> "thank you"
　　　　　　　(동) 감사해하다 (명) 종업원　　　　　　　　　　　　　　　　　(형) 빠른

and be kind and <u>courteous</u>. However, the best <u>way</u> to <u>show</u> <u>appreciation</u> is to
　　　　　　　　(형) 예의 바른　　　　　　　　　　　(명) 방법　(동) 보여주다　(명) 감사

give them a <u>generous</u> tip.
　　　　　　(형) 관대한

STEP 02 구문 분석 훈련 (4형식 동사, 간접목적어, 직접목적어를 표시하고 구문을 분석해보자.)

If you want to thank servers for their services, just tell them a quick "thank you"

and be kind and courteous. However, the best way to show appreciation is to

give them a generous tip.

STEP 03 동의어 훈련

If you want to thank servers for their services, just tell them a quick "thank you" and be kind and <u>courteous</u>. However, the best way to show appreciation is to give them a generous tip.

Q: In the context of the passage, <u>courteous</u> means _____.

(a) rude
(b) polite
(c) patient
(d) stubborn

Day 13

필수문장 123

> A company offers high school students a job and teaches them practical skills suitable for their future profession so that they can gain valuable work experience.
>
> 한 회사는 고등학생들에게 일자리를 제공하고, 그들이 가치 있는 직업 경험을 얻을 수 있도록 그들의 미래 직업에 적합한 소프트 기술을 가르친다.

 단어 암기

A <u>company</u> <u>offers</u> high school students a job and <u>teaches</u> them <u>practical</u> <u>skills</u>
   (명) 회사   (동) 제공하다   (동) 가르치다   (형) 실용적인 (명) 기술

<u>suitable</u> for their <u>future</u> <u>profession</u> <u>so that</u> they can <u>gain</u> <u>valuable</u> work <u>experience</u>.
(형) 적합한   (형) 미래의   (명) 직업   (접) ~하도록   (동) 얻다   (형) 가치 있는   (명) 경험

 구문 분석 훈련 (4형식 동사, 간접목적어, 직접목적어를 표시하고 구문을 분석해보자.)

A company offers high school students a job and teaches them practical skills

suitable for their future profession so that they can gain valuable work experience.

STEP 03 동의어 훈련

A company offers high school students a job and teaches them practical skills suitable for their future profession so that they can <u>gain</u> valuable work experience.

Q: In the context of the passage, <u>gain</u> means _____.

(a) acquire
(b) receive
(c) bestow
(d) confer

Day
13

필수문장 124

Many problems arise with regard to inadequate nutrients for young children. Parents should know the importance of nutrition in early childhood development and teach children healthy eating.

어린아이들에게 불충분한 영양소와 관련하여 많은 문제가 발생한다. 부모들은 유아의 발달 과정에서 영양의 중요성을 알고 아이들에게 건강한 식습관을 가르쳐야 한다.

 단어 암기

Many problems <u>arise</u> <u>with regard to</u> <u>inadequate</u> <u>nutrients</u> for young children.
(동) 발생하다　(전) ~와 관련해서　(형) 불충분한　(명) 영양소

<u>Parents</u> should know the <u>importance</u> of nutrition in <u>early</u> <u>childhood</u> <u>development</u>
(명) 부모　(명) 중요성　(형) 이른, 초기의　(명) 어린 시절　(명) 발달

and teach children <u>healthy</u> <u>eating</u>.
(형) 건강한　(명) 먹기

 구문 분석 훈련 (4형식 동사, 간접목적어, 직접목적어를 표시하고 구문을 분석해보자.)

Many problems arise with regard to inadequate nutrients for young children.

Parents should know the importance of nutrition in early childhood development

and teach children healthy eating.

STEP 03 동의어 훈련

Many problems arise with regard to <u>inadequate</u> nutrients for young children. Parents should know the importance of nutrition in early childhood development and teach children healthy eating.

Q: In the context of the passage, <u>inadequate</u> means _____.

(a) insufficient
(b) ample
(c) moderate
(d) reasonable

Day 13

125

A community center will offer various training programs starting next week to teach women living in the most deprived area skills that they need to get a job and support them.

한 주민센터는 가장 빈곤한 지역에 사는 여성들에게 취업에 필요한 기술을 가르치고 이들을 지원하기 위한 다양한 훈련 프로그램을 다음 주부터 제공할 것이다.

STEP 01 단어 암기

A community center will <u>offer</u> <u>various</u> training programs <u>starting</u> next week to <u>teach</u>
(동) 제공하다 (형) 다양한 ~부터 (동) 가르치다

women living in the <u>most</u> <u>deprived</u> <u>area</u> <u>skills</u> that they need to <u>get</u> a job and
가장 (형) 가난한 (명) 지역 (명) 기술 (동) 얻다

<u>support</u> them.
(동) 지원하다

STEP 02 구문 분석 훈련 (4형식 동사, 간접목적어, 직접목적어를 표시하고 구문을 분석해보자.)

A community center will offer various training programs starting next week to teach

women living in the most deprived area skills that they need to get a job and

support them.

STEP 03 동의어 훈련

A community center will offer various training programs starting next week to teach women living in the most <u>deprived</u> area skills that they need to get a job and support them.

Q: In the context of the passage, <u>deprived</u> means _____.

(a) disadvantaged
(b) affluence
(c) prosperous
(d) untouched

126

> Although Richard tried many different ways to lose weight quickly, a weight loss solution that worked for others didn't work for him and made him unhealthy. A personal trainer told him that he should follow a balanced and healthy diet.
>
> 리차드는 살을 빨리 빼기 위해 많은 다양한 방법들을 시도했지만, 다른 사람들에게 효과가 있는 체중 감량 솔루션이 그에게 효과가 없었고 그를 건강하지 못하게 만들었다. 한 개인 트레이너는 그에게 균형 잡히고 건강한 식단을 따라야 한다고 말했다.

STEP 01 단어 암기

<u>Although</u> Richard <u>tried</u> many <u>different</u> <u>ways</u> to <u>lose</u> <u>weight</u> <u>quickly</u>, a <u>weight</u> <u>loss</u>
(접) 비록 ~일지라도　　　(동) 시도했다　　　(형) 다양한　(명) 방법　(동) 빼다　(명) 몸무게　(부) 빠르게　　(명) 체중 (명) 감량

<u>solution</u> that <u>worked</u> for <u>others</u> didn't work for him and made him <u>unhealthy</u>.
(명) 해결책　　(동) 효과가 있다　(명) 다른 사람들　　　　　　　　　　　　　　(형) 건강하지 못한

A <u>personal</u> trainer told him that he should <u>follow</u> a <u>balanced</u> and <u>healthy</u> <u>diet</u>.
　　(형) 개인의　　　　　　　　　　　　　　　　(동) 따르다　　(형) 균형 잡힌　　　(형) 건강한　(명) 식단

STEP 02 구문 분석 훈련 (4형식 동사, 간접목적어, 직접목적어를 표시하고 구문을 분석해보자.)

Although Richard tried many different ways to lose weight quickly, a weight loss

solution that worked for others didn't work for him and made him unhealthy. A

personal trainer told him that he should follow a balanced and healthy diet.

STEP 03 동의어 훈련

Although Richard tried many different ways to lose weight quickly, a weight loss solution that worked for others didn't work for him and made him unhealthy. A personal trainer told him that he should follow a <u>balanced</u> and healthy diet.

Q: In the context of the passage, <u>balanced</u> means _____.

(a) fair
(b) weighted
(c) mixed
(d) biased

Day 13

필수문장 127

We will send you a copy of the information about a list of tasks that you have to do tomorrow. Because it helps you to create a clear path to accomplishing the project efficiently, your work performance can be improved.

우리는 내일 당신에게 수행해야 하는 작업 목록에 관한 정보의 사본을 보낼 것이다. 그것이 프로젝트를 효율적으로 완수하기 위한 명확한 경로를 만드는 것을 도와주기 때문에, 작업 성과가 개선될 수 있다.

 STEP 01 단어 암기

We will <u>send</u> you a <u>copy</u> of the <u>information</u> about a list of <u>tasks</u> that you have
(동) 보내다   (명) 사본   (명) 정보   (명) 일, 업무

to do tomorrow. Because it helps you to <u>create</u> a <u>clear</u> <u>path</u> to <u>accomplishing</u>
(동) 창조하다 (형) 명확한 (명) 경로 (동) 완성하다, 성취하다

the project <u>efficiently</u>, your work <u>performance</u> can be <u>improved</u>.
(부) 효율적으로   (명) 성과, 수행   (동) 개선시키다

 STEP 02 구문 분석 훈련 (4형식 동사, 간접목적어, 직접목적어를 표시하고 구문을 분석해보자.)

We will send you a copy of the information about a list of tasks that you have

to do tomorrow. Because it helps you to create a clear path to accomplishing the

project efficiently, your work performance can be improved.

STEP 03 동의어 훈련

We will send you a copy of the information about a list of tasks that you have to do tomorrow. Because it helps you to create a clear path to accomplishing the project <u>efficiently</u>, your work performance can be improved.

Q: In the context of the passage, <u>efficiently</u> means _____.

(a) naively
(b) abstractly
(c) productively
(d) flawlessly

Day 13

필수문장 128

Because Mike wanted to reward employees for their work, he offered some employees financial incentives, including cash rewards. Moreover, he gave the best employees extra paid vacation days to recognize their efforts.

마이크는 직원들에게 그들의 일에 대해 보상해주기를 원했기 때문에, 일부 직원들에게 현금 보상을 포함한 금전적 인센티브를 제공했다. 금전적 인센티브와 더불어, 그는 최고의 직원들에게는 그들의 노력을 인정하기 위해 추가 유급 휴가를 주었다.

 STEP 01 단어 암기

Because Mike wanted to reward employees for their work, he offered some
(접) ~ 때문에   (동) 보상해주다   (명) 직원   (동) 제공하다

employees financial incentives, including cash rewards. Moreover, he gave the
(형) 재정적인   (전) ~을 포함하여 (명) 현금 (명) 보상, 보수   (부) 게다가

best employees extra paid vacation days to recognize their efforts.
(형) 추가적인   유급 휴가   (동) 인식하다, 인정하다   (명) 노력

 STEP 02 구문 분석 훈련 (4형식 동사, 간접목적어, 직접목적어를 표시하고 구문을 분석해보자.)

Because Mike wanted to reward employees for their work, he offered some

employees financial incentives, including cash rewards. Moreover, he gave the

best employees extra paid vacation days to recognize their efforts.

276

STEP 03 동의어 훈련

Because Mike wanted to reward employees for their work, he offered some employees <u>financial</u> incentives, including cash rewards. Moreover, he gave the best employees extra paid vacation days to recognize their efforts.

Q: In the context of the passage, <u>financial</u> means _____.

(a) monetary
(b) commercial
(c) alternative
(d) investitive

필수문장 129

Trafficking in wildlife has caused species populations to decline, making some species become extinct. We should fight against illegal wildlife trade across the world and give all species facing threats strict protection.

야생동물 불법 거래는 종의 개체 수를 감소시켰고, 몇몇 종들을 멸종하게 만들었다. 우리는 전 세계의 불법 야생동물 무역에 맞서 싸워야 하고 위협에 직면한 모든 종을 엄격하게 보호해야 한다.

STEP 01 단어 암기

Trafficking in wildlife has caused species populations to decline, making some
(명) 불법거래, 일매   (명) 야생동물   (동) 유발하다   (명) 인구   (동) 감소하다

species become extinct. We should fight against illegal wildlife trade across the
(명) 종   (형) 멸종한   (형) 불법적인   (명) 거래 (전) ~에 걸쳐

world and give all species facing threats strict protection.
(형) 직면한 (명) 위협 (형) 엄격한   (명) 보호

STEP 02 구문 분석 훈련 (4형식 동사, 간접목적어, 직접목적어를 표시하고 구문을 분석해보자.)

Trafficking in wildlife has caused species populations to decline, making some

species become extinct. We should fight against illegal wildlife trade across the

world and give all species facing threats strict protection.

STEP 03 동의어 훈련

Trafficking in wildlife has caused species populations to decline, making some species become extinct. We should fight against illegal wildlife trade across the world and give all species facing threats <u>strict</u> protection.

Q: In the context of the passage, <u>strict</u> means _____.

(a) harsh
(b) rigorous
(c) cruel
(d) accurate

Day 13

필수문장 130

Matthew had a hard time landing the job because he was usually nervous during the interview process. Nevertheless, he struggled to overcome job interview anxiety and prepared for the interview thoroughly. Finally, his dream company hired him and his parents bought him Tesla Model Y as a gift.

매튜는 대개 면접 과정에서 긴장했기 때문에 직장을 잡는 데 어려움을 겪었다. 그럼에도 불구하고 그는 취업 면접 불안을 극복하기 위해 고군분투 했고 면접을 철저히 준비했다. 마침내, 그의 꿈의 회사는 그를 고용했고 그의 부모님은 그에게 테슬라 모델 Y를 선물로 사주었다.

STEP 01 단어 암기

Matthew had a <u>hard</u> time <u>landing</u> the job because he was <u>usually</u> <u>nervous</u> <u>during</u>
　　　　　　(형) 어려운　　(명) 얻다　　　　　　　　　　　(부) 대개　　(형) 긴장한　(전) ~동안

the interview <u>process</u>. <u>Nevertheless</u>, he <u>struggled</u> to <u>overcome</u> job interview <u>anxiety</u>
　　　　　　(명) 과정　　(부) 그럼에도 불구하고　　(동) 고군분투하다　(동) 극복하다　　　　　(명) 불안

and <u>prepared for</u> the interview <u>thoroughly</u>. <u>Finally</u>, his dream <u>company</u> <u>hired</u> him
　　(동) ~을 준비했다　　　　　　(부) 철저하게　(부) 마침내　　　　(명) 회사　(동) 고용하다

and his <u>parents</u> <u>bought</u> him Tesla Model Y <u>as</u> a gift.
　　　　(명) 부모　(동) 사주었다　　　　　　　　　(전) ~로써

STEP 02 구문 분석 훈련 (4형식 동사, 간접목적어, 직접목적어를 표시하고 구문을 분석해보자.)

Matthew had a hard time landing the job because he was usually nervous during

the interview process. Nevertheless, he struggled to overcome job interview

anxiety and prepared for the interview thoroughly. Finally, his dream company

hired him and his parents bought him Tesla Model Y as a gift.

STEP 03 동의어 훈련

Matthew had a hard time landing the job because he was usually nervous during the interview process. Nevertheless, he struggled to overcome job interview anxiety and prepared for the interview <u>thoroughly</u>. Finally, his dream company hired him and his parents bought him Tesla Model Y as a gift.

Day 13

Q: In the context of the passage, <u>thoroughly</u> means _____.

(a) approximately
(b) roughly
(c) strategically
(d) exhaustively

step
04

지텔프 문법 26문항 중 4문항은 연결어와 조동사에서 출제된다. 연결어와 조동사의 경우 다른 문법 문제와 달리 정확히 해석해야 풀리는 문제가 대부분이다. 우리는 지금껏 13가지의 해석 포인트를 활용해 130문장을 해석하는 훈련을 했다. 이제 앞서 학습한 130문장을 가지고 조동사와 연결어를 훈련할 것이다. 그동안 해석이 잘 안 돼서 연결어와 조동사 문제를 푸는 데 어려움이 있었던 수험생들에게 많은 도움이 될 것이다. 문제를 풀기에 앞서 지텔프 문법에 출제되는 연결어와 조동사를 간단히 살펴보자.

1. 연결어

전치사, 접속사, 접속부사가 출제된다. 각 연결어의 문법적 특징과 뜻을 정확히 파악해야 문제를 풀 수 있다. 좀 더 세부적으로 살펴보자.

① 전치사 : 뒤에 명사나 명사구가 나온다.

이유 [~ 때문에]	because of, due to, owing to
~에도 불구하고	in spite of, despite

② 접속사 : 절과 절을 연결해주는 역할을 하며 없앨 경우 문법적으로 오류가 있다.

이유 [~ 때문에, ~라는 점에서]	as, because, in that, now that, since, seeing that
조건	assuming that, as(so) long as, if, provided that, so far as, given that, suppose that, in case that, in the event that [만약 ~라면, ~할 경우, ~라고 가정하면, ~을 고려하면] unless [만약 ~가 아니라면]
양보 [비록 ~일지라도]	even though, even if, although, though, however, no matter how
시간	after [~한 후에] as soon as [~하지마자] as, when [~할 때] before [~하기 전에] once [일단 ~하면] till, until [~할 때까지] while [~하는 동안] whenever [~할 때마다]
목적 [~하기 위하여]	so that in order that
결과 [그 결과 ~하다]	so~that- [너무 ~해서 -하다] such ~that- [너무 ~해서 -하다]
대조 [~하는 반면]	while whereas
기타	as if [마치 ~처럼] whether [~이든 아니든] wherever [~하는 곳은 어디든]

③ 접속부사 : 보통 ,앞에 위치하며 앞 문장과 뒷 문장을 내용적으로 연결해준다. 없앨 경우 문법적으로는
　　　　　 오류가 없다.

인과 [그 결과, 결과적으로]	as a result, accordingly, consequently, for this reason, hence, in conclusion, so, therefore, thus, then, thereby
역접 [그러나, 그럼에도 불구하고]	all the same, even so, however, nevertheless, nonetheless, notwithstanding, still, in fact, yet
대조 [대조적으로, 거꾸로]	conversely, contrarily, in contrast, on the contrary, on the other hand,
예시 [예를 들어]	for example, for instance

유사, 두 번째 예시 [유사하게, 마찬가지로]	in the same way, equally, in the same manner, likewise, similarly,
추가, 첨가 [게다가]	also, additionally, besides, further, furthermore, in addition, moreover
환언 [즉, 다시 말하면]	namely, in other words, that is, that is to say
요약 [간단히 말해, 요약하면]	in a word, in brief, in summary, in short, to sum up
강조	as a matter of fact, actually, certainly, especially, indeed, in fact
기타	afterwards [그 후] above all [무엇보다도] at first [처음에는] eventually, in the end [마침내, 결국] by all means [무슨 일이 있어도] fortunately [다행히도] for one thing, first of all [우선] in the meantime, meanwhile [그러는 동안] instead [대신에] subsequently [그 이후, 계속해서] unfortunately [불행하게도]

2. 조동사

지텔프에서 빈출되는 조동사는 다음과 같다.

can	능력, 가능성, 허가
could	can 보다 가능성이 낮을 때 can의 과거 허가
should	충고, 권유, 도덕성
must	무조건 해야 하는 의무
will	미래에 있을 확실한 일 의지
would	will보다 확실성이 덜한 경우 will의 과거
may	약한 추측

001

The employer reduced my salary _____ the extended work hours.

(a) because of
(b) despite
(c) on the other hand
(d) instead

002

By the age of 5, many children _____ distinguish between reality and

fantasy.

(a) would
(b) must
(c) can
(d) shall

003

Some medical volunteers _____ provide medical care in African communities

next month.

(a) should
(b) must
(c) will
(d) may

004

In the 1990s, in a small town, a man invented numerous instruments for farmers. _____, they were useless.

(a) However

(b) For example

(c) Similarly

(d) Therefore

005

Amy, an English author, born in Leytonstone in 1990, is one of the famous novelists. _____, she is the drummer of a famous band in the city.

(a) On the other hand

(b) In addition

(c) Nevertheless

(d) For example

006

Amy announced her retirement from teaching at the age of forty. _____, her co-worker, Jack, decided to continue his teaching.

(a) On the other hand

(b) Even though

(c) Therefore

(d) Similarly

007

For most people, money is an essential factor in happiness. _____,

people with high incomes are not necessarily satisfied with their lives.

- (a) Though
- (b) While
- (c) However
- (d) Furthemore

008

Flowers use powerful tools for attracting pollinators, including bees and insects.

_____, daylilies use bright colors for attracting bees and insects.

- (a) For example
- (b) Thus
- (c) Similarly
- (d) In other words

009

Fast fashion can have a disastrous impact on humans and our environment.

_____, it is responsible for global carbon emissions because of the use

of fossil fuels like crude oil.

- (a) However
- (b) Instead
- (c) For example
- (d) Nevertheless

010

One of the biggest differences between humans and other animals is the ability of inventing new tools. Also, unlike animals, humans _____ describe thoughts and feelings accurately.

(a) can

(b) would

(c) may

(d) might

011

_____ the boss was sick, he called off an important meeting.

(a) Owing to

(b) As if

(c) Although

(d) Because

012

Police can detain people _____ they fail to provide a valid passport.

(a) in spite of

(b) if

(c) as well as

(d) in order that

013

A study found that outdoor play _____ have a positive impact on children.

(a) should
(b) shall
(c) must
(d) could

014

You need to remember that weather forecasts _____ be wrong.

(a) will
(b) can
(c) shall
(d) must

015

Whenever Jake wanted to spend some quality time with his friends, he

_____ go to the cozy cafe.

(a) shall
(b) must
(c) can
(d) would

016

A school counselor said that Mike _____ earn a bachelor's degree in a related field for his dream.

(a) should
(b) may
(c) will
(d) shall

017

_____ drinking too much carrot juice can be bad for you, some studies showed that carrot juice in your diet could have a health benefit.

(a) Because
(b) In fact
(c) Though
(d) In that

018

A study revealed that people could build a meaningful relationship through adoption. _____, it can be a challenging process.

(a) So
(b) Thus
(c) In addition
(d) However

019

_____ carbohydrates are essential to your diet, the excessive consumption of carbohydrates can result in inconsistent blood sugar levels.

(a) Whenever
(b) Because
(c) Although
(d) Until

020

The impacts of global warming are speeding up _____ concentrations of greenhouse gases in the atmosphere increase.

(a) before
(b) as
(c) wherever
(d) in fact

021

_____ Amy wanted to be slim, she decided to get in shape and lose weight in 7 days.

(a) Because
(b) Though
(c) No matter how
(d) Even though

022

Dogs are the best pet for many reasons. _____, they can bite people and scratch furniture.

(a) Namely
(b) However
(c) In other words
(d) Afterwards

023

April gave up her vacation and canceled the flight ticket _____ she had to finish a project on time.

(a) as soon as
(b) because
(c) whenever
(d) unless

024

Water pollution kills a number of people every year as well as affects the health of animals. _____, most of the people don't do anything to prevent water pollution.

(a) In brief
(b) Subsequently
(c) Nevertheless
(d) In the meantime

025

_____ Rachel met a man in London and had dinner with him at a fancy restaurant last year, she doesn't even remember his name.

(a) As a matter of fact
(b) Now that
(c) Although
(d) As if

026

You _____ present your ID card to attend tomorrow's meeting and take a special lecture. Unless you have an ID card, you can't get in.

(a) can
(b) may
(c) should
(d) must

027

_____ Bill passed his road test and got his driver's license, his sister gave her car to him.

(a) Whether
(b) Above all
(c) At first
(d) When

028

Monica was studying _____ she heard strange sounds and saw something

through the window.

(a) in short

(b) when

(c) conversely

(d) because

029

_____ archaeologists discovered and studied the tomb of a woman, they

found that men and women enjoyed equal rights at that time.

(a) For example

(b) After

(c) Even though

(d) Unless

030

Workout apps gain popularity _____ the interest in health is increasing.

They offer workout videos and training routines for free and provide even

personalized workout plans for all fitness levels.

(a) even though

(b) so that

(c) as

(d) in order that

031

Next week, John _____ donate all of his prize money he received for winning the race to charity.

(a) will
(b) should
(c) shall
(d) would

032

Jason was sure that the mobile app he had created could attract users. _____, the app failed because it was too expensive.

(a) However
(b) Though
(c) In the same way
(d) Contrarily

033

Grace failed to make a delicious pasta dish _____ the recipe she found online was full of errors.

(a) eventually
(b) once
(c) before
(d) because

034

Jason sometimes picks edible mushrooms in the mountains. He _____ make various dishes with the mushrooms he gathers.

(a) can
(b) would
(c) should
(d) shall

035

A few years ago, Amy lost a book her grandfather had given. _____ she searched every corner of the room, she never found the book.

(a) So that
(b) Once
(c) Although
(d) Nevertheless

036

_____ Jane wants to stop wasting money on things she doesn't need and prepare for the future, she puts some money aside every month.

(a) Though
(b) Unless
(c) Because
(d) Thus

037

A boy the babysitter took care of was missing. _____, police found him

in good health and he restored emotional stability after the traumatic event.

(a) Fortunately

(b) As

(c) Certainly

(d) That is

038

One of the reasons consumers shop online is that they _____ compare

a number of products at a time and get instant access to product reviews.

(a) can

(b) shall

(c) may

(d) must

039

Jack thinks that cooking is a waste of time and wants to reduce his cooking

time. _____, he has attempted to halve the time he spends cooking by

preparing the ingredients in advance.

(a) Additionally

(b) On the other hand

(c) Instead

(d) Therefore

040

Technologies have brought so many changes in our lives. For example, computers have changed the way we work significantly. _____, smartphones have changed the way we shop.

(a) For instance
(b) Similarly
(c) On the contrary
(d) Accordingly

041

_____ Molly is not able to sleep well at night, she takes sleeping pills which help to induce sleep.

(a) However
(b) Whenever
(c) So that
(d) Equally

042

People who want to get plastic surgery _____ understand the potential medical risks and get enough information to avoid harmful effects.

(a) shall
(b) will
(c) should
(d) could

043

People who spend long hours on computers _____ experience a headache. You should take a break when you are on a computer.

(a) must
(b) should
(c) will
(d) may

044

Jack is a famous pianist. _____, he is also a comic book writer who has won many awards in comic book contests.

(a) However
(b) In order that
(c) On the other hand
(d) Thereby

045

A boy who physically hurt a man on purpose and went to jail managed to get out of jail _____ he paid the full bail amount.

(a) after
(b) hence
(c) wherever
(d) although

046

Jack is crazy about spicy Mexican food which has a strong flavor from spices. _____, his mom suggested that he avoid eating too much spicy food because it is harmful to his health.

(a) Even though
(b) Besides
(c) In summary
(d) However

047

Ross didn't pay back his student loan when he earned a salary. _____, he bought a company's stock which a colleague recommended.

(a) Instead
(b) All the same
(c) Accordingly
(d) To sum up

048

_____ the girl who had lost three times in a row in a card game suggested changing the rule in her favor, everyone didn't accept her suggestion.

(a) Contrarily
(b) In case that
(c) So far as
(d) Even though

049

The car offers the option to select a driving mode. Those who want to immerse themselves in the exciting driving experience can select sport mode. _____, those who want a smoother ride can select comfort mode.

(a) After
(b) In contrast
(c) Because
(d) In fact

050

Some retail stores that have suffered sharp sales drop because of the emergence of e—commerce are going through tough times. _____. Some retail stores have survived the crisis because they offer things e—commerce cannot replace, including the shopping experience.

(a) Wherever
(b) On the other hand
(c) Similarly
(d) That is to say

051

You _____ choose the right kindergarten if you want your kids to develop valuable social skills.

(a) will
(b) can
(c) should
(d) shall

052

An expert recommends that we stop working from home _____ it could cause the line between our personal lives and work to blur.

(a) furthermore
(b) wherever
(c) because
(d) unless

053

Jane was under stress because of a colleague interfering with her work. _____, she asked her boss to move him to another department.

(a) At first
(b) While
(c) Eventually
(d) For instance

054

_____ many people found harmful materials in a popular convenience food, the local health department required supermarkets to stop the sales of the food.

(a) Because
(b) Afterwards
(c) Provided that
(d) Although

055

Mark assigned too much work to Rachel, which caused her to become depressed. _____, she had a problem with her coworker.

(a) Namely
(b) Furthermore
(c) All the same
(d) As soon as

056

A company _____ release a new version of its software next month. Its various features will allow you to experience amazing things.

(a) will
(b) should
(c) may
(d) must

057

Parents _____ teach their children to respect each other and encourage lifelong friendships between siblings because a positive relationship between siblings can lead to higher levels of self-esteem.

(a) should
(b) must
(c) will
(d) would

058

Employees should attend the training program, which will encourage them to cultivate creativity. _____, the program can motivate employees to increase innovation in products and work hard.

(a) Even so
(b) Moreover
(c) However
(d) By all means

059

Some adoptive parents have urged young couples to adopt a child. However, those who want to adopt a child _____ be financially stable. Unless they meet the financial requirements of adoption, they can't adopt a child.

(a) should
(b) will
(c) can
(d) must

060

Suzy, a wedding florist, takes a lot of pride in her work and tries to make her customers feel special. _____ choosing flowers for the wedding by herself, she always allows brides to choose flowers they want for their wedding.

(a) Moreover
(b) Instead of
(c) In spite of
(d) Despite

061

_____ Mike tried to keep his old dog healthy, the dog vomited several times and refused to eat.

(a) Since
(b) Because
(c) Now that
(d) Although

062

You _____ develop the ability to organize your thoughts and support your point logically to express your ideas clearly.

(a) will
(b) should
(c) shall
(d) would

063

Judy knows that vacation is an excellent opportunity to read books. She ordered some books online and _____ read them all this vacation.

(a) will
(b) might
(c) must
(d) shall

064

Many children who live in extreme poverty struggle to meet the basic living expenses. We _____ take some measures to provide assistance for them.

(a) may
(b) shall
(c) should
(d) might

065

_____ the boss always ignores Amy, she is under too much stress, which is causing hair loss. She is going to buy a special shampoo which strengthens each strand of hair to stop hair loss.

(a) Although
(b) Because
(c) As if
(d) In fact

066

To make the best salad dressing, Ross tried mixing various ingredients such as vinegar and olive oil. _____, he could make the perfect dressing by using yogurt and Dijon mustard.

(a) However
(b) Finally
(c) Nevertheless
(d) On the other hand

067

The doctor recommended that Jenny take essential nutrients through the diet to maintain optimal health and enjoy her life. _____, she keeps on eating only a single food item for each meal to lose weight.

(a) Nevertheless
(b) Thus
(c) While
(d) Similarly

068

My father had wanted to build a factory to make custom furniture in London. However, he gave up _____ he didn't have enough money to build a factory.

(a) while
(b) in addition
(c) even if
(d) because

069

Many small companies need to take a new approach to overcome the financial crisis and achieve their goal. _____, they would stop operating and go out of business.

(a) Nevertheless
(b) On the other hand
(c) Otherwise
(d) In other words

070

_____ Rachel's father promised to give some money to her if she solved a difficult math problem, she made an effort to work through the problem in order to get money.

(a) Until
(b) So
(c) Whereas
(d) Because

071

A doctor warns that drinking too much _____ cause serious health problems.

(a) must
(b) should
(c) shall
(d) can

072

Involving children in household chores has many advantages. _____, getting children to clean their room can make them feel needed.

(a) While
(b) For example
(c) Namely
(d) Meanwhile

073

When you start a restaurant, finding the perfect location for it is so important.

_____ it is in a good location, you will fail to attract many customers.

(a) On the contrary
(b) Even so
(c) Unless
(d) Since

074

_____ a doctor warned that drinking too much coffee could be harmful

to the body by increasing the heartbeat, Judy took in too much caffeine through

coffee. The doctor advised her to find alternatives to coffee.

(a) Until
(b) Provided that
(c) In order that
(d) Wherever

075

Because spending too much time playing computer games could lead to

migraines, Molly advised her brother to stop playing them. _____, he

ignored her advice and played more intensely to escape reality.

(a) In a word
(b) Whereas
(c) For example
(d) Nevertheless

076

Amy helps her son to develop responsibility. _____, she always gets

him to do chores like mowing the lawn and setting the table because she

believes that giving household chores helps him to learn responsibility.

(a) For example

(b) In summary

(c) That is to say

(d) Therefore

077

Taking some time to research a company you want to work for online in advance

is necessary before you attend a job interview. By doing so, you _____ make

a good impression on your potential employer.

(a) must

(b) should

(c) can

(d) shall

078

Because a doctor said that eating too much red meat could increase the risk

of getting heart disease, Judy decided to choose plant-based diets

_____ eating a large amount of meat.

(a) in the same way

(b) despite

(c) in spite of

(d) instead of

079

Because Rachel spent too much money on her hobbies, she was short on rent last month. _____ having a hobby made her happy, her boyfriend asked her to save money instead of spending on expensive hobbies.

(a) Also
(b) Once
(c) Although
(d) Before

080

Molly bans employees from wasting time on social media by blocking social networking sites while they are working _____ she thinks that using social media in the workplace has a negative effect on productivity.

(a) while
(b) because
(c) whether
(d) as if

081

Chris wants to get along with his girlfriend's friends, hoping to meet them. _____, she hides their current relationship from them.

(a) Equally
(b) However
(c) As a result
(d) Hence

082

Amy is eager to travel around the world, experiencing new ways of living and broadening her horizons. _____, she doesn't have enough money to travel.

(a) Unfortunately
(b) In other words
(c) At first
(d) For one thing

083

An aircraft mechanic reported the serious problem with the left engine, adding that the plane _____ make an emergency landing immediately.

(a) should
(b) may
(c) must
(d) could

084

_____ financial problems, E&K has grown into the largest beverage company, generating approximately $500 million of revenue over the last two quarters.

(a) Instead of
(b) Despite
(c) Owing to
(d) Because of

085

The new concealer helps men to cover their skin flaws, addressing the specific needs of men. However, _____ it causes skin irritation, stop using it and consult your doctor.

(a) instead
(b) in case that
(c) before
(d) whereas

086

Using sport mode in your car will make your driving experience more exciting, making your car go faster. _____, leaving your car in sport mode all the time could cause some problems.

(a) While
(b) For instance
(c) However
(d) Moreover

087

Matthew had to cancel his summer vacation to Varanasi due to some reasons, giving up his hope of walking along the Ganges River. _____, he decided to take a break at home, relaxing on the couch and watching movies.

(a) Additionally
(b) Likewise
(c) Instead
(d) Above all

088

Because _____ a man was doing his shopping, his phone was missing, he requested CCTV footage to locate his phone. CCTV footage showed that a little girl glancing around the store and browsing through a magazine stole the phone from his bag.

(a) until
(b) as a matter of fact
(c) whether
(d) while

089

Some people take many different supplements at the same time without thinking, which can increase the risk of adverse drug reactions, leading to dangerous effects. _____, you should be careful when you are taking them, reading the label carefully.

(a) Though
(b) Therefore
(c) Contrarily
(d) In the end

090

A non-profit organization is working to offer various academic programs for the most vulnerable students. _____, many students who otherwise would not have access to quality education have the opportunity to learn.

(a) As a result
(b) For one thing
(c) Further
(d) Fortunately

091

It is well known that the restaurant is good for a first date _____ the perfect lighting.

(a) because of
(b) in that
(c) even though
(d) in spite of

092

Money may be necessary for happiness. _____, it is more important to be satisfied with your life to live a happy life.

(a) However
(b) No matter how
(c) That is to say
(d) To sum up

093

It is necessary to prevent global warming from becoming worse. _____, we should do something to save the planet.

(a) Nevertheless
(b) On the other hand
(c) After
(d) Therefore

094

_____ Kate is wealthy enough not to work, she always works hard instead of being lazy. "It is important to continue working to feel alive.", she says.

(a) Wherever
(b) At first
(c) As
(d) Although

095

It is beneficial to talk and listen to babies. _____, talking to babies from birth makes them hear different and more words, improving their understanding of language and encouraging them to build communication skills.

(a) Even though
(b) Contrarily
(c) For example
(d) All the same

096

It was found that serious problems with tires _____ the car run over a sharp object occurred. Because joey thought that these could cause a car accident, he replaced the tires immediately.

(a) in order that
(b) after
(c) in the same way
(d) till

097

To make a successful presentation, it is especially important to examine information about your listeners and analyze it. In addition, you _____ know how to keep audience's attention during your presentation.

(a) will
(b) should
(c) can
(d) shall

098

It is normal to lose between 50 and 100 hairs a day _____ they are naturally replaced and return to normal levels. However, if you are losing too much hair, see your doctor to do something about it.

(a) because
(b) even if
(c) as if
(d) although

099

It is essential that Betty get some rest because she feels burned out and exhausted after work, losing her passion she once had in her work. Getting more sleep and enough rest _____ relax her mind and body, also improving her mood and relieving stress.

(a) must
(b) can
(c) shall
(d) should

100

It is known that uniforms function as a visual marker of identities and strengthen cohesion among group members. However, people wearing uniforms can lose their individuality _____ others are wearing the same outfit.

(a) nevertheless
(b) so that
(c) because
(d) even though

101

_____ toxic substances found in a processed food, the authority banned the sale of the product.

(a) instead of
(b) despite
(c) in spite of
(d) Because of

102

A company _____ provide cash bonuses next week. That's because sales of products released by the company have been soaring.

(a) will
(b) should
(c) must
(d) might

103

Kevin plans to make a chocolate cake topped with flowers for mom this Mother's Day. _____ he didn't know how to make a cake, he tried finding secrets for a perfect cake online.

(a) Before
(b) However
(c) Because
(d) Whereas

104

Jennifer often goes to a restaurant and enjoys a special meal made by famous chefs with her boyfriend. They drink a glass of wine _____ they go to the restaurant.

(a) as if
(b) whether
(c) whenever
(d) in that

105

We _____ not believe everything presented in the media. Sometimes stories delivered as news can be false information, deliberately deceiving people.

(a) should
(b) must
(c) will
(d) can

106

When a work environment makes workers uncomfortable, creativity is likely to decrease. _____, a comfortable work environment leads to increased creativity and innovation in employees.

(a) Further
(b) On the other hand
(c) Besides
(d) As a matter of fact

107

_____ the devastating earthquake hit the city, Emily tried to provide assistance for people affected by the earthquake. In fact, she always helps others in need.

(a) Provided that
(b) When
(c) Given that
(d) Actually

108

_____ a car hit a boy walking with his mother, she took him to the hospital. Fortunately, he miraculously survived the fatal car accident caused by a drunk driver.

(a) Though
(b) Instead
(c) Right after
(d) Whereas

109

It is debatable whether the ancient city built 1,800 years ago really existed or not. _____ some archeologists can't find written records of the city, they believe that the city really existed.

(a) So that
(b) Although
(c) After
(d) Now that

110

Some organisms called keystone species are essential in determining the structure of the entire ecosystem. _____, we should protect keystone species in order to maintain ecosystems in the right condition.

(a) In contrast
(b) Additionally
(c) However
(d) Therefore

111

_____ more than three people were killed in a house fire, police said that unknown suspects entered the house and lit it on fire, adding that the investigation was still ongoing.

(a) Before

(b) Namely

(c) After

(d) In order that

112

A number of polar bears left in the world have been pushed on the verge of extinction. We _____ do something to protect them from extinction.

(a) should

(b) will

(c) might

(d) may

113

An organization that has been working to safeguard the health of people with disabilities _____ be financed by a conglomerate starting next year.

(a) should

(b) will

(c) must

(d) can

114

To use public spaces as event venues, you _____ register your event with the council and comply with relevant regulations and safety measures. Otherwise, you are not allowed to hold events.

(a) will
(b) should
(c) might
(d) must

115

_____ a leader worked hard to create a positive work environment, making his team members comfortable and encouraging them to achieve the goal they set, productivity was decreased.

(a) Whenever
(b) As
(c) Although
(d) Suppose that

116

Various organizations have been established to cope with food insecurity and provide people in developing countries with food in a sustainable way. _____, they aim to break down the barriers to education by improving the education of poor children.

(a) For instance
(b) However
(c) In addition
(d) Contrarily

117

The scheduled final exam is going to be pushed back _____ teachers need extra teaching time. Some students insist that it follow the original final exam schedule.

(a) in the same way
(b) because
(c) as if
(d) unless

118

Since some parents can't afford to pay for the tuition, a number of students living in poverty are being forced to drop out of school. In fact, the problems persist in poor countries _____ taking measures to reduce school dropout.

(a) in spite of
(b) instead of
(c) while
(d) as soon as

119

Grace had been injured and fallen into a coma in a hit—and—run car accident.

_____ her husband made an effort to find witnesses who saw the accident

and consulted with a car accident attorney, the hit—and—run driver wasn't caught.

(a) Although
(b) As soon as
(c) Because
(d) Till

120

Some pollutants that contain extremely hazardous substances, such as industrial

waste and plastic debris, are being dumped into the ocean. _____ proper

measures to solve this problem are taken, there will be a considerable threat

to the survival of marine mammals.

(a) No matter how
(b) Whether
(c) Once
(d) Unless

121

_____ Amy was so depressed, avoiding contact with people and

isolating herself, Mike gave her some tips for handling depression and

encouraged her to seek therapy.

(a) Because
(b) Before
(c) Even though
(d) In fact

122

If you want to thank servers for their services, just tell them a quick "thank you" and be kind and courteous. _____, the best way to show appreciation is to give them a generous tip.

(a) Accordingly
(b) However
(c) For example
(d) At first

123

A company offers high school students a job and teaches them practical skills suitable for their future profession _____ they can gain valuable work experience.

(a) whereas
(b) so that
(c) although
(d) whenever

124

Many problems arise with regard to inadequate nutrients for young children. Parents _____ know the importance of nutrition in early childhood development and teach children healthy eating.

(a) will
(b) can
(c) would
(d) should

125

A community center _____ offer various training programs starting next week to teach women living in the most deprived area skills that they need to get a job and support them.

(a) might
(b) shall
(c) could
(d) will

126

Although Richard tried many different ways to lose weight quickly, a weight loss solution that worked for others didn't work for him and made him unhealthy. A personal trainer told him that he _____ follow a balanced and healthy diet.

(a) will
(b) shall
(c) should
(d) must

127

We will send you a copy of the information about a list of tasks that you have to do tomorrow. _____ it helps you to create a clear path to accomplishing the project efficiently, your work performance can be improved.

(a) Because
(b) Though
(c) Whether
(d) As if

128

Because Mike wanted to reward employees for their work, he offered some employees financial incentives, including cash rewards. _____, he gave the best employees extra paid vacation days to recognize their efforts.

(a) While
(b) Moreover
(c) Conversely
(d) On the other hand

129

Trafficking in wildlife has caused species populations to decline, making some species become extinct. We _____ fight against illegal wildlife trade across the world and give all species facing threats strict protection.

(a) can
(b) should
(c) would
(d) will

130

Matthew had a hard time landing the job because he was usually nervous during the interview process. _____, he struggled to overcome job interview anxiety and prepared for the interview thoroughly. Finally, his dream company hired him and his parents bought him Tesla Model Y as a gift.

(a) For example
(b) In the end
(c) Nevertheless
(d) Subsequently

켈리지텔프
해석 POINT
13

Day 1 켈리의 지텔프 해석 POINT 1

001

step 2

The employer / reduced / my salary / despite the extended work hours.

사장님은 / 깎았다 / 나의 월급을 / 늘어난 근무시간에도 불구하고.

step 3

문맥상 '삭감하다, 줄이다'를 뜻하는 cut이 적절하다.

cut 줄이다, 삭감하다 minimize 최소화하다 narrow 좁히다 shrink 수축시키다

정답 ⓑ

002

step 2

By the age of 5, / many children / can distinguish / between reality and fantasy.

5살 쯤 되면, / 많은 아이들이 / 구분할 수 있다 / 현실과 환상 사이를.

step 3

문맥상 '구분하다, 구별하다'를 뜻하는 differentiate 이 적절하다.

differentiate 구분하다, 구별하다 observe 관찰하다 acquire 습득하다 consolidate 강화하다

정답 ⓒ

003

step 2

Some medical volunteers / will provide / medical care / in African communities / next month.

몇몇 의료 봉사자들이 / 제공할 것이다 / 의료 서비스를 / 시골의 아프리카 마을에 / 다음 달에.

step 3

문맥상 '제공하다'를 뜻하는 offer이 적절하다.

offer 제공하다 donate 기부하다 anticipate 예상하다 invest 투자하다

정답 ⓑ

004

step 2

In the 1990s /, in a small town, / a man / invented / numerous instrument / for farmers. / However, / they / were useless.

1990년대에 / 한 작은 마을에서, / 한 남자가 / 발명했다 / 수많은 도구들을 / 농부들을 위한. / 그러나, / 그것들은 / 쓸모 없었다.

step 3

문맥상 '만들다'를 뜻하는 made가 적절하다.

make 만들다 adorn 꾸미다 reinforce 강화하다 establish 설립하다

정답 ⓓ

005

step 2

Amy /, an English author, / born / in Leytonstone / in 1990, / is one / of the famous novelists. / In addition, / she / is the drummer / of a famous band / in the city.

에이미는, / 영국의 작가인 / 태어난 / 레이턴스톤에서 / 1990년에, / 하나이다 / 유명한 소설가 중에 / 게다가, / 그녀는 / 드러머이다 / 유명한 밴드의 / 그 도시에서.

step 3

문맥상 '유명한'을 뜻하는 well-known이 적절하다.

well-known 유명한 disreputable 평판이 안 좋은 notorious 악명 높은 dull 따분한

정답 ⓐ

006

step 2

Amy / announced / her retirement / from teaching / at the age of forty. / On the other hand, / her co-worker, Jack, / decided to continue / his teaching.

에이미는 / 선언했다 / 그녀의 은퇴를 / 가르치는 일에서 / 40살 때. / 반면에, / 그녀의 동료인, 잭은, / 계속 하기로 결심했다 / 가르치는 일을.

step 3

문맥상 '선언하다'를 뜻하는 declared가 적절하다.

declare 선언하다 attract 마음을 끌다 reveal 드러내다 plan 계획을 세우다

정답 ⓒ

007

step 2

For most people, / money / is an essential factor / in happiness. / However, / people / with high incomes / are not necessarily satisfied / with their lives.

대부분의 사람들에게. / 돈은 / 필수적인 요소이다 / 행복의. / 그러나. / 사람들이 / 높은 수입을 가진 / 반드시 만족하는 것은 아니다 / 그들의 삶에.

step 3

문맥상 '요소'를 뜻하는 element가 적절하다.

element 요소 material 재료 process 과정 supplier 공급자

정답 ⓒ

008

step 2

Flowers / use / powerful tools / for attracting pollinators, / including bees and insects. / For example, / daylilies / use / bright colors / for attracting bees and insects.

꽃은 / 사용한다 / 강력한 도구를 / 꽃가루 매개자를 끌어들이기 위해. / 벌과 곤충을 포함한. / 예를 들어. / 원추리는 / 사용한다 / 밝은색을 / 벌과 곤충을 유인하기 위해.

step 3

문맥상 '유혹하다'를 뜻하는 enticing이 적절하다.

entice 유혹하다 disturb 불안하게 만들다 involve 포함하다 pose 제기하다

정답 ⓒ

009

step 2

Fast fashion / can have / a disastrous impact / on humans and our environment. / For example, / it / is responsible / for global carbon emissions / because of the use / of fossil fuels / like crude oil.

패스트 패션은 / 가질 수 있다 / 파괴적인 영향을 / 인간과 환경에. / 예를 들어. / 그것은 / 책임이 있다 / 전 세계 탄소 배출에 / 사용 때문에 / 화석연료의 / 원유 같은.

step 3

문맥상 '파괴적인'을 뜻하는 devastating가 적절하다.

devastating 파괴적인 moderate 적당한 unsuccessful 실패한 miscarry 실패하다

정답 ⓓ

010

step 2

One / of the biggest differences / between humans and other animals / is the ability / of inventing new tools.

331

/ Also, / unlike animals, / humans / can describe / thoughts and feelings / accurately.
하나는 / 가장 큰 차이점 중 / 인간과 다른 동물사이에서 / 능력이다 / 새로운 도구를 발명하는. / 또한. / 동물들과 달리, / 인간들은 / 설명할 수 있다 / 생각과 느낌을 / 정확하게.

step 3

문맥상 '정확하게'를 뜻하는 precisely가 적절하다.

precisely 정확하게 carefully 주의하여, 조심스럽게 patiently 끈기 있게 undoubtedly 의심할 여지없이, 확실히

정답 ⓓ

| Day 2 | 켈리의 지텔프 해석 POINT 2 |

011

step 2

Because the boss / was sick, / he / called off / an important meeting.
사장님이 / 아팠기 때문에. / 그는 / 취소했다 / 중요한 회의를.

step 3

문맥상 '취소하다'를 뜻하는 canceled이 적절하다.

cancel 취소하다 delay 미루다 stop 멈추다 hamper 방해하다

정답 ⓒ

012

step 2

Police / can detain / people / if they / fail to provide / a valid passport.

경찰은 / 억류할 수 있다 / 사람들을 / 만약 그들이 / 제공하지 않는다면 / 유효한 여권을.

step 3

문맥상 '억류하다'를 뜻하는 hold가 적절하다.

hold 억류하다, 잡다, 담다 interrupt 방해하다, 차단하다 disturb 방해하다, 불안하게 만들다 defend 방어하다

정답 ⓓ

013

step 2

A study / found / that outdoor play / could have / a positive impact / on children.
한 연구는 / 발견했다 / 야외 활동이 / 줄 수 있다는 것을 / 긍정적인 영향을 / 아이들에게.

step 3

문맥상 '긍정적인, 이로운'을 뜻하는 beneficial이 적절하다.

beneficial 긍정적인, 이로운 confident 자신감 있는 optimistic 낙관적인, 낙관하는 moderate 보통의, 중간의

정답 ⓐ

014

step 2

You / need to remember / that weather forecasts / can be wrong.
당신은 / 기억할 필요가 있다 / 일기 예보가 / 잘못될 수 있다는 것을.

step 3

문맥상 '부정확한, 틀린'을 뜻하는 inaccurate이 적절하다.

inaccurate 부정확한, 틀린 changeable 바뀔 수도 있는, 변덕이 심한 flexible 신축성 있는, 유연한 replaceable 대신할 수 있는

정답 ⓒ

015

step 2

Whenever Jake / **wanted** / to spend / some quality time / with his friends, / he / **would go** / to the cozy cafe.

제이크가 / 원할 때마다 / 보내기를 / 귀중한 시간을 / 그의 친구들과, / 그는 / 가곤 했었다 / 안락한 카페에.

step 3

quality time은 가까운 사람들에게 관심을 기울이면서 보내는 특별하고 중요한 시간을 의미한다. 문맥상 '소중한'를 뜻하는 precious가 적절하다.

precious 소중한 **superior** 우수한 **grade** 등급, 지위 **lazy** 게으른

정답 ⓐ

016

step 2

A school counselor / said / **that** Mike / **should earn** / a bachelor's degree / in a related field / for his dream.

상담 선생님은 / 말했다 / Mike가 / 따야 한다고 / 학사학위를 / 관련 분야에서 / 그의 꿈을 위해

step 3

문맥상 '얻다, 획득하다'를 뜻하는 get이 적절하다.

get 얻다 **collect** 모으다 **produce** 생산하다 **create** 창조하다

정답 ⓐ

017

step 2

Though drinking too much / carrot juice / **can be** bad / for you, / some studies / showed / **that** carrot juice / in your diet / **could have** / a health benefit.

비록 너무 많이 마시는 것은 / 당근쥬스를 / 나쁠 수 있지만 / 너에게, / 몇몇 연구는 / 보여주었다 / 당근쥬스가 / 당신의 식단 안에 / 가질 수 있다는 것을 / 건강상의 이점을.

step 3

문맥상 '이점'을 뜻하는 advantage가 적절하다.

advantage 이점 **welfare** 안녕, 복지 **comfort** 안락, 편안 **usability** 유용성, 편리함

정답 ⓐ

018

step 2

A study / revealed / **that** people / **could build** / a meaningful relationship / through adoption. / However, / it / can be / a challenging process.

한 연구는 / 보여주었다 / 사람들이 / 쌓을 수 있다는 것을 / 의미 있는 관계를 / 입양을 통해. / 그러나, / 그것은 / 될 수 있다 / 힘든 과정이.

step 3

문맥상 '힘든'을 뜻하는 demanding이 적절하다.

demanding 힘든 **inspiring** 고무하는, 격려하는 **energize** 활기를 북돋우다 **purposeful** 목적의식이 있는, 결단력 있는

정답 ⓓ

019

step 2

Although carbohydrates / **are** essential / to your diet, / the excessive consumption / of carbohydrates / can result / in inconsistent blood sugar levels.

비록 탄수화물이 / 필수적이지만 / 당신의 식단에, / 과도한 섭취는 / 탄수화물의 / 유발할 수 있다 / 불안정한 혈당 수치를.

step 3

문맥상 '불안정한'을 뜻하는 unstable이 적절하다.

unstable 불안정한 reconcilable 조정할 수 있는
uncertain 확신이 없는 doubtful 의심을 품은

정답 ⓑ

020

step 2

The impacts / of global warming / are
speeding up / as concentrations / of
greenhouse gases / in the atmosphere
/ increase.

영향이 / 지구 온난화의 / 가속화되고 있다 / 농도
가 / 온실가스의 / 대기 중에 / 증가함에 따라.

step 3

문맥상 '빨라지다'를 뜻하는 accelerating이 적절하다.

accelerate 빨라지다 hasten 서둘러하다, 재촉하다
promote 촉진하다, 고취하다 simplify 간소화하다,
단순화하다

정답 ⓒ

| Day 3 | 켈리의 지텔프 해석 POINT 3 |

021

step 2

Because Amy / wanted to be slim, / she
/ decided / to get in shape / and lose
weight / in 7 days.

에이미는 / 날씬해지고 싶었기 때문에. / 그녀는 /
결심했다 / 몸매를 가꾸기를 / 그리고 살을 빼기로
/ 7일 안에.

step 3

문맥상 '결심하다'를 뜻하는 resolved가 적절하다.

resolve 결심하다 execute 처형하다, 실행하다
prepare 준비하다 accomplish 완수하다, 성취하다

정답 ⓐ

022

step 2

Dogs / are the best pet / for many reasons.
/ However, / they / can bite people / and
scratch furniture.

개는 / 최고의 애완동물이다 / 여러 가지 이유 때문
에. / 그러나. / 그들은 / 사람들을 물 수 있고 /
가구에 긁힌 자국을 낼 수 있다.

step 3

문맥상 '가장 좋은'을 뜻하는 greatest가 적절하다.

greatest 가장 좋은 leading 가장 중요한, 선두적인
principal 주요한 superior 우수한

정답 ⓒ

023

step 2

April / gave up / her vacation / and
canceled / the flight ticket / because she
had to finish / a project / on time.

에이프릴은 / 포기했다 / 휴가를 / 그리고 취소했다
/ 비행기 티켓을 / 그녀는 끝내야 했기 때문에 /
프로젝트를 / 제 시간에.

step 3

문맥상 '완료하다'를 뜻하는 complete가 적절하다.

complete 완료하다 cease 중단시키다 suspend
중단하다, 연기하다 terminate 끝나다, 종료되다

정답 ⓓ

024

step 2

Water pollution / kills / a number of people / every year / as well as affects / the health of animals. / Nevertheless, / most of the people / don't do / anything / to prevent / water pollution.

수질 오염은 / 죽인다 / 수많은 사람들을 / 매년 / 영향을 미칠 뿐만 아니라 / 동물의 건강에. / 그럼에도 불구하고, / 대부분의 사람들은 / 하지 않는다 / 어떤 일도 / 예방하기 위해 / 수질 오염을.

step 3

문맥상 '위협하다'를 뜻하는 threatens가 적절하다.

threaten 위협하다 maintain 유지시키다 profit 이익을 얻다 aid 돕다

정답 ⓐ

025

step 2

Although Rachel / met / him / in London / and had dinner / with him / at a fancy restaurant / last year, / she / doesn't even remember / his name.

비록 레이첼이 / 만났음에도 불구하고 / 그를 / 런던에서 / 그리고 저녁을 먹었음에도 불구하고 / 그와 / 고급 식당에서 / 작년에. / 그녀는 / 기억하지 못한다 / 그의 이름조차.

step 3

문맥상 '고급의'를 뜻하는 luxurious가 적절하다.
luxurious 고급의 affordable 줄 수 있는, 알맞은 cozy 아늑한 reasonable 타당한

정답 ⓒ

026

step 2

You / must present / your ID card / to attend / tomorrow's meeting / and take / a special lecture. / Unless you / have / an ID card, / you / can't get in.

당신은 / 제시해야 한다 / 당신의 신분증을 / 참석하기 위해서 / 내일 회의에 / 그리고 듣기 위해서 / 특별한 강연을. / 만약 당신이 / 가지고 있지 않다면 / 신분증을, / 당신은 / 들어올 수 없다.

step 3

문맥상 '보여주다'를 뜻하는 show가 적절하다.

show 보여주다 appear 나타나다 express 표현하다 release 풀어주다, 놓아주다

정답 ⓐ

027

step 2

When Bill / passed / his road test / and got / his driver's license, / his sister / gave / her car / to him.

빌이 / 통과했을 때 / 그의 도로 주행 테스트를 / 그리고 땄을 때 / 운전면허를. / 그의 누나가 / 주었다 / 그녀의 차를 / 그에게.

step 3

문맥상 '얻다, 획득하다'를 뜻하는 earned가 적절하다.

earn 얻다, 획득하다 develop 발달하다 apply 신청하다, 지원하다 prevail 우세하다, 승리하다, 이기다

정답 ⓑ

028

step 2

Monica / was studying / when she / heard

335

/ strange sounds / and saw / something / through the window.

모니카는 / 공부하는 중이었다 / 그녀가 / 들었을 때 / 이상한 소리를 / 그리고 보았을 때 / 무언가를 / 창문을 통해.

step 3

문맥상 '이상한, 보통이 아닌'을 뜻하는 unusual이 적절하다.

unusual 이상한, 보통이 아닌 unpleasant 불쾌한 typical 전형적인, 대표적인 different 다른

정답 ⓓ

029

step 2

After archaeologists / discovered / and studied / the tomb / of a woman, / they / found / that men and women / enjoyed / equal rights / at that time.

고고학자들이 / 발견한 후에 / 그리고 연구한 후에 / 무덤을 / 한 여성의. / 그들은 / 발견했다 / 남녀가 / 누렸다는 것을 / 동등한 권리를 / 그 당시에.

step 3

문맥상 '가지다'를 뜻하는 had가 적절하다.

have 가지다 divide 나뉘다, 갈라지다 appreciate 진가를 알아보다, 인정하다 allocate 할당하다

정답 ⓐ

030

step 2

Workout apps / gain / popularity / as the interest / in health / is increasing. / They / offer / workout videos and training routines / for free / and provide / even personalized workout plans / for all fitness levels.

운동 어플이 / 얻고 있다 / 인기를 / 흥미가 / 건강에 대한 / 증가하면서. / 그것들은 / 제공한다 / 운동 비디오와 훈련 과정을 / 무료로 / 그리고 제공한다 / 심지어 개인 맞춤화된 계획을 / 모든 건강 수준에 대해.

step 3

문맥상 '개인 맞춤화된'을 뜻하는 personalized가 적절하다.

customized 개인 맞춤화된 formulaic 정형화된 popularized 대중화된 handy 알맞은, 편리한, 쉬운

정답 ⓒ

Day 4	켈리의 지텔프 해석 POINT 4

031

step 2

Next week, / John / will donate / all of his prize money / he received / for winning the race / to charity.

다음 주에. / 존은 / 기부할 것이다 / 모든 상금을 / 그가 받은 / 경주에서 우승해서 / 자선단체에.

step 3

문맥상 '기부하다'를 뜻하는 give가 적절하다.

give 기부하다 transfer 옮기다 return 돌아오다 assign 맡기다, 배정하다

정답 ⓑ

032

step 2

Jason / was sure / that the mobile app / he had created / could attract / users. / However, / the app / failed / because it / was too expensive.

제이슨은 / 확신했다 / 모바일 앱이 / 자신이 만든 / 끌어 모을 수 있다고 / 사용자들을. / 하지만, / 그 앱은 / 실패했다 / 그것이 / 너무 비쌌기 때문에.

step 3

문맥상 '끌다, 끌어들이다'를 뜻하는 draw가 적절하다.

draw 끌다, 끌어들이다 include 포함하다 involve 수반하다 accompany 동반하다

정답 ⓑ

033
step 2

Grace / failed / to make / a delicious pasta dish / because the recipe / she found online / was full of errors.

그레이스는 / 실패했다 / 만드는 데 / 맛있는 파스타 요리를 / 요리법이 / 그녀가 온라인에서 발견한 / 오류로 가득차 있었기 때문에.

step 3

문맥상 '결함, 하자'를 뜻하는 flaws가 적절하다.

flaw 결함, 하자 miscalculation 오산, 잘못 계산함 sufficiency 충분한 양 fragility 부서지기 쉬움, 여림

정답 ⓒ

034
step 2

Jason / sometimes / picks / edible mushrooms / in the mountains. / He / can make / various dishes / with the mushrooms / he gathers.

제이슨은 / 때때로 / 따다 / 식용버섯을 / 산에서. / 그는 / 만들 수 있다 / 다양한 요리를 / 버섯으로 / 그가 채집한.

step 3

문맥상 '다양한'을 뜻하는 different가 적절하다.

different 다양한 dissimilar 같지 않은, 다른 disparate 이질적인 separate 별개의

정답 ⓓ

035
step 2

A few years ago, / Amy / lost / a book / her grandfather had given. / Although she / searched / every corner of the room, / she / never found / the book.

몇 년 전, / 에이미는 / 잃어버렸다 / 책을 / 그녀의 할아버지가 주신. / 비록 그녀가 / 뒤졌지만 / 방 구석구석을, / 그녀는 / 결코 찾지 못했다 / 그 책을.

step 3

문맥상 '알아내다, 찾아내다'를 뜻하는 located가 적절하다.

locate 알아내다, 찾아내다 observe 관찰하다 detect 발견하다 notice 의식하다

정답 ⓒ

036
step 2

Because Jane / wants / to stop wasting / money / on things / she doesn't need / and prepare for the future, / she / puts / some money aside / every month.

제인은 / 원하기 때문에 / 낭비하는 것을 멈추기를 / 돈을 / 물건에 / 그녀가 필요하지 않은 / 그리고 미래를 준비하기를, / 그녀는 / 저축한다 / 약간의 돈을 / 매달.

step 3

put은 aside와 함께 쓰이면 '모으다, 따로 떼어내다'를 뜻한다. set도 aside와 함께 쓰이면 유사한 뜻을 지닌다.

set (aside) 모으다, 따로 떼어내다 earn 벌다 invest 투자하다 fund 자금을 대다

정답 ⓒ

037

step 2

A boy / the babysitter took care of / was missing. / Fortunately, / police / found / him / in good health / and he / restores / emotional stability / after the traumatic event.

소년이 / 베이비시터가 돌보던 / 실종되었다. / 다행히, / 경찰은 / 발견했다 / 그를 / 건강한 상태로 / 그리고 그는 / 되찾았다 / 정서적인 안정을 / 그 충격적인 사건 이후.

step 3

문맥상 '되찾다, 회복하다'를 뜻하는 regained가 적절하다.

regain 되찾다, 회복하다 replace 대신하다 reconstruct 복원하다 reconcile 조화시키다

정답 ⓐ

038

step 2

One / of the reasons / consumers shop / online / is that they / can compare / a number of products / at a time / and get instant access / to product reviews.

하나는 / 이유 중 / 소비자들이 쇼핑을 하는 / 온라인에서 / 그들이 / 비교할 수 있다는 것이다 / 많은 제품을 / 한 번에 / 그리고 즉각적으로 접근할 수 있다는 것이다 / 제품의 후기에.

step 3

문맥상 '즉각적인'를 뜻하는 immediate가 적절하다.

immediate 즉각적인 unexpected 예상 밖의 abrupt 갑작스러운 sudden 급작스러운

정답 ⓓ

039

step 2

Jack / thinks / that cooking / is a waste of time / and wants to reduce / his cooking time. / Therefore, / he / has attempted / to have the time / he spends cooking / by preparing / the ingredients / in advance.

잭은 / 생각한다 / 요리가 / 시간 낭비라고 / 그리고 줄이고 싶어 한다 / 그의 요리하는 시간을. / 그래서, / 그는 / 시도해오고 있다 / 시간을 줄이려고 / 그가 요리하는데 사용하는 / 준비함으로써 / 재료를 / 미리.

step 3

문맥상 '짧게 하다'를 뜻하는 shorten이 적절하다.

shorten 짧게 하다 swell 붓다, 부풀다 remove 치우다 abandon 버리다

정답 ⓐ

040

step 2

Technologies / have brought / so many changes / in our lives. / For example, / computers / have changed / the way / we work / significantly. / Similarly, / smartphones / have changed / the way / we shop.

기술은 / 가져오고 있다 / 너무 많은 변화를 / 우리 삶에. / 예를 들어, / 컴퓨터는 / 변화시켜오고 있다 / 방식을 / 우리가 일하는 / 상당히. / 유사하게, / 스마트폰은 / 변화시켜오고 있다 / 방식을 / 우리가 쇼핑하는.

step 3

문맥상 '상당히'를 뜻하는 considerably가 적절하다.

considerably 상당히 perfectly 완전히 absolutely 전적으로 ideally 이상적으로

정답 ⓒ

Day 5 　켈리의 지텔프 해석 POINT 5

041

step 2

Whenever Molly / is not able to sleep well / at night, / she / takes / sleeping pills / which help / to induce sleep.

몰리는 / 잠을 제대로 잘 수 없을 때마다 / 밤에 / 그녀는 / 먹는다 / 수면제를 / 도움이 되는 / 유도하는데 / 잠을.

step 3

문맥상 '돕다. 촉진하다'를 뜻하는 facilitate가 적절하다.

facilitate 돕다, 촉진하다 persuade 설득하다 inspire 영감을 주다 disdain 무시하다

정답 ⓑ

042

step 2

People / who want / to get plastic surgery / should understand / the potential medical risks / and get / enough information / to avoid / harmful effects.

사람들은 / 원하는 / 성형수술을 받길 / 이해해야 한다 / 잠재적인 의료적인 위협을 / 그리고 얻어야 한다 / 충분한 정보를 / 피하기 위해 / 해로운 영향을.

step 3

문맥상 '해로운'을 뜻하는 detrimental이 적절하다.

detrimental 해로운 painful 고통스러운 bothersome 성가신 irritating 흥분시키는, 자극하는

정답 ⓓ

043

step 2

People / who spend / long hours / on computers / may experience / a headache. / You / should take a break / when you / are on a computer.

사람들은 / 보내는 / 오랜 시간을 / 컴퓨터에서 / 경험할지도 모른다 / 두통을. / 당신은 / 휴식을 취해야 한다 / 당신이 / 컴퓨터를 사용할 때.

step 3

문맥상 '(병이) 있다. 앓다'를 뜻하는 have가 적절하다.

have (병이) 있다, 앓다 confront 닥치다, 맞서다 meet 만나다, 모이다 approach 다가가다

정답 ⓐ

044

step 2

Jack / is a famous pianist. / However, / he / is also a comic book writer / who has won many awards / in comic book contests.

잭은 / 유명한 피아니스트이다. / 하지만, / 그는 / 또한 만화책 작가이다 / 많은 상을 받은 / 만화책 대회에서.

step 3

문맥상 '대회'를 뜻하는 competitions가 적절하다.

competition 대회 final 결승전 game 경기, 시합 occurrence 발생, 존재

정답 ⓒ

045

step 2

A boy / who physically hurt a man / on purpose / and went to jail / managed to get out of jail / after he paid / the full bail amount.

한 소년은 / 한 남자를 다치게 하고 / 고의로 / 그리고 감옥에 간 / 가까스로 감옥에서 나왔다 / 그가 지불한 뒤에 / 보석금 전액을.

step 3

문맥상 '다치게 하다'를 뜻하는 injured가 적절하다.

injure 다치게 하다 destroy 파괴하다 ruined 망치다, 엉망으로 만들다 crash 충돌하다

정답 ⓓ

046

step 2

Jack / is crazy / about spicy Mexican food / which has a strong flavor / from spices. / However, / his mom / suggested / that he avoid / eating / too much spicy food / because it / is harmful / to his health.

잭은 / 열광한다 / 매운 멕시코 음식에 / 강한 향을 가진 / 향신료를 사용한. / 그러나, / 그의 엄마는 / 제안했다 / 그가 피해야 한다고 / 먹는 것을 / 너무 많은 매운 음식을 / 왜냐면 그것은 / 해롭기 때문에 / 그의 건강에.

step 3

문맥상 '멈추다, 중단하다'를 뜻하는 stop이 적절하다.

stop 멈추다, 중단하다 keep 유지하다 illegalize 불법화하다 persist 집요하게 계속하다

정답 ⓐ

047

step 2

Ross didn't pay back / his student loan / when he / earned / a salary. / Instead, / he / bought / a company's stock / which a colleague recommended.

로스는 갚지 않았다. / 그의 학자금 대출금을 / 그

가 / 받았을 때 / 월급을. / 대신, / 그는 / 샀다 / 회사의 주식을 / 동료가 추천한.

step 3

문맥상 '구입하다'를 뜻하는 purchased가 적절하다.

purchase 구입하다 preserve 지키다, 보호하다 secure 안심하는, 획득하다 pick 고르다, 선택하다

정답 ⓒ

048

step 2

Even though the girl / who had lost three times / in a row / in a card game / suggested / changing / the rule / in her favor, / everyone / didn't accept / her suggestion.

비록 소녀가 / 세 번 진 / 연달아 / 카드 게임에서 / 제안했지만 / 바꿀 것을 / 규칙을 / 그녀에게 유리하게, / 모두가 / 받아들이지 않았다 / 그녀의 제안을.

step 3

문맥상 '받아들이다'를 뜻하는 take가 적절하다.

take 받아들이다 obtain 얻다 pick 고르다 determine 알아내다, 밝히다

정답 ⓑ

049

step 2

The car / offers / the option / to select / a driving mode. / Those / who want to immerse themselves / in the exciting driving experience / can select / sport mode. / In contrast, / those / who want a smoother ride / can select / comfort mode.

그 차는 / 제공한다 / 옵션을 / 선택할 수 있는 / 주행 모드를. / 사람들은 / 원하는 / 그들 스스로 몰입하길 / 신나는 운전 경험에 / 선택할 수 있다 / 스포츠 모드를. / 반면, / 사람들은 / 더 부드러운 승차감을 원하는 / 선택할 수 있다 / 컴포트 모드를.

step 3

문맥상 '제공하다'를 뜻하는 provides가 적절하다.

provide 제공하다 support 지지하다, 옹호하다 improve 개선되다, 나아지다 award 수여하다

정답 ⓐ

050

step 2

Some retail stores / that have suffered / sharp sales drop / because of the emergence of e-commerce / are going through tough times. / On the other hand, / some retail stores / have survived the crisis / because they / offer / things / e-commerce cannot replace, / including the shopping experience.

일부 유통업점들은 / 경험하고 있는 / 급격한 매출 감소를 / 전자상거래 등장 때문에 / 힘든 시간을 겪고 있다. / 반면에, / 일부 소매점들은 / 위기에서 살아남았다 / 왜냐하면 그들이 / 제공했기 때문에 / 어떤 것들을 / 전자 상거래가 대체할 수 없는 / 쇼핑 경험을 포함하여.

step 3

문맥상 '힘든'을 뜻하는 hard가 적절하다.

tough 힘든 resistant 저항하는, ~에 잘 견디는 resilient 회복력 있는 destructive 파괴적인

정답 ⓒ

051

step 2

You / should choose / the right kindergarten / if you want / your kids / to develop / valuable social skills.

당신은 / 선택해야 한다 / 올바른 유치원을 / 만약 당신이 원한다면 / 당신의 자녀들이 / 개발하기를 / 가치 있는 유용한 사회적 기술을.

step 3

문맥상 '유용한'을 뜻하는 useful이 적절하다.

useful 유용한 lucrative 수익성이 좋은 profitable 수익성이 있는 extravagant 낭비하는

정답 ⓒ

052

step 2

An expert / recommends / that we stop / working / from home / because it / could cause / the line / between our personal lives and work / to blur.

한 전문가는 / 권한다 / 우리가 그만두어야 한다고 / 일하는 것을 / 집에서 / 그것이 / 야기할 수 있기 때문에 / 경계를 / 우리의 개인적인 삶과 일 사이의 / 흐리게.

step 3

문맥상 '경계'를 뜻하는 boundary가 적절하다.

boundary 경계 frontier 국경 limit 한계 edge 가장자리

정답 ⓒ

053

step 2

Jane / was under stress / because of a colleague / interfering with her work. / Eventually, / she asked / her boss / to move / him / to another department.

제인은 / 스트레스를 받았다 / 동료 때문에 / 그녀의 일에 간섭하는. / 결국, / 그녀는 요청했다. / 그녀의 상사에게 / 옮겨달라고 / 그를 / 다른 부서로.

step 3

문맥상 '요청하다'를 뜻하는 requested가 적절하다.

request 요청하다 inquire 묻다 question 질문하다 force 강요하다

정답 ⓐ

054

step 2

Because many people / found / harmful materials / in a popular convenience food, / the local health department / required / supermarkets / to stop / the sales of the food.

많은 사람들이 / 발견했기 때문에 / 해로운 물질을 / 대중적인 편의 음식에서. / 지역 보건부는 / 요구했다 / 슈퍼마켓이 / 중단하도록 / 음식 판매를

step 3

문맥상 '발견하다'를 뜻하는 detected가 적절하다.

detect 발견하다 diagnose 진단하다 perceive 인식하다, 인지하다 mark 표시하다

정답 ⓓ

055

step 2

Mark / assigned / too much work / to

Rachel, / which caused / her / to become depressed. / Furthermore, / she had / a problem / with her coworker.

마크는 / 할당했다 / 너무 많은 일을 / 레이첼에게. / 그것은 야기했다 / 그녀가 / 우울하도록. / 게다가, / 그녀는 / 가지고 있었다. / 문제를 / 그녀의 동료와.

step 3

문맥상 '주다'를 뜻하는 gave가 적절하다.

give 주다 determine 알아내다 empower 권한을 주다 transfer 이동하다, 옮기다

정답 ⓓ

056

step 2

A company / will release / a new version of its software / next month. / Its various features / will allow / you / to experience / amazing things.

한 회사가 / 출시할 것이다 / 새로운 버전의 소프트웨어를 / 다음 달에. / 그것의 다양한 특징들은 / 허락할 것이다 / 당신이 / 경험할 수 있게 / 놀라운 것들을.

step 3

문맥상 '특징'을 뜻하는 characteristics이 적절하다.

characteristic 특징 drawback 결함, 문제점 theme 주제 appearance 외모, 모습

정답 ⓒ

057

step 2

Parents / should teach / their children / to respect / each other / and encourage / lifelong friendships / between siblings / because a positive relationship /

between siblings / can lead / to higher levels of self−esteem.

부모들은 / 가르쳐야 한다 / 그들의 아이들이 / 존중하도록 / 서로를 / 그리고 장려해야 한다 / 평생의 우정을 / 형제간의 / 왜냐하면 긍정적인 관계가 / 형제간의 / 이어질 수 있기 때문이다 / 더 높은 수준의 자존감으로.

step 3

문맥상 '소중히 여기다'을 뜻하는 value가 적절하다.

value 소중히 여기다 praise 칭찬하다 deify 신격화하다 admire 존경하다

정답 ⓒ

058

step 2

Employees / should attend / the training program, / which will encourage / them / to cultivate / creativity. / Moreover, / the program / can motivate / employees / to increase / innovation / in products / and work hard.

직원들은 / 참석해야 한다 / 연수 프로그램에. / 이것은 장려할 것이다 / 그들이 / 기르도록 / 창의성을. / 게다가. / 이 프로그램은 / 동기를 부여할 수 있다 / 직원들이 / 증가시키도록 / 혁신을 / 제품의 / 그리고 열심히 일하도록.

step 3

문맥상 '발전시키다, 촉진하다'를 뜻하는 foster가 적절하다.

foster 발전시키다, 촉진하다 fertilize 비료를 주다, 비옥하게 하다 learn 학습하다 absorb 흡수하다

정답 ⓑ

059

step 2

Some adoptive parents / have urged /

young couples / to adopt / a child. / However, / those / who want / to adopt a child / must be financially stable. / Unless they / meet / the financial requirements / of adoption,/ they / can't adopt / a child.

일부 양부모들은 / 권해오고 있다 / 젊은 부부들이 / 입양하라고 / 아이를. / 그러나. / 사람들은 / 원하는 / 아이를 입양하기를 / 재정적으로 안정되어야 한다. / 만약 그들이 / 충족시키지 못하면 / 재정적 요구사항을 / 입양의 / 그들은 / 입양할 수 없다 / 아이를.

step 3

문맥상 '장려하다'를 뜻하는 encouraged가 적절하다.

encourage 장려하다 pressure 압력을 주다 plead 애원하다, 변호하다 force 강요하다

정답 ⓐ

060

step 2

Suzy /, a wedding florist, / takes / a lot of pride / in her work / and tries to make / her customers / feel / special. / Instead of choosing flowers / for the wedding / by herself, / she / always / allows / brides / to choose / flowers / they want / for their wedding.

수지는 / 웨딩 플로리스트인. / 가지고 있다 / 큰 자부심을 / 그녀의 일에 / 그리고 만들려고 노력한다 / 그녀의 고객들이 / 느끼도록 / 특별하게. / 꽃을 고르는 대신에 / 결혼식을 위해 / 그녀 스스로. / 그녀는 / 항상 / 허락 한다 / 신부가 / 고르도록 / 꽃들을 / 그들이 원하는 / 그들의 결혼식에서.

step 3

문맥상 '중요한'을 뜻하는 important가 적절하다.

important 중요한 exceptional 극히 예외적인 superb 최고의 arrogant 오만한

정답 ⓓ

061

step 2

Although Mike / tried to keep / his old dog / healthy,/ the dog / vomited / several times / and refused / to eat.

마이크가 / 노력했음에도 불구하고 / 그의 늙은 개를 / 건강하게 하려고, / 그 개는 / 토를 했다 / 여러 번 / 그리고 거부했다 / 먹는 것을.

step 3

문맥상 '시도하다, 애써 해보다'를 뜻하는 attempted가 적절하다.

attempt 시도하다, 애써 해보다 venture (위험을 무릅쓰고 모험하듯) 가다 experiment 실험을 하다 force 강요하다

정답 ⓐ

062

step 2

You / should develop / the ability / to organize / your thoughts / and support / your point / logically / to express / your ideas / clearly.

당신은 / 개발해야 한다 / 능력을 / 정리하는 / 당신의 생각을 / 그리고 뒷받침해야 한다 / 당신이 요점을 / 논리적으로 / 표현하기 위해서 / 당신의 아이디어를 / 분명하게.

step 3

문맥상 '전달하다'를 뜻하는 communicate가 적절하다.

communicate 전달하다 prove 입증하다 extract 추출하다 conceal 숨기다

정답 ⓓ

063

step 2

Judy / knows / that vacation / is an excellent opportunity / to read books. / She / ordered / some books / online / and will read / them all / this vacation.

주디는 / 안다 / 휴가가 / 좋은 기회라는 것을 / 책을 읽을. / 그녀는 / 주문했다 / 책 몇 권을 / 온라인으로 / 그리고 읽을 것이다 / 그것들을 모두 / 이번 휴가 때.

step 3

문맥상 '기회'를 뜻하는 chance가 적절하다.

chance 기회 possibility 가능성, 가능함 prospect 가망, 예상 anticipation 예상, 예측

정답 ⓒ

064

step 2

Many children / who live / in extreme poverty / struggle to meet / the basic living expense. / We / should take / some measures / to provide / assistance / for them.

많은 아이들은 / 사는 / 매우 극심한 빈곤속에서 / 충족시키려 애쓴다 / 기본적인 생활비를. / 우리는 / 취해야 한다 / 몇 가지 조치를 / 제공하기 위해 / 도움을 / 그들에게.

step 3

문맥상 '지원'를 뜻하는 support가 적절하다.

support 지원 intervention 조정, 중재 service 서비스 compensation 보상(금)

정답 ⓓ

065

step 2

Because the boss / always / ignores / Amy, / she / is under too much stress, / which is causing / hair loss. / She / is going to buy / a special shampoo / which strengthens / each strand of hair / to stop / hair loss.

상사가 / 항상 / 무시하기 때문에 / 에이미를. / 그녀는 / 너무 많은 스트레스를 받고 있고, / 이것은 유발하고 있다 / 탈모를. / 그녀는 / 살 것이다 / 특별한 샴푸를 / 강화하는 / 머리카락의 각 가닥을 / 막기 위해 / 탈모를.

step 3

문맥상 '막다'를 뜻하는 prevent가 적절하다.

prevent 막다 finish 끝내다 pause 잠시 멈추다, 정지시키다 complete 완료하다

정답 ⓐ

066

step 2

To make / the best salad dressing, / Ross / tried / mixing / various ingredients / such as vinegar and olive oil. / Finally, / he / could make / the perfect dressing / by using / yogurt and Dijon mustard.

만들기 위해 / 최고의 샐러드 드레싱을. / 로스는 / 시도했다 / 섞는 것을 / 다양한 재료들을 / 식초와 올리브 오일과 같은. / 마침내. / 그는 / 만들 수 있었다 / 완벽한 드레싱을 / 사용함으로써 / 요거트와 디종 머스타드를.

step 3

문맥상 '결합하다'를 뜻하는 combining이 적절하다.

combine 결합하다 shake 흔들리다, 흔들다 construct 건설하다, 구성하다 synthesize 합성하다

정답 ⓐ

067

step 2

The doctor / recommended / that Jenny / take / essential nutrients / through the diet / to maintain / optimal health / and enjoy / her life. / Nevertheless, / she / keeps on eating / only a single food item / for each meal / to lose weight.

의사는 / 추천했다 / 제니가 / 섭취해야 한다고 / 필수적인 영양소를 / 식단을 통해 / 유지하기 위해 / 최적의 건강을 / 그리고 즐기기 위해 / 그녀의 인생을. / 그럼에도 불구하고. / 그녀는 / 계속해서 먹는다 / 단 하나의 음식만을 / 매 끼니마다 / 살을 빼기 위해.

step 3

문맥상 '먹다, 마시다'를 뜻하는 consume이 적절하다.

consume 먹다, 마시다 devour 걸신 들린 듯 먹다 swallow (음식 등을) 삼키다 digest (음식을) 소화하다

정답 ⓒ

068

step 2

My father / had wanted / to build / a factory / to make / custom furniture / in London. / However, / he / gave up / because he / didn't have / enough money / to build / a factory.

나의 아버지는 / 원해왔다 / 짓는 것을 / 공장을 / 만들기 위해 / 맞춤 가구를 / 런던에. / 하지만. / 그는 / 포기했다 / 그는 / 없었기 때문에 / 충분한 돈이 / 지을 / 공장을.

step 3

문맥상 '제작하다, 생산하다'를 뜻하는 manufacture이 적절하다.

manufacture 제작하다, 생산하다 design 설계하다, 도안하다 plan 계획하다 exhibit 전시하다

정답 ⓓ

069

step 2

Many small companies / need to take / a new approach / to overcome / the financial crisis / and achieve / their goal. / Otherwise, / they / would stop / operating / and go out of business.

많은 중소기업들은 / 취해야 한다 / 새로운 접근법을 / 극복하기 위해 / 금융위기를 / 그리고 달성하기 위해 / 그들의 목표를. / 그렇지 않으면, / 그들은 / 멈추게 될 것이다 / 운영하는 것을 / 그리고 폐업할 것이다.

step 3

문맥상 '채택하다'를 뜻하는 adopt가 적절하다.

adopt 채택하다 exclude 제외하다, 배제하다 acquire 습득하다, 얻다 keep 유지하다

정답 ⓑ

070

step 2

Because Rachel's father / promised / to give / some money / to her / if she / solved / a difficult math problem, / she / made / an effort / to work through the problem.

레이첼의 아버지가 / 약속했기 때문에 / 주기로 / 약간의 돈을 / 그녀에게 / 만약 그녀가 / 풀면 / 어려운 수학 문제를. / 그녀는 / 만들었다 / 노력을 / 그 문제를 해결하기 위한.

step 3

문맥상 '힘든'을 뜻하는 challenging이 적절하다.

challenging 힘든 punish 처벌하다, 벌주다 stressful 스트레스가 많은 cruel 잔인한, 괴로운

정답 ⓐ

Day 8 | 켈리의 지텔프 해석 POINT 8

071

step 2

A doctor / warns / that drinking / too much / can cause / serious health problems.

한 의사는 / 경고한다 / 술을 마시는 것이 / 너무 많이 / 일으킬 수 있다고 / 심각한 건강 문제를.

step 3

문맥상 '심각한'을 뜻하는 severe이 적절하다.

severe 심각한 abrupt 돌연한, 갑작스러운 common 흔한 insignificant 대수롭지 않은, 사소한, 하찮은

정답 ⓑ

072

step 2

Involving / children / in household chores / has / many advantages. / For example, / getting / children / to clean / their room / can make / them / feel / needed.

참여시키는 것은 / 아이들을 / 집안일에 / 가지고 있다 / 많은 이점들을. / 예를 들어, / 시키는 것은 / 아이들이 / 청소하도록 / 그들의 방을 / 만들 수 있다 / 그들이 / 느끼도록 / 필요한 존재라고.

step 3

문맥상 '끌어들이다, 관여시키다'를 뜻하는 Engaging이 적절하다.

engage 끌어들이다, 관여시키다 exclude 제외하다, 배제하다 force 강요하다 withdraw 철수하다, 중단하다, 탈퇴하다

정답 ⓑ

073

step 2

When you / start / a restaurant, / finding / the perfect location / for it / is so important. / Unless it / is / in a good location, / you / will fail / to attract / many customers.

당신이 / 시작할 때 / 식당을, / 찾는것은 / 완벽한 장소를 / 식당을 위한 / 매우 중요하다. / 식당이 / 있지 않다면 / 좋은 위치에, / 당신은 / 실패할 것이다 / 끌어들이는 데 / 많은 손님들을.

step 3

문맥상 '이상적인, 더할 나위 없는'을 뜻하는 ideal 이 적절하다.

ideal 이상적인, 더할 나위 없는 **eminent** 저명한, 탁월한 **infamous** 악명높은 **majestic** 장엄한, 위풍당당한

정답 ⓒ

074

step 2

Until a doctor / warned / that drinking / too much coffee / could be harmful / to the body / by increasing / the heartbeat, / Judy / took in too much caffeine / through coffee. / The doctor / advised / her / to find / alternatives / to coffee.

한 의사가 / 경고하기 전까지 / 마시는 것이 / 너무 많은 커피를 / 해로울 수 있다고 / 몸에 / 높임으로써 / 심장 박동을. / 주디는 / 너무 많은 카페인을 섭취했다 / 커피를 통해. / 의사는 / 권고했다. / 그녀에게 / 찾아보라고 / 대체재를 / 커피의.

step 3

문맥상 '대체물'을 뜻하는 replacements이 적절하다.

replacement 대체물 **additive** 첨가물, 첨가제 **complement** 보완물, 덧붙이는 요소 **ingredient** 재료, 구성 요소

정답 ⓒ

075

step 2

Because spending / too much time / playing computer games / could lead to migraines, Molly / advised / her brother / to stop / playing them. / Nevertheless, / he / ignored / her advice / and played / more intensely / to escape / reality.

보내는 것이 / 너무 많은 시간을 / 컴퓨터 게임을 하는 것에 / 편두통으로 이어질 수 있기 때문에, / 편두통을 / 몰리는 / 충고했다 / 그녀의 남동생에게 / 그만하라고 / 게임을 하는 것을. / 그럼에도 불구하고, / 그는 / 무시했다 / 그녀의 충고를 / 그리고 게임을 했다 / 더 치열하게 / 벗어나기 위해 / 현실에서.

step 3

문맥상 '무시하다'를 뜻하는 disregarded가 적절하다.

disregard 무시하다 **forget** 잊다 **overlook** 못 보고 넘어가다, 간과하다 **undertake** (책임을 맡아서) 착수하다

정답 ⓐ

076

step 2

Amy / helps / her son / to develop / responsibility. / For example, / Amy / always / gets / him / to do / chores / like mowing the lawn / and setting the table / because she / believes / that giving / household chores / helps / him / to learn / responsibility.

에이미는 / 돕는다 / 그녀의 아들이 / 기르도록 / 책임감을. / 예를 들어, / 에이미는 / 항상 / 시킨다 / 그가 / 하도록 / 집안일을 / 잔디를 깎는 것과 / 식탁을 차리는 것 같은 / 그녀는 / 믿기 때문이다 / 할당해주는 것이 / 집안일을 / 도움이 된다고 / 그가 / 배우는데 / 책임감을.

step 3

문맥상 '할당하다'를 뜻하는 assigning이 적절하다.

assign 할당하다 determine 결정하다, 알아내다 reserve 예약하다, (자리 등을)따로 잡아 두다 permit 허용하다, 허락하다

정답 ⓒ

077

step 2

Taking / some time / to research a company / you want / to work for / online / in advance / is necessary / before you / attend / a job interview. / By doing so, / you / can make / a good impression / on your potential employer.

갖는 것이 / 시간을 / 회사를 조사하기 위한 / 당신이 원하는 / 일하길 / 온라인으로 / 사전에 / 필수적이다 / 당신이 / 참석하기 전에 / 면접에. / 그렇게 함으로써, / 당신은 / 만들 수 있다 / 좋은 인상을 / 잠재적인 고용주에게.

step 3

문맥상 '장래의, 가망 있는'을 뜻하는 prospective가 적절하다.

prospective 장래의, 가망 있는 capable 유능한 accessible 다가가기 쉬운, 편한 pliable 유연한, 순응적인

정답 ⓐ

078

step 2

Because a doctor / said / that **eating** / too much red meat / could increase / the risk / of **getting** heart disease, / Judy / decided / to choose / plant-based diets / instead of **eating** / a large amount of meat.

한 의사가 / 말했기 때문에 / 먹는 것은 / 너무 많은 육류를 / 증가시킬 수 있다고 / 위험을 / 심장병에 걸릴. / 주디는 / 결정했다 / 선택하기로 / 식물 위주의 식사를 / 먹는 대신에 / 많은 양의 고기를.

step 3

문맥상 '(병)에 걸리다'를 뜻하는 developing이 적절하다.

develop (병)에 걸리다 mitigate 완화시키다 improve 개선되다, 나아지다 flourish 잘 자라다, 잘 지내다

정답 ⓑ

079

step 2

Because Rachel / spent / too much money / on her hobbies, / she / was short on rent / last month. / Although **having** / a hobby / made / her happy, / her boyfriend / asked / her / to save money / instead of **spending** / on expensive hobbies.

레이첼은 / 썼기 때문에 / 너무 많은 돈을 / 그녀의 취미에, / 그녀는 / 집세가 부족했다 / 지난 달에. / 가지는 것이 / 취미를 / 만들었음에도 불구하고 / 그녀를 행복하게, / 그녀의 남자친구는 / 요청했다 / 그녀에게 / 돈을 모으라고 / 돈을 쓰는 대신에 / 비싼 취미에.

step 3

문맥상 '비싼'을 뜻하는 costly가 적절하다.

costly 비싼 abundant 풍부한 economical 경제적인, 알뜰한 moderate 보통의, 중간의

정답 ⓐ

080

step 2

Molly / bans / employees / from **wasting** time / on social media / by blocking / social networking sites / while they / are working / because she / thinks / that using / social media / in the workplace / has / a negative effect / on productivity.

몰리는 / 금지하고 있다 / 직원들을 / 시간 낭비하는 것으로부터 / 소셜 미디어에 / 차단함으로써 / 소셜 네트워킹 사이트를 / 그들이 / 일하는 동안 / 그녀는 / 생각하기 때문이다 / 사용하는 것이 / 소셜 미디어를 / 직장에서 / 가진다고 / 부정적인 영향을 / 생산성에.

step 3

문맥상 '결과'를 뜻하는 result가 적절하다.

result 결과 process 과정 conclusion (최종적인) 판단 evaluation 평가

정답 ⓐ

| Day 9 | 켈리의 지텔프 해석 POINT 9 |

081

step 2

Chris / wants / to get along with his girlfriend's friends, / hoping / to meet / them. / However, / she / hides / their current relationship / from them.

크리스는 / 원한다 / 그의 여자친구의 친구들과 사이좋게 지내는 것을. / 희망하면서 / 만나길 / 그들을. / 하지만, / 그녀는 / 숨긴다 / 그들의 현재 관계를 / 그들로 부터

step 3

문맥상 '숨기다'를 뜻하는 conceals이 적절하다.

conceal 숨기다 cease 중단시키다 suspend 매달다, 중단하다, 유보하다 deteriorate 약화되다, 더 나빠지다

정답 ⓐ

082

step 2

Amy / is eager / to travel / around the world, / experiencing / new ways of living / and broadening / her horizons. / Unfortunately, / she / doesn't have / enough money / to travel.

에이미는 / 열망한다 / 여행하기를 / 세계를, / 경험하면서 / 새로운 삶의 방식을 / 그리고 넓히면서 / 그녀의 시야를. / 안타깝게도, / 그녀는 / 가지고 있지 않다 / 충분한 돈을 / 여행을 갈.

step 3

문맥상 '넓히다, 확장하다'를 뜻하는 expanding이 적절하다.

expand 넓히다, 확장하다 inflate 부풀리다, 과장하다 fill 채우다, 메우다 contract 수축시키다, 줄이다

정답 ⓓ

083

step 2

An aircraft mechanic / reported / the serious problem / with the left engine, / adding / that the plane / must make an emergency landing / immediately.

한 항공기 정비사는 / 보고했다 / 심각한 문제를 / 왼쪽 엔진에. / 덧붙이면서 / 비행기가 / 비상 착륙해야 한다고 / 즉시.

step 3

문맥상 '즉시'를 뜻하는 instantly가 적절하다.

instantly 즉시 punctually 정각에, 시간대로, 엄수하여 diligently 부지런히, 열심히 prudently 신중하게

정답 ⓑ

084

step 2

Despite financial problems, / E&K has grown / into the largest beverage company, / generating / approximately $500 million of revenue / over the last two quarters.

재정적인 문제에도 불구하고, / E&K는 성장했다 / 가장 큰 음료 회사로, / 만들어 내면서 / 약 5억 달러의 수익을 / 지난 2분기 동안.

step 3

문맥상 '대략'을 뜻하는 roughly가 적절하다.

roughly 대략 precisely 정확하게 exactly 정확히, 틀림없이 conservatively 보수적으로, 줄잡아 말해서

정답 ⓑ

085

step 2

The new concealer / helps / men / to cover / their skin flaws, / addressing / the specific needs / of men. / However, / in case that it / causes / skin irritation, / stop / using / it / and consult / your doctor.

그 새로운 컨실러는 / 돕는다 / 남성들이 / 커버하도록 / 그들의 피부 결점을. / 다루면서 / 특별한 요구를 / 남성들의. / 그러나. / 그것이 / 일으키는 경우에는 / 피부 염증을. / 중지해라 / 사용하는 것을 / 그것을 / 그리고 상담해라 / 의사와.

step 3

문맥상 '다루다'를 뜻하는 treating이 적절하다.

treat 다루다 withstand 견뎌 내다 neglect 방치하다, 도외시하다 maintain 유지하다

정답 ⓑ

086

step 2

Using / sport mode / in your car / will make / your driving experience / more exciting, / making / your car / go faster. / However, / leaving / your car / in sport mode / all the time / could cause / some problems.

사용하는 것은 / 스포츠 모드를 / 자동차에서 / 만들 것이다 / 당신의 운전 경험을 / 더욱 흥미롭게. / 만들면서 / 당신의 차가 / 더 빨리가도록 / 하지만. / 두는 것은 / 당신의 차를 / 스포츠 모드로 / 항상 / 일으킬 수 있다 / 문제를.

step 3

문맥상 '만들다'를 뜻하는 make가 적절하다.

make 만들다 discover 발견하다 find 찾다 resolve 해결하다

정답 ⓐ

087

step 2

Matthew / had to cancel / his summer vacation / to Varanasi / due to some reasons, / giving up / his hope / of walking / along the Ganges River. / Instead, / he / decided / to take a break / at home, / relaxing / on the couch / and watching / movies.

매튜는 / 취소해야만 했다 / 그의 여름 휴가를 / 바라나시로 가는 / 몇몇 이유 때문에. / 포기하면서 / 희망을 / 걷겠다는 / 갠지스 강을 따라. / 대신. / 그는 / 결심했다 / 휴식을 취하기로 / 집에서. / 쉬면서 / 소파 위에서 / 그리고 보면서 / 영화를.

step 3

정답 ⓐ

문맥상 '선택하다'를 뜻하는 chose가 적절하다.

choose 선택하다 execute 실행하다, 수행하다
implement 실행하다 proceed 진행하다

088

step 2

Bacause while a man / was doing / his shopping, / his phone / was missing, / he / requested / CCTV footage / to locate / his phone. / CCTV footage / showed / that a little girl / glancing around the store / and browsing through a magazine / stole / the phone / from his bag,

한 남성이 / 하는 동안 / 그의 쇼핑을. / 그의 휴대전화가 / 없어졌기 때문에. / 그는 / 요청했다 / CCTV 영상을 / 찾기 위해 / 그의 휴대전화를. / CCTV 영상은 / 보여주었다 / 한 소녀가 / 가게를 둘러보던 / 그리고 잡지를 여기저기 훑던 / 훔친 것을 / 전화기를 / 그의 가방에서.

step 3

정답 ⓑ

문맥상 '가져가다'를 뜻하는 took가 적절하다.

take 가져가다 detect 발견하다 survey 조사하다
observe 관찰하다

089

step 2

Some people / take / many different supplements / at the same time / without thinking, / which can increase / the risk / of adverse drug reactions, / leading / to dangerous effects. / Therefore, / you / should be careful / when you / are taking / them, / reading / the label / carefully.

몇몇 사람들은 / 복용한다 / 많은 다양한 보충제를 / 동시에 / 생각하지 않고, / 이것은 증가시킬 수 있다 / 위험을 / 약물유해반응의. / 이어지면서 / 위험한 결과로. / 그러므로. / 당신은 / 조심해야 한다 / 당신이 / 복용할 때 / 그것들을. / 읽으면서 / 라벨을 / 주의 깊게.

step 3

문맥상 '매우 해로운'를 뜻하는 devastating이 적절하다.

devastating 매우 해로운 unpleasant 불쾌한, 불편한 prospective 장래의, 유망한 adequate 충분한

정답 ⓐ

090

step 2

A non-profit organization / is working / to offer / various academic programs / for the most vulnerable students. / As a result, / many students / who otherwise would not have access / to quality education / have / the opportunity / to learn.

한 비영리 단체가 / 노력하는 중이다 / 제공하기 위해 / 다양한 학술 프로그램을 / 가장 취약한 학생들에게. / 그 결과. / 많은 학생들이 / 그렇게 하지 않았다면 접근할 수가 없었던 / 양질의 교육에 / 가진다 / 기회를 / 배울.

step 3

문맥상 '애쓰다'를 뜻하는 trying이 적절하다.

try 애쓰다 toil 고생스럽게 일하다 unwilling 마지못해 하는, 싫어하는 reluctant 꺼리는, 마지못한

정답 ⓐ

Day 10 · 켈리의 지텔프 해석 POINT 10

091

step 2

It is well known / that the restaurant / is good / for a first date / because of the perfect lighting.

잘 알려져 있다 / 그 식당이 / 좋다고 / 첫 데이트에 / 완벽한 조명 때문에.

step 3

문맥상 '적합한'을 뜻하는 suitable이 적절하다.

suitable 적합한 efficient 능률적인, 유능한, 효율적인 admissible 인정되는 precious 귀한, 소중한

정답 ⓐ

092

step 2

Money / may be necessary / for happiness. / However, / it is more important / to be satisfied / with your life / to live / a happy life.

돈은 / 필요지도 모른다 / 행복을 위해. / 하지만. / 더 중요하다 / 만족하는 것이 / 당신의 삶에 / 살기 위해서 / 행복한 삶을.

step 3

문맥상 '만족한'을 뜻하는 contented가 적절하다.

contented 만족한 proud 자랑스러운 prominent 중요한, 유명한 plentiful 풍부한

정답 ⓓ

093

step 2

It is necessary / to prevent / global warming / from becoming worse. Therefore, / we / should do / something / to save / the planet.

필수적이다. / 막는것이 / 지구 온난화를 / 더 심해 지는 것으로부터 / 그러므로. / 우리는 / 해야 한다 / 무언가를 / 지키기 위해 / 지구를.

step 3

문맥상 '구하다. 보호하다'를 뜻하는 rescue가 적절 하다.

rescue 구하다, 보호하다 reserve 예약하다 retain 유지하다, 보유하다 conquer 정복하다

정답 ⓓ

094

step 2

Although Kate / is wealthy / enough / not to work, / she / always / works hard / instead of being lazy. / "It is important / to continue / working / to feel / alive.", / she / says.

케이트는 / 부유함에도 불구하고 / 충분히 / 일을 하지 않아도 될 만큼. / 그녀는 / 항상 / 열심히 일 한다 / 게으름을 피우는 대신에. / "중요합니다 / 계속 하는 것이 / 일하는 것을 / 느끼기 위해 / 살아 있다고". / 그녀는 / 말한다.

step 3

문맥상 '열심히. 부지런히'를 뜻하는 diligently가 적 절하다.

diligently 열심히, 부지런히 necessarily 어쩔 수 없이, 필연적으로 roughly 거칠게, 험하게, 대략 accurately 정확히

정답 ⓑ

095

step 2

It is beneficial / to talk / and listen / to babies. / For example, / talking / to babies / from birth / makes / them / hear / different and more words, / improving / their understanding / of language / and encouraging / them / to build / communication skills.

이롭다 / 말하는 것은 / 그리고 귀를 귀울이는 것은 / 아기들에게. / 예를 들어, / 말하는 것은 / 아기들에게 / 태어날 때부터 / 만든다 / 그들이 / 듣도록 / 다양하고 많은 단어들을, / 향상시키면서 / 그들의 이해를 / 언어에 대한 / 그리고 장려하면서 / 그들이 / 쌓도록 / 의사소통 기술을.

step 3

문맥상 '이로운'을 뜻하는 advantageous가 적절하다.

advantageous 이로운 fundamental 근본적인, 필수적인 evitable 피할 수 있는 outstanding 뛰어난

정답 ⓐ

096

step 2

It was found / that serious problems / with tires / after the car / run over a sharp object / occurred. / Because joey / thought / that these / could cause / a car accident, / he / replaced / the tires / immediately.

발견되었다 / 심각한 문제가 / 타이어에 / 차가 / 날카로운 물체에 부딪힌 뒤 / 발생한 것이. / 조이가 / 생각했기 때문에 / 이런 것들이 / 유발할 수 있다는 것을 / 교통사고를, / 그는 / 교체했다 / 타이어를 / 즉시.

step 3

문맥상 '문제, 곤란, 골칫거리'를 뜻하는 troubles가

적절하다.

trouble 문제, 곤란, 골칫거리 obstacle 장애 eradication 근절, 박멸 feature 특징, 특색

정답 ⓒ

097

step 2

To make / a successful presentation, / it is especially important / to examine / information / about your listeners / and analyze / it. / In addition, / you / should know / how to keep audience's attention / during your presentation.

만들기 위해서 / 성공적인 발표를. / 특히 중요하다 / 조사하는 것이 / 정보를 / 청중에 대해 / 그리고 분석하는 것이 / 그것을. / 게다가, / 당신은 / 알아야 한다 / 청중들의 관심을 유지시키는 방법을 / 당신이 발표하는 동안.

step 3

문맥상 '유지하다, 지속하다'를 뜻하는 maintain이 적절하다.

maintain 유지하다, 지속하다 prove 입증하다, 드러나다 support 지지하다, 옹호하다 establish 설립하다, 수립하다

정답 ⓐ

098

step 2

It is normal / to lose / between 50 and 100 hairs / a day / because they / are naturally replaced / and return / to normal levels. / However, / if you / are losing / too much hair, / see / your doctor / to do / something / about it.

정상이다 / 잃는 것은 / 50에서 100개의 머리카락을 / 하루에 / 그것들은 / 자연스럽게 대체되기 때

문에 / 그리고 돌아오기 때문이다 / 정상 수준으로. / 그러나, / 당신이 / 잃고 있다면 / 너무 많은 머리카락을, / 봐라 / 의사를 / 하기 위해 / 무엇인가를 / 그것에 대해.

step 3

문맥상 '보통의, 전형적인'을 뜻하는 typical이 적절하다.

typical 보통의, 전형적인 **peculiar** 이상한, 독특한 **primary** 기본적인, 중요한 **grave** 심각한

정답 ⓐ

099

step 2

It is essential / **that** Betty / get some rest / because she / feels / burned out / and exhausts / after work, / losing / her passion / she once had / in her work. / Getting / more sleep and enough rest / can relax / her mind and body, / also improving / her mood / and relieving / stress.

필수적이다 / 베티가 / 휴식을 취하는 것은 / 그녀는 / 느끼기 때문이다 / 지침을 / 그리고 지쳤기 때문에 / 일을 마친 후, / 잃어버리면서 / 그녀의 열정을 / 그녀가 한때 가졌던 / 그녀의 일에서. / 취하는 것은 / 더 많은 잠과 충분한 휴식을 / 쉽게 할 수 있다 / 그녀의 몸과 마음을, / 향상시키면서 / 그녀의 기분을 / 그리고 완화시키면서 / 스트레스를.

step 3

문맥상 '충분한'을 뜻하는 adequate이 적절하다.

adequate 충분한 **expand** 확장시키다 **brief** 짧은, 잠시 동안의, 간단한 **compulsory** 강제적인, 의무적인, 필수의

정답 ⓐ

100

step 2

It is known / **that** uniforms / function / as a visual marker / of identities / and strengthen / cohesion / among group members. / However, / people / wearing uniforms / can lose / their individuality / because others / are wearing / the same outfit.

알려져있다 / 유니폼은 / 기능 한다고 / 시각적인 표시기로써 / 신분의 / 그리고 강화한다고 / 결속력을 / 단체 구성원 간에. / 하지만, / 사람들은 / 유니폼을 입는 / 잃을 수 있다 / 그들의 개성을 / 다른 사람들도 / 입기 때문이다 / 같은 옷을.

step 3

문맥상 '결속성, 단일성'을 뜻하는 unity가 적절하다.

unity 결속성, 단일성 **separation** 분리 **combination** 조합물, 결합물 **cooperation** 협력, 협동, 합동

정답 ⓓ

Day 11 켈리의 지텔프 해석 POINT 11

101

step 2

Because of toxic substances / found / in a processed food, / the authority / banned / the sale / of the product.

독성물질 때문에 / 발견된 / 한 가공식품에서, / 당국은 / 금지했다 / 판매를 / 그 제품의.

step 3

문맥상 '금지하다'를 뜻하는 prohibited가 적절하다.

prohibit 금지하다 **renovate** 개조하다, 보수하다 **inspect** 점검하다, 검사하다 **facilitate** 가능하게 하다, 용이하게 하다

정답 ⓑ

102

step 2

A company / will provide / cash bonuses / next week. / That's because / sales / of products / released / by the company / have been soaring.

한 회사는 / 제공할 것이다. / 현금 보너스를 / 다음 주에. / 그것은 왜냐하면 / 판매가 / 제품의 / 출시된 / 그 회사에 의해 / 급증하고 있기 때문이다.

step 3

문맥상 '급등하다'을 뜻하는 skyrocketing이 적절하다.

skyrocket 급등하다 **develop** 성장하다, 발달하다 **reinforce** 강화하다, 보강하다 **support** 지지하다, 지원하다

정답 ⓑ

103

step 2

Kevin / plans / to make / a chocolate cake / topped with flowers / for mom / this Mother's Day. / Because he / didn't know / how to make a cake, / he / tried / finding / secrets / for a perfect cake / online.

케빈은 / 계획하고 있다 / 만들것을 / 초콜릿 케이크를 / 꽃으로 토핑된 / 엄마를 위해 / 이번 어머니날에. / 그가 / 몰랐기 때문에 / 케이크 만드는 방법을, / 그는 / 시도했다 / 발견하려고 / 비법을 / 완벽한 케이크를 위한 / 온라인에서.

step 3

문맥상 '정보, 비결'을 뜻하는 tips가 적절하다.

tip 정보, 비결 **procedure** 절차 **instruction** 설명 **strategy** 계획, 전략

정답 ⓐ

104

step 2

Jennifer / often / goes / to a restaurant / and enjoys / a special meal / made / by famous chefs / with her boyfriend. / They / drink / a glass of wine / whenever they / go / to the restaurant.

제니퍼는 / 종종 / 간다 / 레스토랑에 / 그리고 즐긴다 / 특별한 식사를 / 만들어진 / 유명한 요리사들에 의해 / 그녀의 남자친구와. / 그들은 / 마신다 / 와인 한 잔을 / 그들이 / 갈 때마다 / 레스토랑에.

step 3

문맥상 '준비된'을 뜻하는 prepared가 적절하다.

prepared 준비된 **manufactured** 제작된 **generated** 발생된, 만들어진 **constructed** 건설된, 구성된

정답 ⓐ

105

step 2

We / should not believe / everything / presented / in the media. / Sometimes / stories / delivered / as news / can be false information, / deliberately deceiving / people.

우리는 / 믿어서는 안 된다 / 모든 것을 / 보여진 / 매체에. / 때때로 / 이야기들은 / 전달된 / 뉴스로 / 잘못된 정보일 수 있다 / 고의로 속이면서 / 사람들을.

step 3

문맥상 '의도적으로'를 뜻하는 intentionally가 적절하다.

intentionally 의도적으로 unknowingly 모르고, 알아채지 못하고 accidentally 우연히, 뜻하지 않게 systematically 질서 정연하게

정답 ⓐ

106

step 2

When a work environment / makes / workers / uncomfortable, / creativity / is likely to decrease. / On the other hand, / a comfortable work environment / leads to increased creativity and innovation / in employees.

근무환경이 / 만들 때 / 근로자들을 / 불편하게, / 창의력은 / 감소할 가능성이 있다. / 반면에, / 편안한 근무 환경은 / 증진된 창의력과 혁신으로 이어진다 / 근로자들에게.

step 3

문맥상 '～하는 경향이 있는'을 뜻하는 apt가 적절하다.

apt ～하는 경향이 있는 reasonable 타당한, 합리적인 suitable 적합한, 적절한 acceptable 용인되는, 받아들일 수 있는

정답 ⓐ

107

step 2

When the devastating earthquake / hit / the city, / Emily / tried to provide / assistance / for people / affected / by the earthquake. / In fact, / she / always / helps / others / in need.

파괴적인 지진이 / 강타했을 때 / 도시를, / 에밀리는 / 제공하려 노력했다 / 도움을 / 사람들에게 / 영향을 받은 / 지진의. / 사실, / 그녀는 / 항상 / 돕는다 / 다른 사람들을 / 어려움에 처한.

step 3

문맥상 '원조, 도움, 조력'을 뜻하는 aid가 적절하다.

aid 원조, 도움, 조력 instruction 설명 inspiration 영감, 자극 endurance 인내(력), 참을성

정답 ⓓ

108

step 2

Right after a car / hit / a boy / walking / with his mother, / she / took / him / to the hospital. / Fortunately, / he / miraculously / survived / the fatal car accident / caused / by a drunk driver.

차가 / 친 직후 / 소년을 / 걷던 / 그의 엄마와, / 그녀는 / 데려갔다 / 그를 / 병원으로. / 다행히, / 그는 / 기적적으로 / 살아남았다 / 치명적인 교통사고에서 / 발생된 / 음주 운전자에 의해.

step 3

문맥상 '치명적인'을 뜻하는 deadly가 적절하다.

deadly 치명적인 tolerable 견딜 만한, 참을 수 있는 trivial 사소한, 하찮은 superficial 표면적인, 얄팍한

정답 ⓓ

109

step 2

It is debatable / whether the ancient city / built / 1,800 years ago / really existed or not. / Although some archeologists / can't find / written records / of the city, / they / believe / that the city / really existed.

논쟁의 여지가 있다 / 고대 도시가 / 지어진 / 1800년 전에 / 실제로 존재했는지 아닌지는. / 어떤

고고학자들이 / 찾을 수 없음에도 불구하고 / 쓰여진 기록을 / 그 도시에 대한. / 그들은 / 믿는다 / 그 도시가 / 실제로 존재했다고.

step 3

문맥상 '논쟁의 여지가 있는'을 뜻하는 arguable이 적절하다.

arguable 논쟁의 여지가 있는 resistant 반대하는 advocate 지지하다, 옹호하다 agreeable 선뜻 동의하는

정답 ⓒ

110

step 2

Some organisms / called a keystone species / are essential / in determining / the structure / of the entire ecosystem. / Therefore, / we / should protect / keystone species / in order to maintain / ecosystems / in the right condition.

어떤 유기체들은 / 핵심종이라고 불리는 / 필수적이다 / 결정하는데 / 구조를 / 생태계 전체의. / 그러므로. / 우리는 / 보호해야 한다. / 핵심종을 / 유지하기 위해서 / 생태계를 / 적절한 상태로.

step 3

문맥상 '적합한'을 뜻하는 appropriate가 적절하다.

appropriate 적합한 significant 중요한 vicious 잔인한 unrivaled 경쟁자가 없는, 무쌍의, 비할 데 없는

정답 ⓓ

111

step 2

After more than three people / were killed / in a house fire, / police / said / that unknown suspects / entered / the house / and lit / it / on fire, / adding / that the investigation / was still ongoing.

세 명 이상이 / 죽임을 당한 뒤에 / 주택화재로. / 경찰이 / 말했다 / 알려지지 않은 용의자들이 / 들어왔다고 / 집에 / 그리고 붙였다고 / 그것에 / 불을. / 덧붙이면서 / 수사가 / 아직 진행 중이라고.

step 3

문맥상 '진행 중인'을 뜻하는 underway가 적절하다.

underway 진행 중인 emerging 최근 생겨난 consistent 한결같은, 거듭되는 persistent 끈질긴, 끊임없이 지속되는

정답 ⓓ

112

step 2

A number of polar bears / left / in the world / have been pushed / on the verge of extinction. / We / should do / something / to protect / them / from extinction.

수많은 북극곰들이 / 남겨진 / 세계에 / 압박받아오고 있다 / 멸종 직전에 처하도록 / 우리는 / 해야 한다 / 무언가를 / 보호하기 위해 / 그들을 / 멸종으로부터.

step 3

문맥상 '구하다'를 뜻하는 save가 적절하다.

save 구하다 maintain 유지하다 increase 증가하다, 인상시키다 breed 재배하다

정답 ⓑ

113

step 2

An organization / that has been working / to safeguard / the health / of people / with disabilities / **will be financed** / by a conglomerate / starting next year.

단체가 / 노력해 온 / 지키기 위해 / 건강을 / 사람들의 / 장애가 있는 / 자금을 받게 된다 / 한 대기업으로부터 / 내년부터.

step 3

문맥상 '후원하다'를 뜻하는 sponsored가 적절하다.

sponsor 후원하다 operate 운영하다, 작동하다 invest 투자하다 regulate 규제하다

정답 ⓒ

114

step 2

To use / public spaces / as event venues, / you / must register / your event / with the council / and comply / with relevant regulations and safety measures. / Otherwise, / you / **are not allowed** / to hold / events.

사용하기 위해 / 공공장소를 / 행사장소로써, / 당신은 / 등록해야 한다 / 당신의 행사를 / 시의회에 / 그리고 준수해야 한다 / 관련 규정과 안전조치를. / 그렇지 않으면, / 당신은 / 허락되지 않는다 / 개최하는 것이 / 행사를.

step 3

문맥상 '허락하다'를 뜻하는 permitted가 적절하다.

permit 허락하다 legal 합법적인 contract 계약, 줄어들다, 수축하다 advise 충고하다, 조언하다

정답 ⓐ

115

step 2

Although a leader / worked hard / to create / a positive work environment, / making / his team members / comfortable / and encouraging / them / to achieve / the goal / they set, / productivity / **was decreased**.

리더가 / 열심히 노력했음에도 불구하고 / 만들기 위해 / 긍정적인 업무 환경을. / 만들면서 / 그의 팀원들을 / 편안하게 / 그리고 격려하면서 / 그들이 / 달성하도록 / 목표를 / 그들이 설정한, / 생산성이 / 감소되었다.

step 3

문맥상 '이루다, 달성하다, 성취하다'를 뜻하는 accomplish가 적절하다.

accomplish 이루다, 달성하다, 성취하다 acquire 습득하다 secure 안심하는 cease 중단되다

정답 ⓒ

116

step 2

Various organizations / **have been established** / to cope with food insecurity / and provide / people / in developing countries / with food / in a sustainable way. / In addition, / they / aim / to break down / the barriers / to education / by improving / the education / of poor children.

많은 기관들이 / 설립되어오고 있다 / 식량 불안에 대처하기 위해서 / 그리고 제공하기 위해서 / 사람들에게 / 개발도상국의 / 식량을 / 지속 가능한 방법으로. / 게다가, / 그들은 / 목표로 하고 있다 / 무너뜨리는 것을 / 장벽을 / 교육의 / 향상함으로써 / 교육을 / 가난한 아이들의.

step 3

문맥상 '다루다, 처리하다'를 뜻하는 deal (with) 이 적절하다.

deal (with) 다루다, 처리하다 solve 해결하다, 타결하다 get 받다, 마련하다 remove 치우다, 내보내다, 제거하다

정답 ⓐ

117

step 2

The scheduled final exam / is going to **be pushed back** / because teachers / need / extra teaching time. / Some students / insist / that it / follow / the original final exam schedule.

예정된 기말고사는 / 연기될 것이다 / 왜냐하면 교사들이 / 필요로 하기 때문이다 / 추가 수업 시간을. / 일부 학생들은 / 주장한다 / 기말고사가 / 따라야 한다고 / 원래의 기말고사 일정을.

step 3

문맥상 '필요로 하다, 요구하다'를 뜻하는 require 이 적절하다.

require 필요로 하다, 요구하다 force 강요하다 entail 수반하다, 포함하다 inquire 질문을 하다, 알아보다

정답 ⓑ

118

step 2

Since some parents / can't afford / to pay / for the tuition, / a number of students / living / in poverty / **are being forced** / to drop out of school. / In fact, / the problems / persist / in poor countries / in spite of taking / measures / to reduce / school dropout.

일부 부모님들이 / 여유가 없기 때문에 / 지불할 / 등록금을. / 많은 학생들이 / 사는 / 빈곤 속에 / 강요받고 있다 / 학교를 중퇴하도록. / 사실, / 그 문제는 / 지속되고 있다 / 가난한 나라들에서 / 취했음에도 불구하고 / 조치를 / 줄이기 위한 / 학교 중퇴자를.

step 3

문맥상 '조치'를 뜻하는 steps가 적절하다.

step 조치 deed 행위, 행동, 증서 operation 작전(활동), 수술 standard 수준, 기준

정답 ⓓ

119

step 2

Grace / **had been injured** / and fallen / into a coma / in a hit-and-run car accident. / Although her husband / made / efforts / to find / witnesses / who saw / the accident / and consulted / with a car accident attorney, / the hit-and-run driver / wasn't caught.

그레이스는 / 부상을 입었다 / 그리고 빠졌다 / 혼수상태에 / 뺑소니 교통사고로. / 그녀의 남편이 / 만들었음에도 불구하고 / 노력을 / 찾기 위한 / 목격자를 / 본 / 그 사고를 / 그리고 상담했음에도 불구하고 / 교통사고 변호사와, / 뺑소니 운전자는 / 잡히지 않았다.

step 3

문맥상 '노력'을 뜻하는 endeavor가 적절하다.

endeavor 노력 fruitful 생산적인, 유익한 labor (임금을 얻기 위한) 노동, 근로 toil 노역, 고역

정답 ⓐ

120

step 2

Some pollutants / that contain / extremely hazardous substances, / such as

359

industrial waste and plastic debris, / are being dumped / into the ocean. / Unless proper measures / to solve / this problem / are taken, / there will be / a considerable threat / to the survival / of marine mammals.

일부 오염물질들이 / 포함한 / 극히 유해한 물질들을, / 산업폐기물과 플라스틱 파편 등과 같은 / 버려지고 있다 / 바다에. / 적절한 조치가 / 해결하기 위한 / 이 문제를 / 취해지지 않으면, / 있을 것이다 / 상당한 위협이 / 생존에 / 해양 포유류의.

step 3

문맥상 '엄청난, 거대한'을 뜻하는 huge가 적절하다.

huge 엄청난, 거대한 important 중요한 fancy 원하다 persistent 끈질긴, 집요한

정답 ⓑ

Day 13 켈리의 지텔프 해석 POINT 13

121

step 2

Because Amy / was so depressed, / avoiding / contact / with people / and isolating herself, / Mike / gave / her / some tips / for handling depression / and encouraged / her / to seek therapy.

에이미가 / 너무 우울했기 때문에, / 피하면서 / 접촉을 / 사람들과 / 그리고 자신을 고립시키면서, / 마이크는 / 주었다 / 그녀에게 / 몇 가지 팁을 / 우울증을 다루기 위한 / 그리고 권했다 / 그녀가 / 치료를 받으라고

step 3

문맥상 '다루는 것'을 뜻하는 addressing이 적절하다.

address 다루다 operate (기계를) 작동하다, 가동하다 manipulate 조종하다, 조작하다, 처리하다 react 반응을 보이다, 반응하다

정답 ⓑ

122

step 2

If you / want / to thank / servers / for their services, / just tell / them / a quick "thank you" / and be kind and courteous. / However, / the best way / to show appreciation / is to give / them / a generous tip.

만약 당신이 / 원한다면 / 감사하길 / 종업원에게 / 그들의 서비스에 대해, / 단지 말해라 / 그들에게 / 빠르게 "감사합니다"라고 / 그리고 친절하고 공손해라. / 그러나, / 가장 좋은 방법은 / 감사를 보여주는 / 주는 것이다 / 그들에게 / 후한 팁을.

step 3

문맥상 '공손한, 예의바른'을 뜻하는 polite가 적절하다.

polite 공손한, 예의바른 rude 무례한, 예의 없는 patient 참을성 있는, 인내심 있는 stubborn 완고한, 고집스러운, 완강한

정답 ⓑ

123

step 2

A company / offers / high school students / a job / and teaches / them / practical skills / suitable / for their future profession / so that they / can gain / valuable work experience.

한 회사는 / 제공한다 / 고등학교 학생들에게 / 일

자리를 / 그리고 가르친다 / 그들에게 / 실용적인 기술을 / 적합한 / 그들의 미래 직업에 / 그들이 / 얻을 수 있도록 / 귀중한 직업 경험을.

step 3

문맥상 '얻다, 습득하다'를 뜻하는 acquire가 적절하다.

acquire 얻다, 습득하다 receive 받다, 받아들이다 bestow 수여하다 confer 상의하다, 수여하다

정답 ⓐ

124

step 2

Many problems / arise / with regard to inadequate nutrients / for young children. / Parents / should know / the importance / of nutrition / in early childhood development / and teach / children / healthy eating.

많은 문제들이 / 발생한다 / 부족한 영양소와 관련하여 / 어린 아이들에게. / 부모들은 / 알아야 한다 / 중요성을 / 영양의 / 초기 유아의 발달 과정에서 / 그리고 가르쳐야 한다 / 아이들에게 / 건강한 식습관을.

step 3

문맥상 '불충분한, 부족한'을 뜻하는 insufficient가 적절하다.

insufficient 불충분한, 부족한 ample 충분한, 풍만한 moderate 보통의, 중간의 reasonable 타당한, 합리적인

정답 ⓐ

125

step 2

A community center / will offer / various training programs / starting next week / to teach / women / living / in the most deprived area / skills / that they need / to get a job / and support / them.

한 주민센터는 / 제공할 것이다 / 다양한 훈련 프로그램들을 / 다음 주부터 / 가르치기 위해서 / 여성들에게 / 사는 / 가장 빈곤한 지역에 / 기술들을 / 그들이 필요로 하는 / 직장을 얻기 위해서 / 그리고 지원하기 위해서 / 그들을.

step 3

문맥상 '불우한'을 뜻하는 disadvantaged가 적절하다.

disadvantaged 불우한 affluence 풍부함, 풍족 prosperous 번영한, 번창한 untouched 훼손되지 않은, 본래 그대로의

정답 ⓐ

126

step 2

Although Richard / tried / many different ways / to lose / weight / quickly, / a weight loss solution / that worked / for others / didn't work / for him / and made / him / unhealthy. / A personal trainer / told / him / that he / should follow / a balanced and healthy diet.

비록 리차드가 / 시도했지만 / 많은 다양한 방법들을 / 줄이기 위해 / 몸무게를 / 빠르게. / 체중 감량 솔루션이 / 효과가 있었던 / 다른 사람들에게 / 효과가 없었다 / 그에게 / 그리고 만들었다 / 그를 / 건강하지 못하게. / 한 개인 트레이너는 / 말했다 / 그에게 / 그가 / 따라야 한다고 / 균형 잡히고 건강한 식단을.

step 3

문맥상 '다양한 것이 섞인'을 뜻하는 mixed가 적절하다.

mixed 다양한 것이 섞인 fair 타당한, 공평한 weighted 치우친, 편중된 bias 편견, 편견을 갖게 하다

정답 ⓒ

127

step 2

We / will send / you / a copy of the information / about a list of tasks / that you have to do / tomorrow. / Because it / helps / you / to create / a clear path / to accomplishing the project / efficiently, / your work perfor mance / can be improved.

우리는 / 보낼 것이다 / 당신에게 / 정보의 사본을 / 작업목록에 관하여 / 당신이 수행해야 하는 / 내일. / 그것이 / 도와주기 때문에, / 당신이 / 만들도록 / 명확한 경로를 / 프로젝트를 완수하기 위한 / 효율적으로, / 당신의 작업 성과가 / 개선될 수 있다.

step 3

문맥상 '생산적으로'를 뜻하는 productively가 적절하다.

productively 생산적으로 naively 순진하게 abstractly 추상적으로 flawlessly 흠 없이, 완전하게

정답 ⓒ

128

step 2

Because Mike / wanted / to reward / employees / for their work, / he / offered / some employees / financial incentives, / including cash rewards. / Moreover, / he / gave / the best employees / extra paid vacation days / to recognize / their efforts.

마이크가 / 원했기 때문에 / 보상해주기를 / 직원들에게 / 그들의 일에 대해, / 그는 / 제공했다 / 일부 직원들에게 / 금전적 인센티브를, / 현금 보상을 포함하여. / 게다가, / 그는 / 주었다 / 최고의 직원들에게 / 추가 유급 휴가를 / 인정하기 위해 / 그들의 노력을.

step 3

문맥상 '금전의, 금전상의'를 뜻하는 monetary가 적절하다.

monetary 금전의, 금전상의 commercial 상업의, 상업적인 alternative 대체 가능한, 대안이 되는 investitive 투자의, 자격을 수여하는

정답 ⓐ

129

step 2

Trafficking / in wildlife / has caused / species populations / to decline, / making / some species / become extinct. / We / should fight / against illegal wildlife trade / across the world / and give / all species / facing threats / strict protection.

불법 거래는 / 야생동물의 / 유발해오고 있다 / 종의 개체 수가 / 감소하도록, / 만들면서 / 몇몇 종들이 / 멸종하게. / 우리는 / 싸워야 한다 / 불법 야생동물 거래에 맞서 / 전 세계의 / 그리고 주어야 한다 / 모든 종들에게 / 위협에 직면한 / 엄격한 보호를.

step 3

문맥상 '엄격한'을 뜻하는 rigorous가 적절하다.

rigorous 엄격한 harsh 가혹한, 냉혹한, 혹독한 cruel 잔혹한, 잔인한 accurate 정확한, 정밀한

정답 ⓑ

130

step 2

Matthew / had a hard time / landing the job / because he / was usually nervous / during the interview process. / Nevertheless, / he / struggled / to overcome / job interview anxiety / and prepared / for the interview / thoroughly. / Finally, / his dream company / hired / him / and his parents / bought / him / Tesla Model Y / as a gift.

매튜는 / 어려움을 겪었다 / 직장을 잡는데 / 왜냐하면 그가 / 대개 긴장했기 때문에 / 면접 과정에서. / 그럼에도 불구하고, / 그는 / 고분분투했다 / 극복하려고 / 면접 불안을 / 그리고 준비했다 / 면접을 / 철저히. / 마침내, / 그의 꿈의 회사는 / 고용했다 / 그를 / 그리고 그의 부모님은 / 사주었다 / 그에게 / 테슬라 모델 Y를 / 선물로.

step 3

문맥상 '철저하게, 속속들이'를 뜻하는 exhaustively 가 적절하다.

exhaustively 철저하게, 속속들이
approximately 거의 (정확하게) **roughly** 대략, 거의
strategically 전략적으로, 전략상으로

정답 ⓓ

STEP 4 | 조동사와 연결어 훈련

001

전치사 자리이므로 접속부사인 (c)와 (d)를 소거한다. 월급의 감소와 늘어난 노동 시간은 역접의 관계이므로 '~에도 불구하고'를 뜻하는 despite가 적절하다.

정답 (b)

002

현실과 환상을 구분하는 능력에 대해 말하고 있으므로 can이 적절하다.

정답 (c)

003

정확한 미래시점(next month)이 나와 있으므로 미래에 있을 일을 나타내는 조동사 will이 적절하다.

정답 (c)

004

접속부사 자리이다. 발명한 도구가 쓸모없었으므로 '그러나'를 뜻하는 however가 적절하다.

정답 (a)

005

접속부사 자리이다. 에이미는 소설가일 뿐 아니라 드러머이기도 하다. 따라서 '게다가'를 뜻하는 접속부사 in addition이 적절하다.

정답 (b)

006

접속부사 자리이므로 접속사인 (b)를 소거한다. 에이미와 책을 대조하고 있으므로 '반면에'를 뜻하는 on the other hand가 적절하다.

정답 (a)

007

접속부사 자리이므로 접속사인 (a)와 (b)를 소거한

다. 앞 문장과 뒷 문장이 역접이므로 '그러나'를 뜻하는 however가 적절하다.

정답 (c)

008

접속부사 자리이다. 꽃 중에서 원추리를 구체적인 사례로 언급하고 있으므로 '예를 들어'를 뜻하는 for example이 적절하다.

정답 (a)

009

접속부사 자리이다. 패스트 패션의 파괴적인 영향 중 이산화탄소 배출을 구체적인 사례로 언급하고 있으므로 '예를 들어'를 뜻하는 for example이 적절하다.

정답 (c)

010

생각과 감정을 정확히 묘사할 수 있는 인간의 능력에 대해 말하고 있으므로 can이 적절하다.

정답 (a)

011

접속사 자리이므로 전치사인 (a)를 소거한다. 사장님이 미팅을 취소한 이유에 대해 언급하고 있으므로 '~ 때문에'를 뜻하는 because가 적절하다.

정답 (d)

012

접속사 자리이므로 전치사인 (a)를 소거한다. 해석상 '만약 ~라면'을 뜻하는 if가 적절하다.

정답 (b)

013

가능성을 나타내는 can이 적절하다.

정답 (d)

014

가능성을 나타내는 can이 적절하다.

정답 (b)

015

'~하곤 했었다'를 뜻하면서 과거의 습관을 나타내는 조동사 would가 적절하다.

정답 (d)

016

조언, 권고를 나타내는 조동사 should가 적절하다.

정답 (a)

017

접속사 자리이므로 접속부사인 (b)를 소거한다. 주절과 종속절의 관계가 역접이므로 '비록 ~일지라도'를 뜻하는 though가 적절하다.

정답 (c)

018

접속부사 자리이다. 의미 있는 관계 형성이 어려운 과정이 될 수도 있다고 하고 있으므로 '그러나'를 뜻하는 however가 적절하다.

정답 (d)

019

접속사 자리이다. 주절과 종속절의 관계가 역접이므로 '비록 ~일지라도'를 뜻하는 although가 적절하다.

정답 (c)

020

접속사 자리이므로 접속부사인 (d)를 소거한다. 해석상 '~함에 따라'를 뜻하는 as가 적절하다.

정답 (b)

021

접속사 자리이다. 에이미가 다이어트를 결심한 이유에 대해 언급하고 있으므로 '~ 때문에'를 뜻하는 because가 적절하다.

정답 (a)

022

접속부사 자리이다. 앞 문장과 뒷 문장의 관계가 역접이므로 '그러나'를 뜻하는 however가 적절하다.

정답 (b)

023

접속사 자리이다. 에이프릴이 휴가를 취소한 이유에 대해 언급하고 있으므로 '∼ 때문에'를 뜻하는 because가 적절하다.

정답 (b)

024

접속부사 자리이다. 앞 문장에서 수질오염의 부정적 영향에 대해 언급했고 뒷 문장에서는 수질 오염 예방을 위해 아무것도 하지 않는다고 했으므로 '그럼에도 불구하고'를 뜻하는 nevertheless가 적절하다.

정답 (c)

025

접속사 자리이므로 접속부사인 (a)를 소거한다. 레이첼이 한 남자와 만나 저녁 식사까지 했지만 이름조차 기억하지 못한다고 했으므로 '비록 ∼일지라도'를 뜻하는 although가 적절하다.

정답 (c)

026

미팅 참석을 위해서는 내 의지와 상관없이 무조건 신분증을 제시해야 한다. 따라서 must가 적절하다.

정답 (d)

027

접속사 자리이므로 접속부사인 (b)와 (c)를 소거한다. 해석상 '∼할 때'를 뜻하는 when이 적절하다.

정답 (d)

028

접속사 자리이므로 접속부사인 (a)와 (c)를 소거한다. 해석상 '∼할 때'를 뜻하는 when이 적절하다.

정답 (b)

029

접속사 자리이므로 접속부사인 (a)와 (c)를 소거한다. 해석상 '∼후에'를 뜻하는 after가 적절하다.

정답 (b)

030

접속사 자리이다. 해석상 '∼함에 따라'를 뜻하는 as가 적절하다.

정답 (c)

031

정확한 미래시점(next week)이 나와 있으므로 미래에 있을 일을 나타내는 조동사 will이 적절하다.

정답 (a)

032

접속부사 자리이다. 앱을 개발했지만 실패했으므로 '그러나'를 뜻하는 however가 적절하다.

정답 (a)

033

접속사 자리이므로 접속부사인 (a)를 소거한다. 그레이스가 파스타 요리에 실패한 이유에 대해 언급하고 있으므로 '∼ 때문에'를 뜻하는 because가 적절하다.

정답 (d)

034

버섯으로 다양한 요리를 만들 수 있는 능력에 대해 말하고 있으므로 can이 적절하다.

정답 (a)

035

접속사 자리이므로 접속부사인 (d)를 소거한다. 책을 찾으려 했으나 발견할 수 없었으므로 '비록 ∼일지라도'를 뜻하는 although가 적절하다.

정답 (c)

036

접속사 자리이다. 제인이 저축한 이유에 대해 언급하고 있으므로 '～ 때문에'를 뜻하는 because가 적절하다.

정답 (c)

037

접속부사 자리이므로 접속사나 전치사 역할을 하는 (b)를 소거한다. 해석상 '다행히도'를 뜻하는 fortunately가 적절하다.

정답 (a)

038

능력, 가능성을 나타내는 can이 적절하다.

정답 (a)

039

접속부사 자리이다. 앞 문장과 뒷 문장이 원인과 결과의 관계이므로 '그러므로'를 뜻하는 therefore가 적절하다.

정답 (d)

040

접속부사 자리이다. 두 번째 사례가 언급되고 있으므로 '유사하게'를 뜻하는 simiraly가 적절하다.

정답 (b)

041

접속사 자리이므로 접속부사인 (d)를 소거한다. 해석상 '～할 때마다'를 뜻하는 whenever가 적절하다.

정답 (b)

042

조언, 권고를 나타내는 조동사 should가 적절하다.

정답 (c)

043

추측을 나타내는 may가 적절하다.

정답 (d)

044

접속부사 자리이므로 접속사인 (b)를 소거한다. also와 함께 쓰이는 however는 역접의 의미가 아니다. 잭이 피아니스트이기도 하지만 또한 만화책 작가이므로 '그러나'를 뜻하는 however가 적절하다.

정답 (a)

045

접속사 자리이므로 접속부사인 (b)를 소거한다. 해석상 '～한 후에'를 뜻하는 after가 적절하다.

정답 (a)

046

접속부사 자리이므로 접속사인 (a)를 소거한다. 앞 문장과 뒷 문장이 역접의 관계이므로 '그러나'를 뜻하는 however가 적절하다.

정답 (d)

047

접속부사 자리이다. 월급을 학자금을 갚는 데 쓰는 대신 주식을 사는 데 썼으므로 '대신에'를 뜻하는 instead가 적절하다.

정답 (a)

048

접속사 자리이므로 접속부사인 (a)를 소거한다. 해석상 '～에도 불구하고'를 뜻하는 even though가 적절하다.

정답 (d)

049

접속부사 자리이므로 접속사나 전치사 역할을 하는 (a)와 접속사 (c)를 소거한다. 스포츠 모드를 선택하는 사람과 컴포트 모드를 사용하는 사람을 대조하고 있으므로 '대조적으로'를 뜻하는 in contrast가 적절하다.

정답 (b)

050

접속부사 자리이므로 접속사인 (a)를 소거한다. 판매량의 하락을 겪은 소매점과 위기에서 살아남은 소매점을 대조하고 있으므로 '반면에'를 뜻하는 on the other hand가 적절하다.

정답 (b)

051

조언, 권고를 나타내는 조동사 should가 적절하다.

정답 (c)

052

접속사 자리이므로 접속부사인 (a)를 소거한다. 집에서 일하는 것을 멈춰야 하는 이유에 대해 언급하고 있으므로 '~ 때문에'를 뜻하는 because가 적절하다.

정답 (c)

053

접속부사 자리이므로 접속사인 (b)를 소거한다. 해석상 '결국, 마침내'를 뜻하는 eventually가 적절하다.

정답 (c)

054

접속사 자리이므로 접속부사인 (b)를 소거한다. 음식판매를 중지한 이유에 대해 언급하고 있으므로 '~ 때문에'를 뜻하는 because가 적절하다.

정답 (a)

055

접속부사 자리이므로 접속사인 (d)를 소거한다. 과중한 업무로 인한 우울감에 동료와의 문제까지 더해졌으므로 '게다가'를 뜻하는 furthermore이 적절하다.

정답 (b)

056

정확한 미래시점(next month)이 나와 있으므로 미래에 있을 일을 나타내는 조동사 will이 적절하다.

정답 (a)

057

조언, 권고를 나타내는 조동사 should가 적절하다.

정답 (a)

058

접속부사 자리이다. 훈련 프로그램의 추가적인 장점이 언급되어 있으므로 '게다가'를 뜻하는 moreover이 적절하다.

정답 (b)

059

입양을 원하는 부모는 재정적 안정성을 무조건 충족시켜야 한다. 따라서 must가 적절하다.

정답 (d)

060

전치사 자리이므로 접속부사인 (a)를 소거한다. 수지가 꽃을 고르는 대신 신부들이 직접 꽃을 고른다고 언급되어 있으므로 '~대신에'를 뜻하는 instead of가 적절하다.

정답 (b)

061

접속사 자리이다. 주절과 종속절이 역접의 관계이므로 '비록 ~일지라도'를 뜻하는 although가 적절하다.

정답 (d)

062

조언, 권고를 나타내는 조동사 should가 적절하다.

정답 (b)

063

휴가 때 책을 읽겠다는 의지가 담겨 있으므로 will이 적절하다.

정답 (a)

064

조언, 권고를 나타내는 조동사 should가 적절하다.

정답 (c)

065

접속사 자리이므로 접속부사인 (d)를 소거한다. 에이미가 스트레스를 받은 이유에 대해 언급하고 있으므로 '~ 때문에'를 뜻하는 because가 적절하다.

정답 (b)

066

접속부사 자리이다. 해석상 '마침내'를 뜻하는 finally가 적절하다.

정답 (b)

067

접속부사 자리이므로 접속사인 (c)를 소거한다. 앞 문장과 뒷 문장이 역접의 관계이므로 '그럼에도 불구하고'를 뜻하는 nevertheless가 적절하다.

정답 (a)

068

접속사 자리이므로 접속부사인 (b)를 소거한다. 아버지가 공장 설립을 포기한 이유에 대해 언급하고 있으므로 '~ 때문에'를 뜻하는 because가 적절하다.

정답 (d)

069

접속부사 자리이다. 해석상 '만약 그렇지 않으면'을 뜻하는 otherwise가 적절하다.

정답 (c)

070

접속사 자리이다. 레이첼이 수학 문제를 풀기 위해 노력한 이유에 대해 언급하고 있으므로 '~ 때문에'를 뜻하는 because가 적절하다.

정답 (d)

071

가능성을 나타내는 can이 적절하다.

정답 (d)

072

접속부사 자리이므로 접속사인 (a)를 소거한다. 아이들에게 집안일을 시키는 것에 대한 장점의 사례가 구체적으로 언급되어 있으므로 '예를 들어'를 뜻하는 for example이 적절하다.

정답 (b)

073

접속사 자리이므로 접속부사인 (a)와 (b)를 소거한다. 해석상 '~하지 않는다면'을 뜻하는 unless가 적절하다.

정답 (c)

074

접속사 자리이다. 해석상 '~까지'를 뜻하는 until이 적절하다.

정답 (a)

075

접속부사 자리이므로 접속사인 (b)를 소거한다. 앞 문장과 뒷 문장이 역접의 관계이므로 '그럼에도 불구하고'를 뜻하는 nevertheless가 적절하다.

정답 (d)

076

접속부사 자리이다. 에이미가 아들의 책임감 발달에 도움을 주는 사례가 구체적으로 언급되어 있으므로 '예를 들어'를 뜻하는 for example이 적절하다.

정답 (a)

077

능력, 가능성을 나타내는 can이 적절하다.

정답 (c)

078

전치사 자리이므로 접속부사인 (a)를 소거한다. 주 디가 고기를 먹는 대신 채소 식단을 먹는다고 언급 되어 있으므로 '~대신에'를 뜻하는 instead of가 적절하다.

정답 (d)

079

접속사 자리이므로 접속부사인 (a)를 소거한다. 주 절과 종속절의 관계가 역접이므로 '비록 ~일지라 도'를 뜻하는 although가 적절하다.

정답 (c)

080

접속사 자리이다. 몰리가 SNS 사용을 금지한 이유 에 대해 언급하고 있으므로 '~ 때문에'를 뜻하는 because가 적절하다.

정답 (b)

081

접속부사 자리이다. 앞 문장과 뒷 문장의 관계가 역 접이므로 '그러나'를 뜻하는 however가 적절하다.

정답 (b)

082

접속부사 자리이다. 해석상 '다행히도'를 뜻하 는 unfortunately가 적절하다.

정답 (a)

083

비행기가 즉시 착륙해야 하는 것은 반드시 이루어 져야 한다. 따라서 must가 적절하다.

정답 (c)

084

전치사 자리이다. 재정적 문제에도 불구하고 성장 했으므로 '~에도 불구하고'를 뜻하는 despite가 적 절하다.

정답 (b)

085

접속사 자리이므로 접속부사인 (a)를 소거한다. 해 석상 '~하는 경우에'를 뜻하는 in case that이 적절 하다.

정답 (b)

086

접속부사 자리이므로 접속사인 (a)를 소거한다. 앞 문장과 뒷 문장의 관계가 역접이므로 '그러나'를 뜻 하는 however가 적절하다.

정답 (c)

087

접속부사 자리이다. 바라나시로 가는 여름휴가를 포기하는 대신 집에서 쉬기로 결정했으므로 '대신 에'를 뜻하는 instead가 적절하다.

정답 (c)

088

접속사 자리이므로 접속부사인 (b)를 소거한다. 해 석상 '~하는 동안'을 뜻하는 while이 적절하다.

정답 (d)

089

접속부사 자리이므로 접속사인 (a)를 소거한다. 앞 문장과 뒷 문장이 원인과 결과의 관계이므로 '그러 므로'를 뜻하는 therefore가 적절하다.

정답 (b)

090

접속부사 자리이다. 앞문장과 뒷문장이 원인과 결 과의 관계이므로 '그 결과'를 뜻하는 as a result가 적절하다.

정답 (a)

091

전치사 자리이므로 접속사인 (b)와 (c)를 소거한다. 레스토랑이 유명한 이유에 대해 언급하고 있으므로 '~때문에'를 뜻하는 because of가 적절하다.

정답 (a)

092

접속부사 자리이므로 접속사인 (b)를 소거한다. 앞 문장과 뒷 문장의 관계가 역접이므로 '그러나'를 뜻하는 however가 적절하다.

정답 (a)

093

접속부사 자리이므로 접속사와 전치사 역할을 하는 (c)를 소거한다. 해석상 '그러므로'를 뜻하는 therefore가 적절하다.

정답 (d)

094

접속사 자리이므로 접속부사인 (b)를 소거한다. 해석상 '비록 ~일지라도'를 뜻하는 although가 적절하다.

정답 (d)

095

접속부사 자리이므로 접속사인 (a)를 소거한다. 아기에게 말을 하는 것의 장점에 대한 사례가 구체적으로 언급되어 있으므로 '예를 들어'를 뜻하는 for example이 적절하다.

정답 (c)

096

접속사 자리이므로 접속부사인 (c)를 소거한다. 해석상 '~후에'를 뜻하는 after가 적절하다.

정답 (b)

097

조언, 권고를 나타내는 조동사 should가 적절하다.

정답 (b)

098

접속사 자리이다. 하루에 50~100개의 머리카락이 빠지는 것이 정상인 이유에 대해 언급하고 있으므로 '~ 때문에'를 뜻하는 because가 적절하다.

정답 (a)

099

가능성을 나타내는 can이 적절하다.

정답 (b)

100

접속사 자리이므로 접속부사인 (a)를 소거한다. 유니폼을 입는 것이 개성을 없애는 이유에 대해 언급하고 있으므로 '~ 때문에'를 뜻하는 because가 적절하다.

정답 (c)

101

전치사 자리이다. 제품판매를 금지한 이유에 대해 언급하고 있으므로 '~때문에'를 뜻하는 because of가 적절하다.

정답 (d)

102

정확한 미래시점(next week)이 나와 있으므로 미래에 있을 일을 나타내는 조동사 will이 적절하다.

정답 (a)

103

접속사 자리이다. 온라인에서 케이크를 만들기 위한 비법을 찾은 이유에 대해 언급하고 있으므로 '~ 때문에'를 뜻하는 because가 적절하다.

정답 (c)

104

접속사 자리이다. 해석상 '~할 때마다'를 뜻하는 whenever가 적절하다.

정답 (c)

105

조언, 권고를 나타내는 조동사 should가 적절하다.

정답 (a)

106

접속부사 자리이다. 직원을 불편하게 만드는 작업환경과 편안하게 만드는 작업환경을 대조하고 있으므로 '반면에'를 뜻하는 on the other hand가 적절하다.

정답 (b)

107

접속사 자리이므로 접속부사인 (d)를 소거한다. 해석상 '~할 때'를 뜻하는 when이 적절하다.

정답 (b)

108

접속사 자리이므로 접속부사인 (b)를 소거한다. 해석상 '~한 직후'를 뜻하는 right after가 적절하다.

정답 (c)

109

접속사 자리이다. 주절과 종속절의 관계가 역접이므로 '비록 ~일지라도'를 뜻하는 although가 적절하다.

정답 (b)

110

접속부사 자리이다. 앞 문장과 뒷 문장이 원인과 결과의 관계이므로 '그러므로'를 뜻하는 therefore가 적절하다.

정답 (d)

111

접속사 자리이므로 접속부사인 (b)를 소거한다. 해석상 '~한 후'를 뜻하는 after가 적절하다.

정답 (c)

112

조언, 권고를 나타내는 조동사 should가 적절하다.

정답 (a)

113

정확한 미래시점(next year)이 나와 있으므로 미래에 있을 일을 나타내는 조동사 will이 적절하다.

정답 (b)

114

공공장소를 행사 장소로 사용하려 할 때 무조건 해야 하는 의무가 언급되어 있으므로 must가 적절하다.

정답 (d)

115

접속사 자리이다. 주절과 종속절의 관계가 역접이므로 '비록 ~일지라도'를 뜻하는 although가 적절하다.

정답 (c)

116

접속부사 자리이다. 다양한 조직이 하는 일들이 추가적으로 언급되어 있으므로 '게다가'를 뜻하는 in addition이 적절하다.

정답 (c)

117

접속사 자리이므로 접속부사인 (a)를 소거한다. 시험이 미뤄진 이유에 대해 언급하고 있으므로 '~ 때문에'를 뜻하는 because가 적절하다.

정답 (b)

118

전치사 자리이므로 접속사인 (c)와 (d)를 소거한다. 조치를 취했음에도 문제가 지속되었으므로 '~에도 불구하고'를 뜻하는 in spite of가 적절하다.

정답 (a)

Answer

119

접속사 자리이다. 주절과 종속절의 관계가 역접이므로 '비록 ~일지라도'를 뜻하는 although가 적절하다.

정답 (a)

120

접속사 자리이다. 해석상 '~하지 않는다면'을 뜻하는 unless가 적절하다.

정답 (d)

121

접속사 자리이므로 접속부사인 (d)를 소거한다. 에이미가 사람과의 접촉을 피하는 이유에 대해 언급하고 있으므로 '~ 때문에'를 뜻하는 because가 적절하다.

정답 (a)

122

접속부사 자리이다. 최상급과 함께 쓰이는 however는 강조할 때 사용하기도 한다. 직원에게 감사함을 보여주는 최고의 방법을 강조하고 있으므로 '그러나'를 뜻하는 however가 적절하다.

정답 (b)

123

접속사 자리이다. 해석상 '~하기 위해'를 뜻하는 so that이 적절하다.

정답 (b)

124

조언, 권고를 나타내는 조동사 should가 적절하다.

정답 (d)

125

정확한 미래시점(next week)이 나와 있으므로 미래에 있을 일을 나타내는 조동사 will이 적절하다.

정답 (d)

126

조언, 권고를 나타내는 조동사 should가 적절하다.

정답 (c)

127

접속사 자리이다. 업무성과가 향상될 수 있는 이유에 대해 언급하고 있으므로 '~ 때문에'를 뜻하는 because가 적절하다.

정답 (a)

128

접속부사 자리이므로 접속사인 (a)를 소거한다. 직원에게 보상을 주는 수단이 추가적으로 언급되어 있으므로 '게다가'를 뜻하는 moreover가 적절하다.

정답 (b)

129

조언, 권고를 나타내는 조동사 should가 적절하다.

정답 (b)

130

접속부사 자리이다. 앞 문장과 뒷 문장의 역접의 관계이므로 '그럼에도 불구하고'를 뜻하는 nevertheless가 적절하다.

정답 (c)

켈리지텔프
해석 POINT
13

동의어
모의고사

그동안 공부했던 동의어 중에서 30문제를 선별하였습니다. 복습이 제대로 되었는지 점검해 보세요.

01

You need to remember that weather forecasts can be <u>wrong</u>.

> Q
>
> In the context of the passage, wrong means _____.

(a) changeable　(b) flexible　(c) inaccurate　(d) replaceable

02

Because Amy wanted to be slim, she <u>decided</u> to get in shape and lose weight in 7 days.

> Q
>
> In the context of the passage, decided means _____.

(a) resolved　(b) executed　(c) prepared　(d) accomplished

03

It is well known that the restaurant is <u>good</u> for a first date because of the perfect lighting.

> Q
>
> In the context of the passage, good means _____.

(a) suitable　(b) efficient　(c) admissible　(d) precious

04

Mark <u>assigned</u> too much work to Rachel, which caused her to become depressed. Furthermore, she had a problem with her coworker.

> Q
>
> In the context of the passage, assigned means _____.

(a) determined (b) empowered (c) transferred (d) gave

05

You must <u>present</u> your ID card to attend tomorrow's meeting and take a special lecture. Unless you have an ID card, you can't get in.

> Q
>
> In the context of the passage, present means _____.

(a) show (b) appear (c) express (d) release

06

Money may be necessary for happiness. However, it is more important to be <u>satisfied</u> with your life to live a happy life.

> Q
>
> In the context of the passage, satisfied means _____.

(a) proud (b) prominent (c) plentiful (d) contented

07

The new concealer helps men to cover their skin flaws, <u>addressing</u> the specific needs of men. However, in case that it causes skin irritation, stop using it and consult your doctor.

Q

In the context of the passage, addressing means _____.

(a) withstanding   (b) treating   (c) neglecting   (d) maintaining

08

A study revealed that people could build a meaningful relationship through adoption. However, it can be a <u>challenging</u> process.

Q

In the context of the passage, challenging means _____.

(a) inspiring   (b) energizing   (c) purposeful   (d) demanding

09

Using sport mode in your car will make your driving experience more exciting, making your car go faster. However, leaving your car in sport mode all the time can <u>cause</u> some problems.

Q

In the context of the passage, cause means _____.

(a) make   (b) discover   (c) find   (d) resolve

10

Workout apps gain popularity as the interest in health is increasing. They offer workout videos and training routines for free and provide even <u>personalized</u> workout plans for all fitness levels.

> Q
>
> In the context of the passage, personalized means _____.

(a) formulaic   (b) popularized   (c) customized   (d) handy

11

One of the reasons consumers shop online is that they can compare a number of products at a time and get <u>instant</u> access to product reviews.

> Q
>
> In the context of the passage, instant means _____.

(a) unexpected   (b) abrupt   (c) sudden   (d) immediate

12

A company will provide cash bonuses next week. That's because sales of products released by the company have been <u>soaring</u>.

> Q
>
> In the context of the passage, soaring means _____.

(a) developing   (b) skyrocketing   (c) reinforcing   (d) supporting

13

Because Rachel spent too much on her hobbies, she was short on rent last month. Although having a hobby made her happy, her boyfriend asked her to save money instead of spending on <u>expensive</u> hobbies.

> Q
>
> In the context of the passage, expensive means _____.

(a) costly (b) abundant (c) economical (d) moderate

14

People who want to get plastic surgery should understand the potential medical risks and get enough information to avoid <u>harmful</u> effects.

> Q
>
> In the context of the passage, harmful means _____.

(a) painful (b) bothersome (c) irritating (d) detrimental

15

Employees should attend the training program, which will encourage them to <u>cultivate</u> creativity. Moreover, the program can motivate employees to increase innovation in products and work hard.

> Q
>
> In the context of the passage, cultivate means _____.

(a) fertilize (b) foster (c) learn (d) absorb

16

A non-profit organization is <u>working</u> to offer various academic programs for the most vulnerable students. As a result, many students who otherwise would not have access to quality education have the opportunity to learn.

Q

In the context of the passage, working means _____.

(a) trying   (b) toiling   (c) unwilling   (d) reluctant

17

Because the boss always ignores Amy, she is under too much stress, which is causing hair loss. She is going to buy a special shampoo which strengthens each strand of hair to <u>stop</u> hair loss.

Q

In the context of the passage, stop means _____.

(a) prevent   (b) finish   (c) pause   (d) complete

18

Many small companies need to <u>take</u> a new approach to overcome the financial crisis and achieve their goal. Otherwise, they would stop operating and go out of business.

Q

In the context of the passage, take means _____.

(a) exclude   (b) adopt   (c) acquire   (d) keep

19

<u>Involving</u> children in household chores has many advantages. For example, getting children to clean their room can make them feel needed.

> Q
>
> In the context of the passage, Involving means _____.

(a) Excluding   (b) Engaging   (c) Forcing   (d) Withdrawing

20

Water pollution kills a number of people every year as well as <u>affects</u> the health of animals. Nevertheless, most of the people don't do anything to prevent water pollution.

> Q
>
> In the context of the passage, affects means _____.

(a) threatens   (b) maintains   (c) profits   (d) aids

21

It is essential that Betty get some rest because she feels burned out and exhausted after work, losing her passion she once had in her work. Getting more sleep and <u>enough</u> rest can relax her mind and body, also improving her mood and relieving stress.

> Q
>
> In the context of the passage, enough means _____.

(a) adequate   (b) expanding   (c) brief   (d) compulsory

22

One of the biggest differences between humans and other animals is the ability of inventing new tools. Also, unlike animals, humans can describe thoughts and feelings accurately.

Q

In the context of the passage, accurately means _____.

(a) carefully (b) patiently (c) undoubtedly (d) precisely

23

Taking some time to research a company you want to work for online in advance is necessary before you attend a job interview. By doing so, you can make a good impression on your potential employer.

Q

In the context of the passage, potential means _____.

(a) prospective (b) capable (c) accessible (d) pliable

24

The car offers the option to select a driving mode. Those who want to immerse themselves in the exciting driving experience can select sport mode. In contrast, those who want a smoother ride can select comfort mode.

Q

In the context of the passage, offers means _____.

(a) provides (b) supports (c) improves (d) awards

381

25

Molly bans employees from wasting time on social media by blocking social networking sites while they are working because she thinks that using social media in the workplace has a negative <u>effect</u> on productivity.

> Q
> In the context of the passage, effect means _____.

(a) result   (b) process   (c) conclusion   (d) evaluation

26

Until a doctor warned that drinking too much coffee could be harmful to the body by increasing the heartbeat, Judy took in too much caffeine through coffee. The doctor advised her to find <u>alternatives</u> to coffee.

> Q
> In the context of the passage, alternatives means _____.

(a) additives   (b) complements   (c) replacements   (d) ingredients

27

After more than three people were killed in a house fire, police said that unknown suspects entered the house and lit it on fire, adding that the investigation was still <u>ongoing</u>.

> Q
> In the context of the passage, ongoing means _____.

(a) emerging   (b) consistent   (c) persistent   (d) underway

28

Because Amy was so depressed, avoiding contact with people and isolating herself, Mike gave her some tips for <u>handling</u> depression and encouraged her to seek therapy.

Q

In the context of the passage, handling means _____.

(a) operating (b) addressing (c) manipulating (d) reacting

29

Many problems arise with regard to <u>inadequate</u> nutrients for young children. Parents should know the importance of nutrition in early childhood development and teach children healthy eating.

Q

In the context of the passage, inadequate means _____.

(a) insufficient (b) ample (c) moderate (d) reasonable

30

Trafficking in wildlife has caused species populations to decline, making some species become extinct. We should fight against illegal wildlife trade across the world and give all species facing threats <u>strict</u> protection.

Q

In the context of the passage, strict means _____.

(a) harsh (b) rigorous (c) cruel (d) accurate

켈리지텔프
해석POINT
13

켈리지텔프
해석POINT
13

동의어
모의고사

| 정답 및 해설&해석 |

01

문맥상 '부정확한, 틀린'을 뜻하는 inaccurate이 적절하다.

inaccurate 부정확한, 틀린 changeable 바뀔 수도 있는, 변덕이 심한 flexible 신축성 있는, 유연한 replaceable 대신할 수 있는

정답 ⓒ

02

문맥상 '결심하다'를 뜻하는 resolved가 적절하다.

resolve 결심하다 execute 처형하다, 실행하다 prepare 준비하다 accomplish 완수하다, 성취하다

정답 ⓐ

03

문맥상 '적합한'을 뜻하는 suitable이 적절하다.

suitable 적합한 efficient 능률적인, 유능한, 효율적인 admissible 인정되는 precious 귀한, 소중한

정답 ⓐ

04

문맥상 '주다'를 뜻하는 gave가 적절하다.

give 주다 determine 알아내다 empower 권한을 주다 transfer 이동하다, 옮기다

정답 ⓓ

05

문맥상 '보여주다'를 뜻하는 show가 적절하다.

show 보여주다 appear 나타나다 express 표현하다 release 풀어주다, 놓아주다

정답 ⓐ

06

문맥상 '만족한'을 뜻하는 contented가 적절하다.

contented 만족한 proud 자랑스러운 prominent 중요한, 유명한 plentiful 풍부한

정답 ⓓ

07

문맥상 '다루다'를 뜻하는 treating이 적절하다.

treat 다루다 withstand 견뎌 내다 neglect 방치하다, 도외시하다 maintain 유지하다

정답 ⓑ

08

문맥상 '힘든'을 뜻하는 demanding이 적절하다.

demanding 힘든 inspiring 고무하는, 격려하는 energize 활기를 북돋우다 purposeful 목적의식이 있는, 결단력 있는

정답 ⓓ

09

문맥상 '만들다'를 뜻하는 make가 적절하다.

make 만들다 discover 발견하다 find 찾다 resolve 해결하다

정답 ⓐ

10

문맥상 '개인 맞춤화된'을 뜻하는 personalized가 적절하다.

customized 개인 맞춤된 formulaic 정형화된 popularized 대중화된 handy 알맞은, 편리한, 쉬운

정답 ⓒ

11

문맥상 '즉각적인'을 뜻하는 immediate가 적절하다.

immediate 즉각적인 unexpected 예상 밖의 abrupt 갑작스러운 sudden 급작스러운

정답 ⓓ

12

문맥상 '급등하다'을 뜻하는 skyrocketing이 적절하다.

skyrocket 급등하다 develop 성장하다, 발달하다 reinforce 강화하다, 보강하다 support 지지하다, 지원하다

정답 ⓑ

13

문맥상 '비싼'을 뜻하는 costly가 적절하다.

costly 비싼 abundant 풍부한 economical
경제적인, 알뜰한 moderate 보통의, 중간의

정답 ⓐ

14

문맥상 '해로운'을 뜻하는 detrimental이 적절하다.

detrimental 해로운 painful 고통스러운
bothersome 성가신 irritating 흥분시키는,
자극하는

정답 ⓓ

15

문맥상 '발전시키다, 촉진하다'를 뜻하는 foster가
적절하다.

foster 발전시키다, 촉진하다 fertilize 비료를 주다,
비옥하게 하다 learn 학습하다 absorb 흡수하다

정답 ⓑ

16

문맥상 '애쓰다'를 뜻하는 trying이 적절하다.

try 애쓰다 toil 고생스럽게 일하다 unwilling 마지못해
하는, 싫어하는 reluctant 꺼리는, 마지못한

정답 ⓐ

17

문맥상 '막다'를 뜻하는 prevent가 적절하다.

prevent 막다 finish 끝내다 pause 잠시 멈추다,
정지시키다 complete 완료하다

정답 ⓐ

18

문맥상 '채택하다'를 뜻하는 adopt가 적절하다.
adopt 채택하다 exclude 제외하다, 배제하다
acquire 습득하다, 얻다 keep 유지하다

정답 ⓑ

19

문맥상 '끌어들이다, 관여시키다'를 뜻하는 Engaging
이 적절하다.

engage 끌어들이다, 관여시키다 exclude 제외하다,
배제하다 force 강요하다 withdraw 철수하다,
중단하다, 탈퇴하다

정답 ⓑ

20

문맥상 '위협하다'를 뜻하는 threatens가 적절하다.

threaten 위협하다 maintain 유지시키다 profit
이익을 얻다 aid 돕다

정답 ⓐ

21

문맥상 '충분한'을 뜻하는 adequate이 적절하다.

adequate 충분한 expand 확장시키다 brief 짧은,
잠시 동안의, 간단한 compulsory 강제적인, 의무적인,
필수의

정답 ⓐ

22

문맥상 '정확하게'를 뜻하는 precisely가 적절하다.

precisely 정확하게 carefully 주의하여, 조심스럽게
patiently 끈기 있게 undoubtedly 의심할 여지없이,
확실히

정답 ⓓ

23

문맥상 '장래의, 가망 있는'을 뜻하는 prospective
가 적절하다.

prospective 장래의, 가망 있는 capable 유능한
accessible 다가가기 쉬운, 편한 pliable 유연한,
순응적인

정답 ⓐ

24

문맥상 '제공하다'를 뜻하는 provides가 적절하다.

provide 제공하다 support 지지하다, 옹호하다

improve 개선되다, 나아지다 award 수여하다

정답 ⓐ

25

문맥상 '결과'를 뜻하는 result가 적절하다.

result 결과 process 과정 conclusion (최종적인) 판단 evaluation 평가

정답 ⓐ

26

문맥상 '대체물'을 뜻하는 replacements이 적절하다.

replacement 대체물 addictive 중독성의, 중독성이 있는 complement 보완물, 덧붙이는 요소 ingredient 재료, 구성 요소

정답 ⓒ

27

문맥상 '진행 중인'을 뜻하는 underway가 적절하다.

underway 진행 중인 emerging 최근 생겨난 consistent 한결같은, 거듭되는 persistent 끈질긴, 끊임없이 지속되는

정답 ⓓ

28

문맥상 '다루는 것'을 뜻하는 addressing이 적절하다.

address 다루다 operate (기계를) 작동하다, 가동하다 manipulate 조종하다, 조작하다, 처리하다 react 반응을 보이다, 반응하다

정답 ⓑ

29

문맥상 '불충분한, 부족한'을 뜻하는 insufficient 가 적절하다.

insufficient 불충분한, 부족한 ample 충분한, 풍만한 moderate 보통의, 중간의 reasonable 타당한, 합리적인

정답 ⓐ

30

문맥상 '엄격한'을 뜻하는 rigorous가 적절하다.

rigorous 엄격한 harsh 가혹한, 냉혹한, 혹독한 cruel 잔혹한, 잔인한 accurate 정확한, 정밀한

정답 ⓑ

켈리지텔프
해석POINT
13

켈리지텔프 해석포인트 13　　　　　　　ISBN 979-11-6049-206-4

발　　　　행	2021년 8월 25일
1 판 3 쇄	2022년 2월 21일
1 판 4 쇄	2022년 8월 20일
1 판 5 쇄	2023년 5월 30일
1 판 6 쇄	2024년12월 13일
1 판 7 쇄	2025년 1월 10일

저자와의
협의하에
인지생략

저　　　자	켈리
발 행 인	금병희
발 행 처	멘토링
출 판 등 록	319-26-60호
주　　　소	서울시 동작구 노량진로 16길 30
주　　　문	Tel 02) 825-0606 / Fax 02) 6499-3195

정가 25,000원